The Guardian Year '97

Introduction by **Alan Rusbridger**
Edited by **John Ezard**

FOURTH ESTATE ● *London*

First published in Great Britain in 1997 by
Fourth Estate Limited
6 Salem Road
London W2 4BU

Copyright © 1997 by Guardian Newspapers Ltd
Introduction © 1997 by Alan Rusbridger
1 3 5 7 9 10 8 6 4 2
The right of John Ezard to be identified as the editor of this work has been asserted
by him in accordance with the Copyright, Designs and Patents Act 1988.

A catalogue record for this book is available from the British Library.

ISBN 1-85702-776-0

Typesetting and layout by Clare Bell
Printed in Great Britain by Bath Press

Contents

Contents

Contents

Contents

Foreign parts

Sex and shopping

Contents

Final calls

Voices from elsewhere

Contents

The Arts: ancient faces and lonesome songs

More important than life and death

Alan Rusbridger
Introduction

A daily newspaper is sometimes said to be the first draft of history. An anthology of journalism is not quite the same: what you read in these pages is a moving picture, not a still one. It is, if you like, a rough cut of history.

And sometimes even the rough cut of an anthology is interrupted – as newspapers often are – by a gigantic new event. This book was going to press when the most piteous, globally mourned British event of 1997 occurred: the death of Diana, Princess of Wales, in a Paris car crash at the age of 36. She left two sons and a nation which discovered a new spontaneity of sustained, wonderfully demonstrative public grief in her passing.

'Her sun is gone down while it was yet day,' as the prophet Jeremiah in the Bible wrote. Diana taught us that many of us have changed, become more demonstrative, perhaps more mindful of others than collectively we used to be. The story of that extraordinary, endearing, sometimes disturbing autumn week is told and studied as it happened in the opening section of this anthology. Its legacy, developing with the months, will be with you as you read these pages. The other sections – since life has to go on – are a picture of other, less impassioned yet often central ways in which our public world has changed over the year: often for the better.

To see how this picture moves consider two pieces, barely eleven weeks apart, on Tony Blair. The first, a leader written the morning after the Wirral South by-election in late March, states as a matter of certainty that there will soon be a Labour government. So far so prescient. But it ends by asking: Where's the buzz for Blair? It observes that there is no enthusiasm around the country for what the future Prime Minister is offering. His impending victory will be more to do with a determination to get rid of the Tories than any illusions about the alternative.

Splice that together with Mark Lawson, five weeks after May Day, on 'Our never-ending love affair with Blair'. The piece begins by describing a country wildly, passionately, elatedly in love with its new Prime Minister. The Gallup ratings are off any known scale; the honeymoon has been prolonged indefinitely and all anyone can talk of is Camelot (as in JFK, not fat cats). A moving picture. Was the leader writer wrong in March? Not as I remember it. We were at that stage about to embark on the longest – and, in many ways, most dispiriting – campaign in modern history. Labour were, at that stage of the game, quite happy to sit back and let the Tories lose the election. They had no intention of going out to inspire the voters with visionary schemes of their own which would only be ritually costed and disembowelled by a Naughtie or Paxman. New – certainly. Young – certainly. Reassuring – yes please. Cynical and dull – if you must.

Two pieces in opposition, but both right. The leader writer in March was right to ask where the buzz was for Blair. And Mark Lawson, too, captured the national mood – call it euphoria, call it relief – that we had picked the right man, if for scarcely guessed

reasons. The first draft of history is only that: a series of snapshots or freeze frames –
a rough stab at pinpointing the facts, or the political mood, or the national tempera-
ture, or the cultural drift, at the point of deadline. Of course, it is crude. Of course we
get things wrong. But at the end of the day – the end, even, of a year – I am generally
surprised by how much we get right.

It would be a poor historian who relied solely on newspapers for his grander project:
for one thing, the annual 1 January trip to the Public Records Office in Kew is always
a salutary reminder of how much – thirty years ago, as now – is hidden and how much
manipulated. Newspapers are often poor at sifting nuances and identifying cultural
trends outside (sometimes, alas, even inside) their staked-out territory. The pressures
of the clock push them towards the smaller picture, not the bigger picture. But, for all
that, newspapers are not a bad start.

This is the forty-fifth annual collection of *Guardian* writing. I have all but two volumes on my shelves. You can open any one at random and read something fresh and
valid about the events of the year in question. There is a clear continuity running
through them: a continuity of writing, attitude, values, individuality and wit. Call it
Guardianesque for shorthand's sake. There is also a continuity of writers. Here in 1997's
collection is Harry Jackson, who first made an appearance in the 1966 *Bedside
Guardian*. Here is David McKie (first appearance 1977), Peter Preston (1965), Peter
Lennon and Simon Hoggart (1970). Alongside them are journalists in their early and
mid-twenties who have only just joined the paper, together with one who is still a
trainee.

That mix goes some way to explaining the Guardianesque quality of the *Guardian*.
How else can new recruits absorb the values and style of a newspaper unless through
osmosis from the old hands around them? You watch other newspapers, with their regular Augean purgings each time an editor or proprietor comes or goes, and wonder what
they are, beyond a masthead or a 'brand'. The *Guardian* has effectively been under the
same ownership since 1821. Its editors have traditionally been expected to stay the
course. That stability matters. One rival editor – beset by budget cuts, regular re-
launches and violent lurches up and down market in search of a viable circulation – said
that he had always imagined the entire staff of the *Guardian* could walk out at tea-time
and the paper would still appear: the building itself would produce it. There was both
frustration and envy behind the thought.

As these pages show, the year in question was a momentous one in the political life
of the country. It was also a pretty significant one in the life of the *Guardian* – a fact that
was not unrelated to the political climate. In the space of eight months – from November 1996 to June 1997 – the paper was at the centre of half a dozen bruising political and
legal battles, each one of which led to banner headlines throughout the country. The
period in question was the culmination of three years of reporting that saw the resignation of two Cabinet ministers and two junior ministers, and a flurry of official reports
and courtroom dramas which will keep the revisers of libel textbooks busy for a little
while yet. Five policemen tried, and failed, to recover damages against a newspaper for

having the temerity to report allegations of police corruption. Five former MPs were told that they would have been suspended from the Commons had they still been in office.

The sequence began, as it ended, with Neil Hamilton who, with his dynamic wife Christine, were surely the couple of the year. Mr Hamilton managed to overturn the 1689 Bill of Rights in order to sue the *Guardian*. His intention, along with his fellow conspirator, Ian Greer, had been to deprive the paper of £10 million in aggravated damages. Sadly, the two men fell out along the way. Documents obtained on discovery contained embarrassing material for both men. Their lawyers resigned and the case collapsed at the court door. Mr Hamilton announced that he would take his case instead to Sir Gordon Downey, the new Parliamentary Commissioner. Mr Greer turned to autobiography for his catharsis.

One of the documents turned up during the case seemed to show a former government whip – the then Financial Secretary, David Willetts – as having interfered in an earlier parliamentary inquiry into Mr Hamilton's affairs. Mr Willetts turned up to be quizzed by his colleagues armed with both brains but in want of common survival skills, or even common sense. He found himself skewered by one of his own side, the admirable Quentin Davies, and another ministerial career had bitten the dust.

The policemen came next. A massive inquiry into corruption in a single police station in London. Officers transferred, two eventually sent to jail. Cases overturned in the Court of Appeal. Huge damages paid out by the Metropolitan Police. And a trade union – the Police Federation – determined that newspapers should write about as little of this as possible. We were the ninety-sixth action the union had brought. The score in the previous ninety-five cases was 95 to the police: 0 to the media. It was a clear, and hitherto successful, policy of intimidation with a view to shutting down reporting the Police Federation disapproved of. With no thanks to the judge, but all thanks to a London jury, we won. Score: 95–1.

The election intervened. For reasons still never explained Mr Major arranged the proroguing of Parliament so that the Downey Report would tick away in a Whitehall safe rather than explode shrapnel over his party a month before polling day. The suspect MPs standing again were thus free to present themselves to the electorate claiming utter innocence even though we already knew that some of them had made significant confessions to Sir Gordon in private.

The *Guardian*, in the innocent belief that democracy depends on voting in the light, not the dark, decided to risk breaching parliamentary privilege by publishing those confessions. Sleaze thereby became the *leitmotif* of the first fortnight of the extended election campaign. Tim Smith resigned from his seat at Beaconsfield, but Neil and Christine Hamilton battled on, a decision which was to have a startling impact on the life and career of a white-suited BBC war correspondent.

Next came Jonathan Aitken with his trusty sword of truth intent on cutting out the cancer of bent and twisted journalism. This, like Hamilton, was a case due to last several weeks at the High Court. Like Hamilton, it collapsed suddenly with the plaintiff ignominiously withdrawing. Mr Aitken found himself impaled on his own trusty sword and fled to America, while here the police waited to interview him about his own understanding of the concept of truth.

Finally, there came the Downey Report – all 900 doorstopping pages of it. The man Hamilton said would vindicate him instead condemned him. The evidence that the Tatton MP had taken considerable sums of money from Mohamed Al Fayed was, he said, compelling, 'and I so conclude'. He painted a picture of greed and laxity at Westminster which should have made uncomfortable reading for those who had shrugged their shoulders all along. What we had been writing about was not corruption on a grand scale, but it was not nothing, either.

Mention should be made here of my predecessor, Peter Preston, who will surely be remembered not only as one of the great editors of the *Guardian*, but also as one of the great editors of the post-war period. These battles all had their roots in his editorship. He conducted them with a courteous but gritty resolve and those – such as Sir Robin Butler or Jonathan Aitken – who thought they could out-flank him or out-fox him severely misread the man. Lord Nolan and Sir Gordon Downey will have played their part in ensuring that British political life remains remarkably clean, but it was Peter who began it all.

In continuing and winning these wars I think we managed something else: a slight, but significant shift in perceptions of the press. Discussion of the media in Britain tends to be narcissistic and cynical. The narcissism is perhaps inevitable, the cynicism not always unhealthy. But months and years in which the overwhelming balance of commentary dwells on circulation wars, pricing strategies, marketing campaigns and tabloid excesses do little to nourish any sense that journalists can be motivated by considerations of public interest.

It helps if reporters and editors have some sense of history. There were plenty of lonely moments during this eight-month climax of scraps and battles, just as there were for Peter during the previous two years. The *Guardian* received much support from fellow journalists – but also, from others, a surprising trickle of toxic denigration. We learned the hard way that the sort of judges who sit in libel trials – and even in the higher courts – have given little thought to the press's role in keeping society informed about itself. In the same respect, politicians almost invariably disappoint. Any newspaper which directly challenges both Prime Minister and Parliament itself is in for a bumpy ride. It is some comfort for editors as they jolt along to be able to draw on the honourable history of the press in this country at other periods when newspapers have been pitched into conflict with Parliament or the courts. The letters of Junius – a contemporary of another formidable fighter, John Wilkes – are as resonant today as they were 200 years ago: 'They who conceive that our newspapers are no restraint upon bad men, or impediment to the execution of bad measures, know nothing of this country.' •

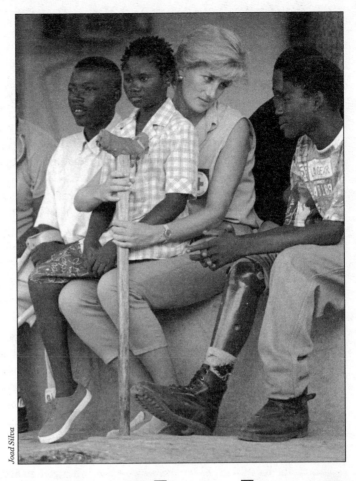

Diana: the last day of summer

1 September 1997

Lawrence Donegan
William, Harry and Charles

Three black limousines crawled up the hill to Crathie kirk at 11.30 a.m. In the first the Queen and Prince Philip, followed by a Daimler carrying the Prince of Wales and his sons, then the Queen Mother and other members of the royal family in the third.

Sunday mornings in Scotland have a long tradition for the royals. In the valley below the church, Balmoral castle's royal standard flapped at full mast. A spokesman explained that the Balmoral flag is never lowered, even for the death of the monarch.

Two small bunches of carnations, one red, one yellow, had been laid against the steps of the kirk's front door by members of the congregation.

The Queen was wearing a knee-length coat and simple hat, both in Presbyterian black, the Queen Mother too; Prince Charles, in full highland regalia and coping manfully with his emotions, wore a black tie, as did princes William and Harry. The other family members present, the Duke of York and Peter Phillips, sombrely and slowly helped the Queen Mother into the church.

As always the Queen stopped by the side door for a brief conversation with the royal chaplain, the Reverend Robert Sloan. Prince William stole a quick glance over his shoulder at the watching crowd. Prince Harry stared at the ground.

'I can't imagine that I would be so brave,' said Dorothy Brown, a regular visitor to Crathie in the summer months. 'I saw Diana here a few times. She was such a beautiful, wonderful woman – I will never forget her as long as I live.'

Inside the half-filled church, the service was conducted in an eerie normality, with notices about the open day which raised £2,100 for church funds, and a musical event in the parish later this week.

The Reverend Adrian Varwell, a visiting minister from the island of Benbecula, began proceedings with a prayer.

Mr Sloan took over, alluding immediately to the events in Paris in remembering 'all of those who at this time need to know your presence, God, all those whose lives are darkened by tragedy and grief, who need now more than human comfort and service. Where there is weakness you are our strength, in our darkness you are our light, in our sorrows you are our comfort and peace,' he said, bringing the service to an end.

But there was no mention of Princess Diana's name, an otherworldly omission on a day when her death dominated church services throughout the world.

Then the 100-strong congregation began to sing 'God Save the Queen' and Mr Sloan put his hands to his face in an effort to hold back tears. •

1 September 1997

Jonathan Freedland
The homecoming

I n the end, they let her go quietly. No drum, no funeral note – only a dumb silence as the body of Diana, Princess of Wales, returned to the land she might have ruled as queen.

There was no crowd to meet her, none of the hordes of flag-wavers she so delighted in life. Instead the flat, grey tarmac of RAF Northolt, windy as a prairie, a line-up of dignitaries – and a hearse.

She had made the journey from Paris by plane, on an RAF BAe 146. They kept the coffin in the passenger cabin, within sight of her two sisters, Lady Jane Fellowes and Lady Sarah McCorquodale, and her former husband, the Prince of Wales.

The skies themselves seemed to make way for her arrival, the clouds parting like an honour guard. Once the plane had landed, it nudged toward the welcoming party hesitantly, as if weighed down by its tragic cargo. Waiting there was the kind of receiving line Diana met every day. In the middle, arms by his sides, fists clenched tight, the Prime Minister. A cleric stood close by, bright in scarlet cassock. None of them said a word.

Eventually the plane door opened, and the Prince appeared head down, hands clasped behind his back. He was guided by the Lord Chamberlain, the Earl of Airlie. In another context it might have been a standard royal visit: Charles shown round a new factory or hospital wing. But he had come on a more baleful duty. He took his place in line – as he has done so often.

By now, the team of coffin bearers, each one in the crisp uniform of the Queen's Colour Squadron, had completed its precise march toward the other side of the aircraft. At the stroke of seven o'clock, the hatch opened revealing a glimpse of colour, the Royal Standard clinging to the hard, square outline of the coffin. It seemed an unforgiving shape: just a box, with none of the curve or sparkle of the woman whose body lay within.

The silence of the air was cut, and not just by the sound of distant traffic – which rumbled on, as if to prove that the clocks never stop, even for the death of a princess.

The air was filled with the *chickageev, chickageev* of the thousand camera lenses pointed at the scene ahead. Even now the world's telephoto eye was still staring at her, more focused than ever. Despite everything, everyone still wanted a piece of Diana. The cameras kept up their din, but there was an eerie silence from the men who held them. Once they would cry out, 'Diana! Diana!' – urging her to look their way or to flash just one more of those million-dollar smiles. But there was no shouting yesterday. And no smiles either.

The bearers of the body inched their way to the hearse. They stood, swivelled on their heels, and clasping tight with their white-gloved hands, lowered the coffin as smoothly as a hydraulic pump. They were about to turn away, but a bit of the flag was still spilling out; it had to be tucked in, just like the train of one of Diana's more lavish ball gowns.

The sisters stepped forward, each one turning to curtsy for the man whom Diana had once loved. Charles kissed each one before they stepped into the royal Daimler. The next car was filled with bouquets.

The Prince himself did his duty, talking to each one of the VIPs who had stood beside him. Tony Blair clasped both royal hands in a double handshake, nodding intently. Charles made a gesture with upturned palms, as if to say 'What can I do?' He thanked the RAF guard and disappeared back inside the plane, heading for Balmoral and his newly bereaved young sons. 'He's going back to the boys,' said his spokesman.

And then, on the final day of August, the sky darkened, and the wind whipped harder. It felt like the last day of summer, and the beginning of a long winter. •

1 September 1997

Ben Pimlott
'One of us'

I t is probably too early to get the whole thing into perspective. But one thing is clear. You cannot be a sentient human being and not feel grief and horror at Diana's death – the suddenness of it, the folly of it. The shots of people weeping in the streets spoke for many tears privately shed.

Too soon for profundity, but early enough to reflect on the meaning of the Princess's tragically brief life.

She was a very ordinary person. Ordinary in the sense that the neglect of her formal education had left her much closer in her attitudes to the majority than many cultured professionals, but also in the sense that she lacked preconceptions or pretensions – she took people, and the world, as she found them, and responded instinctively. Indeed, despite her own aristocratic origins, she lacked visible snobbery of any sort. An early, self-deprecating remark about being 'as thick as a plank' was far from the truth – everybody who knew her recalls the six-shooter precision of her wit, which may have been one of the problems with the slower Prince Charles. However, it expressed part of her appeal: she could talk directly to millions of people who, like her, seldom read the broadsheets.

Part of the appeal was a tactile quality. She was a toucher and a hugger. It is hard for a royal to be a good and close parent but she seemed to manage it. 'I hug my children to death and get into bed with them at night,' she was quoted as saying. People who saw her as a fantasy girlfriend or mistress, perhaps also really saw her as a fantasy mum. If there was a mawkish side to this image (cuddling a tearful Elton John at the Versace funeral), there was also a political one. At a time when American policemen broke up gay demonstrations wearing rubber gloves, she touched Aids victims without revulsion. Later, she reminded the world of the misery caused by landmines by sitting maimed Angolan children on her knee. The fact that she picked rough, controversial campaigns – not namby-pamby ones – irritated some politicians. But it gained her headlines, and fed public interest.

The woman whose faintly mocking smile launched a thousand glossy magazines, in her vanity and vulnerability and warmth, was one of us. She was part of the currency of everybody's social intercourse. People talked about her, as of nobody else, on the tops of buses, and at chattering classes' dinner parties. To lose her is to lose part of our collective selves.

Thus her death will affect how we view the royal family. It may briefly affect the media's treatment of royals, especially the younger ones least able to care for themselves. There are also constitutional implications, yet to be pondered. •

6 September 1997

John Vidal
The vigil

The traffic has calmed, the city lights have dimmed, and there is a profound stillness in central London as the long vigil continues into the small hours. Here at four in the morning in Kensington Gardens, thousands of people are walking slowly, arm in arm and in small groups, threading between the many thousands of impromptu candlelit shrines that have been created in every bowl of tree and on every crowd barrier.

The park has become an open-air temple for every denomination and creed. Its pillars and vaulted ceilings are the garlanded trees in full summer leaf, its walls the great black and gold railings, its transept an ocean of flowers in front of the main gates of the palace.

Every living thing has been dressed in freesias, dahlias, carnations, roses and sunflowers. The incense of 10,000 candles and joss sticks below the trees mixes with the blossom of a million blooms. London, the great maw of bustle, noise and diesel, is private and fragrant.

Ten thousand people, the police estimate, are queueing through the night and 10,000 more bunches of flowers line the Mall, adorning the statues, the Inigo Jones church and the roadside.

The Jones family came down from Birmingham, just jumped in the car at 11 p.m., no sleeping bags, blankets, thermos or umbrellas. Why? 'We had to be here.'

And so, via Buckingham Palace, pale and monstrous in the dying night, to the last station in the pilgrimage, Westminster Abbey. Here, the halogen bulbs that bathed the great entrance in a sepulchral light until midnight have been turned off.

One man has left his father in hospital and is praying his condition does not worsen. Jeffrey Fletcher has travelled all day from France. He has cancelled his wedding to an understanding French girl. Why is he here on the pavement? Because he was homeless and living on the London streets for four years and once Diana talked to him when the politicians, the state, the council, the institutions and everyone else who said they cared had failed him.

And here, at the last, is the touchstone of the phenomenon. The vigil is nearly over and a pale dawn comes over the Thames. We will never see this again, says one woman as she adjusts her blankets. 'It's a tidal wave we're seeing. Who knows where it will end?' •

8 September 1997

Nancy Banks-Smith
Hush, you team . . .

'Cover her face.
Mine eyes dazzle.
She died young.'
The Duchess of Malfi (by John Webster)

For the first time I remember, television seemed a second best. I would have liked to be part of it, to take part in it. Be where a million people were moving together, being moved together.

You can't, for instance, throw flowers at a TV screen. I have thrown ping-pong balls at it but that is another story.

Flowers were a powerful symbol of the public sorrow. Diana, like Proserpina, kidnapped by death, left a trail of fallen flowers which could be followed.

At Kensington Palace where, in a classically Freudian slip, David Dimbleby said, 'The Queen's body has been lying all night', the bees were having a bonanza in the sudden herbaceous border.

Somewhere en route to St James's one brash, pink, proletarian carnation, thrown at the gun carriage, stuck among the magnificent wreath of lilies. You could hear them putting their heads together. 'Who is it? Don't talk to it, Muriel. You don't know where it's been.'

Nothing abashed it or shook it off. Pink and perky, it was there as the six-foot guardsmen shouldered the lead coffin. It entered the Abbey without a by-your-leave. It left for Althorp in the hearse. For all I know, it is lying on the grave on the island in the lake. Somebody's thoroughly common or garden carnation.

As the hearse headed home surrounded – your skin prickled – by seven motorcyclists, showers of flowers were thrown like confetti. It soon began to wear a rackety hat like a battered Easter bonnet with all the flowers upon it. The driver, who seemed on the small side, was bouncing up and down trying to look over or peer through the flowers his windscreen wipers could not shift.

At Lord's, young lads, who will give Australia a fright one day, flung gladdies with wicket-shattering accuracy. At the start of the M1, startled road workers had an impromptu bouquet laid at their feet as the hearse's windscreen was cleared. The whole day was impromptu. 'We've been caught by surprise by everything,' said ITN.

Where Have All The Flowers Gone? could be rewritten as Where Did They All Come From? They all came from the people. Even on the inhuman motorway flowers rained on, fell off, fell under the hearse. Arthur C. Clarke, who ponders the mysteries of this and other worlds, might like to look into it.

The horses that pulled the gun carriage had had flowers thrown at them all week – and that is something else I would have liked to see – to accustom them to a rose up the nose. They advanced with muffled hooves like the surrey with the fringe on top bringing home a tired girl in Oklahoma. ('Hush, you team, my baby's a-sleeping. Hush, you team, and just keep a-creeping with a slow clip clop.') Prince Harry's round wreath, stuffed with plump buds and with Mummy written on it, looked like a child's cake. Sixteen years ago, when Lady Diana and Prince Charles did their first television interview, she talked about being sent small iced cakes from children. 'Covered with Smarties,' she said and laughed, being too young then, too young always, to know that one doesn't mention brand names.

Thinking themselves unobserved in the darkness of an arch, Earl Spencer patted Harry's shoulder encouragingly. Prince Philip touched William and snatched his hand away as if stung. (It may be said, on behalf of old-style stoicism, that this walk was not easy for him either. He is 75 and arthritic.)

There were four sudden bursts of applause from the congregation outside the Abbey. For Richard Branson, striding along on foot, waving cheerfully, wearing the tie no one knew he possessed. For Pavarotti, leaning heavily on two stick-thin young women and wearing an expression no one knew he possessed. For the Union Jack being lowered to half mast at Buckingham Palace. And for Earl Spencer, who has leaped on to the public stage with an exhilarating flash and bang.

After his speech (in which press and royals, to their mutual embarrassment, both got a piece of his mind), the crowd outside stood up and applauded with their hands above their heads. In the Abbey, Chris de Burgh, who had been giving a comradely thumbs-up to Elton John, heard the sound coming in the west door like a wave and rushing up the nave to the coffin. 'It made,' he said, 'your hair stand on end.' Unless, of course, you were Elton John.

People had been extremely quiet, all the reporters remarked on it. When they raised their voice, it raised your hair. There's a story in the Bible about Paul trying to preach in Ephesus but the Ephesians already had their own goddess. 'And all with one voice about the space of two hours cried out *Great is Diana of the Ephesians.*' And Paul gave up and got out. •

· ·

8 September 1997

John Ezard

Althorp

The A428, flanked by handsome parkland, was a world away from the intensity of London; but the people on it had the hallmark of great determination. To reach the two-mile stretch to Althorp for the end of Diana's consecrated journey, they first had to walk two miles from parking spots on remote lane verges. And their legs knew they faced the same trek back – elderly couples using sticks, quiet teenagers, mothers with wreaths, supermarket bags full of food, and already irritable children.

These were the townies among the 300,000 people on the seven-mile route from the M1. The locals infiltrated the traffic exclusion zone along bridle paths, under railway bridges and across ploughed fields.

Virtually all were unused to hiking. Although they joked as they went, they were driven by an impulse – part pious, part atavistic – like that which first wore a network of tracks along the ridgeways from northern England to Canterbury after Thomas à Becket was murdered in 1170. The English countryside was seeing a true pilgrimage: a journey by citizens in search of a meaning, or anxious to pay respect, or both.

At the Fox and Hounds pub in Harlestone, Colin Mold, 42, who works in double glazing, and his friend Mark Springett, 27, a used car dealer, said that seeing the Westminster Abbey service on television had helped ease what Colin called 'a sense of emptiness – absolutely amazing emptiness. All week I have felt I'm going to wake up and say, "What a horrible dream I've just had". A friend said it was like splitting up from the best girlfriend you've ever had and knowing you will never see her again.'

At the roadside near the gates of Althorp, a woman stood with her arm poised on the crush barrier ready to throw a posy of white flowers when the hearse passed. She stood like that, barely moving, for two hours.

At last a police escort helicopter appeared in the sky. Stillness and silence swept through the crowd like a cold wind. The hearse came down the hill; the woman cast her posy. To applause, the car vanished into the estate. The quarry for whom they had waited so decorously, so tenderly and with such effortful patience had gone to earth.

It was all over in 10 seconds. The crowd poured down the hill to the gates of Althorp, trying not to tread on the last, thrown roses. •

Wizards, bogeys and sinful breakfasts

....

17 December 1996

Matthew Norman
Diary of a hypochondriac

Tuesday: Once again, my medical dictionary has vanished. I last consulted it on Thursday regarding fascioliasis, a disease caused by liver fluke which occurs in sheep, cattle and other herbivorous animals. Now, however, when I have located a lump in the neck, the book has gone. My wife denies all knowledge. It is very odd: this is the third to disappear since March, without any logical explanation. Sometimes, it feels as though I am trapped inside an episode of *The Twilight Zone.*

Wednesday: More like a nodule than anything, the growth is to the right of the neck bone, an inch and a half from the base of the head. It moves horizontally when pressure is applied, and I fear it is a symptom of non-Hodgkin's lymphoma, the cancer that killed Marti Caine and that marvellous journalist (and gifted hypochondriac) Martyn Harris. But without the dictionary, however, it is hard to be certain.

Thursday: I have passed a deeply troubled night, riddled with nightmares from the specialists' consulting room. Martyn Harris described it brilliantly in the *Spectator* soon after he was diagnosed ... that classic Woody Allen scene in which the doctor snaps the X-ray on the light machine, and says, 'Well, Mr Allen, as you can see we have found something ...' And then Woody wakes from his daydream to hear that he is perfectly well. Only in his consultation, there was no daydream for Harris to wake from. This is the truly agonising thing about hypochondria: it is no defence whatever against illness and death.

Friday: I have passed another troubled night. In one dream, the doctor points at the X-ray and says, 'As you can see, Mr Norman, I'm afraid we have discovered three large tumours. I can't be certain until we have the results of the tests, but I'm pretty sure they are malignant medical dictionaries.'

Saturday: To begin the Christmas shopping, I go to a bookshop and return with a large carrier bag. 'Oh, what's this?' asks my wife, picking it up. 'No, don't look in there,' I say. 'It's presents for you.' But I am too late, and as she very slowly removes the books, one of our murderous silences descends. Finally, it is broken. 'For me, are they?' she says. '*Stop Ageing Now!* by Jean Carper. That's for me, is it? *Black's Medical Dictionary*, edited by G. Macpherson. For me?' She pauses for a moment and languidly cups the third, a paperback, in her left hand. 'Oh, you are clever, darling, it's just what I wanted,' she says. '*Living with Angina*, by Dr Tom Smith.' I begin to explain about the need to be prepared, but she is swift to leave the room.

Sunday: Tomorrow sees my second appointment with Dr Neil Frazer, who has taken over while my regular physician, Dr Sarah Jarvis, is off having her baby. During my first consultation, he told me that he is the doctor to nearby Queens Park Rangers FC. QPR, I recall, were relegated last season. What kind of omen is that?

Monday: A medical student in corduroy trousers sits in Dr Frazer's room when I arrive. Since the appointment will not involve disposable gloves, I do not object. Although already developing the glazed look familiar to Dr Jarvis, Dr Frazer is extremely thorough, examining the neck and then under each arm at some length. 'Nope,' he eventually declares, 'nothing at all. In fact, you're unusually gland-less. The lump in your neck,' he adds, 'is what we doctors call muscle.' Asked to be more specific, he mutters something that sounds like sternocleidomastoid. Concerned, I rush home to look this up. But the medical dictionary – which I last saw this morning at 4.30, when I put it down to go to bed – has gone. A weird sound pervades the sitting room. Do do doo dooooo, do do doo doooo, do do doo dooooo . . . Is it the wind swirling through an air vent, or the early stirrings of tinnitus? Or could it be the theme tune from *The Twilight Zone?* ●

30 December 1996

Veronica Horwell

Rebeccaaaagh!

My mother owned only one book, besides the Bible and a few film annuals, a novel, tiny print on cheap paper, with the incriminating remains of a date stamp for Plymouth Public Libraries stuck to its fly-leaf: *Rebecca*, byDaphne du Maurier. Mother knew it line by line; I took it up repeatedly. It was – it still is – our book in common.

Except for this: she adores it; I think it malign. I hated it at nine, 13, 17 and while re-reading it last Tuesday. She still pitches it as the perfect female romance. Since it has sold over a million copies in hardback, been in print almost 60 years, and is yet again a pop-prestige TV drama, hers is the majority, even official line. Only one friend has never read it, though she has seen Alfred Hitchcock's 1940 film. It is so familiar that Maureen Freely's ingenious novel, *The Other Rebecca*, reuses it as if it were fairy-tale.

So why do I loathe the 'perfect female romance'?

A smidgeon of background first. Daphne du Maurier was the daughter of the charismatic stage actor Gerald du Maurier. His casual mannerisms had enormous, subtle influence for other actors – including Laurence Olivier, the lead in Hitchcock's *Rebecca* – who adopted and adapted his nonchalance (used to express power), even his tap of a cigarette's end before lighting. Gerald's public style became a national, even an international, brand of masculinity.

But Daphne also knew his private moods of despondency and anger. Father and daughter were very close. He encouraged her to write. To do so, she stayed secluded in their country home, Ferryside, at Bodinnick-by-Fowey, in Cornwall. Smitten by desire for light, for melodramatic climate and for a cityless landscape, early-twentieth-century English painters settled on Cornwall's emphatic north coast, while celebrities who followed after preferred the warmth and lush growth of deep, sheltered south-coast estuaries. Daphne's first novel was a Cornish family saga; her second – a best-seller – *Jamaica Inn*, was very exact about brutal Bodmin Moor.

When it was published in 1936, Gerald was dead, Daphne married. Her husband, Major Frederick 'Boy' Browning, was a character Gerald might have aspired to play: a ruthless, reticent trench hero of the First World War (and an airborne commander in the Second – on landing near Nijmegen, it was Boy who said that the Arnhem operation had gone 'a bridge too far'). Beautiful, clever, insecure Daphne was wife to the best-turned-out officer in the British army, and a disciplinarian to (polished) boot. In England she coped, but in 1936 Boy was posted to Egypt. She had to go too. Unsociable Daphne was obliged to live by the rituals of a peacetime army. She knew that Boy's first fiancée, Jan Ricardo, had been better suited to the ceremonial life, and she was sick at heart for the gulls and rhododendrons of the Fowey estuary. So she wrote to escape the grit, Blancoed belts and bad cocktails, her jealousy, resentments and pregnancy. More than that, she wrote to release her 'No. 2 self', dark and violent. Her fantasies were more real than Egypt glaring outside the window. She wrote *Rebecca*.

That's why it leaves even resisting readers entranced: it must have been written in a self-hypnotic state. It is urgently told by a nameless narrator, a young, poor paid companion to a Riviera vulgarian. She is befriended by Maxim de Winter, twice her age, inheritor of the ancient Cornish house of Manderley, and whose celebrated wife Rebecca died in an accident. The narrator becomes the second Mrs de Winter, unhappy mistress of Manderley, where the housekeeper is Rebecca's devotee, Mrs Danvers. The narrator is told – she does nothing so active as discover – that the admired first marriage was a sham, agreed upon to prevent shaming the name of Manderley; that Rebecca was a sexual tramp whom Max shot when she tormented him with her pregnancy – not his baby. Maxim, at risk from a murder charge when a sabotaged boat and Rebecca's skeleton surfaces, learns that she despised sexual relationships; that she was not pregnant but terminally cancerous, and had goaded him into euthanasia. Suicide is publicly assumed; Mrs Danvers burns Manderley; the de Winters exit, subdued, to exile.

The book's lineage is interesting. It shares its snobbery about ownership and name with half the novels in *The Oxford Companion to Eng Lit*. Its old house of honour and secrets, set in a landscape now mist, now sun, now rose garden, now rocks, was patented by Mrs Radcliffe, the eighteenth-century Gothic novelist with a talent for literary property (let's be tolerant about Manderley being too stately and Knole-like to be plausibly on the Cornish coast). The hero whose desirability is in his pride and discretion about tragic secrets is ultimately derived from Byron. Rebecca is an early – and English – version of a character familiar from American pop literature (and film noir) – the femme fatale, her beauty alluring despite, perhaps because of, her sexual predatoriness and cruelty: the 'she was evil, I tell you, evil, so I killed her' style flashback predates most other print or film examples. And the narrator is usually thought a reworking of Charlotte Brontë's Jane Eyre.

Well, perhaps Daphne did borrow plain clothes and uncurled hair from Jane. But Jane Eyre, like her creator, was a woman made fierce by privation, passion, information gleaned from books and knowledge painfully gained from observation and experience. In poverty and isolation, Jane is stronger, more generous than any man she meets. *Rebecca*'s narrator is the most passive of print females, a masochistic drip who makes Joan Didion's zonked zombies read like Joan of Arc.

Margaret Forster, in her biography of Daphne, perceived that the latter believed she should have been a boy but felt compelled to hide her masculine aspects, revealing them only in writing. And I suppose that is why I hate *Rebecca* so. Every woman in it is despised by its true authorial voice. The narrator is made to hate herself for her virginity, which Max de Winter uses as solace and restorative; her sole later purpose is to comfort him, to prevent remembrance past clouding his face. Rebecca behaves as boldly and bravely as a man, and pays for it not only by death but in the contempt readers are conned into pouring on her. Mrs Danvers is a sinister manipulator and broken but vengeful woman. No female – bluff sister, petulant grandmother, frivolous bishop's wife – is spared the author's scorn; yet the men – a murderer, a blackmailer and official perverters of justice – are all let off. They're decent, sexy, or both; it was the woman did tempt them, and they did eat . . .

Mother, next time there's an amnesty on library books, send that copy back – it's only 50 years overdue. And as for a perfect female romance – can I recommend *The Silence of the Lambs*? ●

· ·

8 January 1997

Francis Wheen

We're not off to see the Wizard after all

Dozens of readers have written in to confirm my suspicion that *The Wizard of Oz* is a far more dangerous and subversive film than *Crash*. 'Did you know,' asks Ted Wilson, a history lecturer at Manchester Metropolitan University, 'that

Wizards, bogeys and sinful breakfasts

The Wizard of Oz was written as an allegory of the Democratic campaign of 1896?' I'm ashamed to say that I didn't.

L. Frank Baum, the author, was a bimetallist – a supporter of the reintroduction of silver into the American currency – and thus an opponent of monetary union with Britain via the gold standard. According to Wilson, the Lion represents William Jennings Bryan, the radical Democratic Party candidate of 1896, who 'roared' his speeches against British imperialism, the gold standard and alcohol. Dorothy (the spirit of the West) and her dog Toto (an abbreviation of 'teetotaller') join the scarecrow (an agricultural worker) and the tin man (an industrial worker who has been unemployed for so long that his joints have seized up) on the Yellow Brick Road (gold, geddit?) to the Emerald City (New York and its greenback dollars) to plead for reform.

The Wizard, in case you were wondering, probably represents Marcus Hannah, the original Republican spin doctor, and Dorothy's silver slippers – changed to ruby by Hollywood – denote the bimetallic ratio which can solve all the country's economic problems. Rather ingeniously, Wilson suggests that the film ought to appeal to Eurosceptics, since Dorothy and her mates are intent on detaching the great republic from the grasping hands of European bankers and financiers, who were responsible for the depressions of the 1990s.

While I am digesting this allegorical banquet – and trying to picture Bill Cash, John Redwood and Teresa Gorman as a chorus of Munchkins – another letter arrives. 'Did you know,' asks Peter White, a reader from Leicester, 'that showings of *The Wizard of Oz* have been stopped in this country?' Shortly before Christmas he took his daughters to a long-advertised Saturday afternoon showing at a local cinema, the Phoenix, only to discover that it had been cancelled. The explanation was that the American media mogul Ted Turner had recently acquired the rights and was refusing all requests for screenings.

By happy coincidence, Turner also owns the firm that distributes *Crash* in America and for a few weeks last autumn he banned all screenings of that as well. The canny fellow then cashed in on the ensuing publicity by allowing the film to go out after all, while continuing to insist that it was a despicable piece of work. He claimed, feebly, that the decision to release *Crash* had been taken over his head – as if he were some mere understrapper or boxwallah.

Why does he now wish to suppress *The Wizard of Oz*? Is he, perhaps, a secret supporter of the gold standard? Alas, no: he simply realised that he could boost his profits by flogging the movie exclusively to American cable and satellite channels. 'Personally, I am at a bit of a loss to know how he can make money in the States by stopping my daughters in Leicester seeing a film,' White adds. 'But I dare say that is just one of the reasons why I am not a billionaire.'

I dare say it is also why Peter White is not married to Jane Fonda. •

16 April 1997

Peter Lennon
Just an average punchbag

Every day I came home from school my parents would ask, 'How many biffs did you get today?' It was the 1940s and I was going to one of the most celebrated Christian Brothers' schools in Ireland, Dublin's Synge Street. I was not an unruly pupil, nor was I slow to learn. I was just your average punching bag for Edmund Ignatius Rice's band of unpolished pedagogues.

Physical collision was their preferred method of terrifying knowledge into you. The entire nation accepted this behaviour and, when it occasionally got out of hand, the explanation was that the poor men (not the unfortunate victim) 'didn't have the consolation of the Mass' and they were exonerated. People were more discreet about the fact that neither did they have the consolation of a concubine.

In those days we would have gone white and called a doctor if a Christian Brother apologised for past aggression and abuse, like the new leader of the order, Edmund Garvey, yesterday. I am sure all us ex-Synge Street boys appreciate the symbolism of making the statement in Drogheda, renowned for having displayed the Blessed Oliver Plunkett's head on a spike, a position I had reserved for many years for brothers Phelan, Ryan, Kelly and 'Winkles'. The routine instrument of punishment was 'the leather', a stocky object about eight inches long, made of four or five layers of tightly stitched leathers. When it became flabby they would stitch in coins to harden the tip.

You would stand out in front of the class, the brother swinging his fist high, skirts and sleeves flying like Mandrake the Magician. Then you had a sensation on your palm of being stung by a dozen bees. More dreaded was the pointer, a long polished wooden stick, thick at one end, pointed at the other. This would be brought down on your fingers with a crack that shot agony from skull to heel.

The beatings went on from the age of about seven to 13. The reason it stopped at 13 was tactical: by 14, boys were big, broad, muscular and bolshie, and stories of a heroic adolescent finally flooring a Christian Brother were undoubtedly behind the sudden man-to-man relationship in senior school.

Since this was a day school, there were no instances of serious sexual abuse, but some teachers were known 'messers'. One came a cropper publicly. He was one of those ingratiating creatures with an oily benevolence who liked to make boys who did not know their lessons stand with him at his desk and, cooing reproaches, he would put his hand up your short trousers. One day he chose the wrong boy: a big lad, redoing his year for about the third time. Standing half hidden by the desk beside the stooping, fawning brother, he suddenly roared out, 'Jaysus, he's got me by the bollicks.'

The unfortunate man had a nervous breakdown. I can't say I wish for Edmund Ignatius Rice's band of terrorists a fate worse than that which, by now, has no doubt befallen many of them: oblivion. •

. . . .

17 February 1997

Matthew Norman
Diary

With the anniversary of rail privatisation comes evidence that service on trains is better than ever. For some, at least. A reader travelling to Plymouth on the 6.15 a.m. from Paddington walked into a first-class compartment and found Rail minister John Watts eating breakfast with his civil servants. Dining-car staff were not normally on the train, a steward explained, but an exception had been made for the minister. In Plymouth, and on a full stomach, Mr Watts treated the Valentine's Day conference (Shagger Norris would have gone, of course, were he still at Transport) to ecstatic praise of the railways' improved performance in the last year. And no wonder. After all, for transport ministers, the service could scarcely be better. •

. . . .

1 March 1997

Keith Harper
Rail firms aim to lure travellers with sinful breakfast

Forget the traditional English breakfast on the newly privatised railway. Welcome aboard to the breakfast of the future, the Ten Deadly Sins, a magnificent blow-out for the traveller at around £14. Kidney and liver will be added to the eight ingredients already familiar to the 400,000 people who eat breakfast on the train each year.

The new menu was revealed yesterday on platform one at Euston station by the company which is developing services for train-operating companies in the UK and Europe. Mike Smith, marketing director of European Catering Services, said there was enough room on the plate for the new ingredients to sit alongside bacon, sausage, scrambled egg, black pudding, mushrooms, sauté potatoes, grilled steak and fried bread. 'It's a meal to last the whole day,' he said.

Before Ten Deadly Sins comes the Prego express trolley, a new concept in hot food which can be brought to the passenger's seat. Trials begin on South West Trains' services between Waterloo and Southampton.

For between £75,000 and £100,000, enterprising train operators can fit out their carriages with an on-board continental-style café. But if that is too expensive, they will be able to lease the equipment or sign a contract.

ECS's managing director, Terry Coyle, said that the café 'boasts the smells, sounds and atmosphere of an Italian coffee bar, serving authentic espressos, plus delicious different bread products prepared at on-station bakeries'. SWT has already signed up to this idea, said Mr Coyle. 'It means that their passengers will be able to board the train, put down their luggage and relax at the bar without having to rush for a coffee in the station. It will make the journey more fun.'

One of his colleagues said, 'We have come a long way from the curled-up sandwich and the stewed cup of tea.' •

1 February 1997

Stephen Bates
New Euro-myth from Old Hack

Deep in the bowels of the Old Hack pub in the seedy part of Brussels' European district, Dennis Newson, a veteran correspondent for Britain's tabloid papers, was yesterday celebrating a triple triumph in the creation of yet another Euro-myth.

Three British tabloids took his story about the European Union insisting on statues of former Commission president Jacques Delors being erected all along Britain's motorways.

Dennis explained, 'I wrote a piece of whimsy. It's legitimate to speculate, isn't it?'

Nevertheless, the piece of whimsy made the *Daily Star* ('Statue Up There Jacques?') and a page lead in the *Daily Mail* ('Danger – Statue of Delors Ahead'), together with an incongruous photograph of Delors's head superimposed on a classical statue.

Most satisfactory of all, there was a splash in the *Sun* under the heading 'You Daft Bustards', together with a leader suggesting, 'They've finally gone off their rockers in Brussels' and an article in which former Tory leadership contender John Redwood speculated that Brussels might force British taxpayers to pay for a statue of the European Commissioner and former Labour leader Neil Kinnock.

Even the BBC picked up the story for a time. The only niggling trouble was that, as with previous tabloid tales such as the straight banana story (about the Commission allegedly insisting that bananas should not bend) and the fable about fishermen being forced to wear hairnets, it was, as the *Sun* might say, complete B*******s.

The story arose out of Resolution 18, passed by the European Parliament, including British MEPs, the previous day, which calls on the Commission to regulate that up to 1 per cent of the funding for public works receiving EU money should go towards art-works to embellish the project.

It is an old idea already in force in parts of Europe, such as Germany, and might on the face of it be considered a harmless wheeze. The Victorians after all used to decorate their town halls with statuary. There is nothing about statues, or about great Europeans, not even about Monsieur Delors.

Nor was it an idea dreamed up by bureaucrats. Nor will it necessarily come to pass. It has to go before the Commission, which is highly unlikely to take it up. But if the Commission did do so it would then have to be passed to a Council of Ministers' meeting, for approval by, among others, a British cabinet minister, before getting the go-ahead.

A Commission spokesman said yesterday, 'It stands as much chance of becoming law as Jacques Delors does of becoming the British prime minister. The story is potty.'

Dennis, who owns the Old Hack, said, 'My story was a report of the parliament's vote. From that it is not a very large step to say that it may just be possible that the works of art might just possibly be of Euro-worthies, and who might be considered more of a Euro-worthy than Jacques Delors?' •

* *

3 April 1997

Lisa Buckingham
Insurer zaps its alien cover

The company which insured the 39 members of the Heaven's Gate cult against being abducted by aliens said yesterday it would stop offering the extraordinary cover because of feelings of guilt.

Simon Burgess, managing director of the insurance broker which has made a spe-ciality of bizarre covers, such as policies against immaculate conception, said he was saddened at the loss of life.

The members of the Heaven's Gate cult died in an apparent mass suicide last week at a multi-million-dollar mansion on the outskirts of San Diego, California, in the hope of being transported to another planet by aliens following in the trail of the Hale-Bopp comet.

According to Mr Burgess's company, Goodfellow Rebecca Ingrams Pearson (GRIP), the members of the cult took out their insurance cover on 10 October in the name of The Higher Source, the name of its Internet web-site, at a $1,000-a-year premium.

Mr Burgess told the Press Association that the group of big British insurers who back his policies could lose $39 million (£24 million) if a US coroner's court delivers an open verdict on the affair, opening the way for families of the cult members to claim up to $1 million per head.

GRIP – which has provided weird insurance for the past 15 years, such as cover against turning into a vampire or werewolf – said the cult members had probably found out about the policy from its site on the Internet.

According to Mr Burgess, about 4,000 clients around the world have taken out policies for eventualities involving aliens, though others took advantage of earthier protection, such as loss-of-earnings insurance for prostitutes who have been stricken by headaches and backaches.

Unfaithful husbands have also been signing up to protect themselves against 'Bobbitting' – a policy developed after John Bobbitt of Virginia had his penis severed by his wife in 1993.

Mr Burgess said withdrawal of the more outlandish covers would cut income by £1 million a year but the group was happier concentrating on its mainstream redundancy and disability business. •

••

4 August 1997

Dan Atkinson
Mutton dressed up as lamb

One definition of ageing may be the sensation of realising that what at first seems a novel development is, in fact, the opening phase of a revival of something, the fag-end of which one can just about remember.

Such a dud goes under the name of regional development agencies. Last week, the big news of the moment was the new 'strategic' (expensive and useless) authority for London and a beefed-up, 'accountable' identity for the English economic regions.

Apparently, the agencies will be held to account by indirectly elected councillors representing the constituent authorities of each zone. On hearing this, the old dodderers among us blew the dust from an HMSO document dated June 1969, titled Royal Commission on Local Government in England, chairman the Rt Hon Lord Redcliffe-Maud. Word for word, dot for dot, it is all in there, with the exception that John Prescott's 'regions' were then called 'provinces'. And what wonderful things these provinces would do for their local economies! Declining industries would be monitored, new universities sited, airports opened, economic growth sponsored and a 'strategic plan' would pull it all together, simultaneously settling 'the framework and order of priorities' while consisting of an 'evolving series of objectives and policies'.

Just as with today's regional development agencies, the provincial councils would be made up of indirectly elected local councillors and, just as must be suspected with today's authorities, the provinces 'must have their own staff, in their direct employment'. Well, of course, and the more the merrier. One sure way to arrest declining employment prospects in a depressed region is to take on lots of people to monitor . . . declining employment prospects. In 1969 and 1997, the idea is the same: big is beautiful. One thing hasn't changed. Twenty-eight years ago, as now, we learned: 'The work at provincial level will not call for large staffs.'

It's the way they tell them. •

....

30 April 1997

David McKie

One jump ahead of the queue

Thehe civic authorities in decorous Thameside Abingdon have published a brochure offering advice to foreign visitors on how to comport themselves in this ancient town. One local convention forcefully emphasised is the British belief in the queue. 'In Britain it is traditional to queue for buses and for service in shops and cafés,' says the guide. 'Ignoring queues is seen as very bad manners and may cause problems.'

That may still apply in Abingdon, but to anyone who lives in London, or probably any town of substantial size, it reads like something out of the 1940s. The institution of queueing smacks of the post-war settlement, the Labour victory of '45, food rationing, Sir Stafford Cripps's austerity programme, and men in hats with cigarettes gripped between nicotined fingers speculating on Burnley's chances of winning the Cup.

The queue speaks of egalitarian values, not much in vogue today. It is predicated not just on equality of opportunity, but on equality of outcome, a phrase which in this election has not crossed the lips of anyone much younger than the new Lord Hattersley.

Observe any handy bus stop, once a place where people queued in orderly fashion. The stop bore the legend 'Queue this side' and everyone dutifully did. The bus stop will still have a queue, made up of the old and weary. But several related clusters will have gathered about it. Over there, pretending to gaze acquisitively at the windows of Freeman, Hardy and Willis – no, that's probably closed; make it Shellys – is a gaggle of schoolgirls. Watch what they do as the bus approaches at last (it is 10 minutes late and virtually full already). Do they barge their way to the front of the queue? No, they're much more subtle than that. They take up their station a pace or two beyond it and wave the first half-dozen legitimate queuers ahead in a manner which indicates both courtesy and eagerness to comply. Then, as if at a given signal, they queue-jump the rest.

There used to be in privileged Esher, Surrey, an old-fashioned Sainsbury's, the kind where the counters had marble tops and you queued first for bacon, then further along the counter for butter and finally a third time for jam. The élite of Esher would swan their way to the front of these queues where the counter staff would greet them, not with rebuke, but with grovelling servility.

That kind of thing is less easy to practise in supermarkets, but it still seems to work on the roads. Where an outbreak of cones obstructs a highway and a rash of notices warns that two carriageways will shortly reduce to one, most motorists, brought up in the tradition of queueing, let their vehicles interweave: one from our queue, then one from yours. There is always someone, however, who roars past in the outside lane with the bass on the CD player pumping away and then tries to barge in at the last possible moment. The odd brave soul attempts to strike a blow for egalitarian values by trying to squeeze him out. But you know he will always succeed: if he didn't, he wouldn't do it.

It is time for the rest of continental Europe, which used to admire our stoic self-discipline, to abandon such romantic delusions. The spokesman for St Niklaas in Belgium, for instance, which is one of five towns twinned with Abingdon. 'I have always been astonished at the well-mannered way in which the English wait to have their turn,' he told the *European* the other day. 'The English system is a way of showing respect to other people.' In his own country, 'when a bus arrives, 10 youngsters attack it, and the old lady who has been waiting half an hour is the last to get on'.

Get off your knees, you Belgians. Perhaps in the era of ration books and Burnley winning the Cup you had something to learn from the British in this context. But not, I fear, for much longer. •

* * *

6 December 1996

Stuart Millar

Last march of Colonel Bogey

Colonel Bogey was a staple of Northlew Silver Band's concert repertoire for more than 60 years. But the north Devon church concert and summer fête circuit will never be the same after a coup by young members ousted the definitive military march and the village band's veteran musical director in the name of progress.

In a classic example of 'artistic differences', rebels told Percy Adams, aged 78, he would have to go because his old-fashioned tastes were putting off new recruits and forcing the band into stagnation. Mr Adams, a farmer and grandfather, had devoted his

Wizards, bogeys and sinful breakfasts

entire life to the band since joining in the 1930s. He rose through the ranks, playing cornet, tenor horn and trombone before taking over as bandmaster in 1971. Since then he has chosen every tune the 20-piece band played.

The dispute came to a head at a meeting to plan the Christmas concert in the village hall, the most

Brassed off

Top five brass band tunes

Percy Adams	The Young Turks
1: Colonel Bogey	1: All You Need is Love, *The Beatles*
2: Onward Christian Soldiers	2: Let It Be, *The Beatles*
3: Jerusalem	3: YMCA, *Village People*
4: Old Rugged Cross	4: Eye of the Tiger, *Survivor*
5: How Great Thou Art	5: Super Trooper, *Abba*

glittering date in the band's calendar. The youngsters demanded that they be allowed to play dangerously modern music such as the Beatles and Village People, but Mr Adams insisted they stick to military marches and rousing hymns. They responded by offering to draw up his resignation letter.

Yesterday, Mr Adams announced he would boycott the concert. 'I am upset and disappointed at the way they have done it,' he said. 'I'm not young and if they waited I could not have gone on for much longer. When they asked me to resign it came as a shock . . . I think one or two of them wanted my job and that is why they kicked me out.'

He said he preferred 'proper' old brass band music. 'There are no tunes in the stuff they wanted to play. I don't remember much of what they asked for, but there was stuff from the Beatles and a pop song called "YMCA". It was all the new-fangled pop stuff they wanted.'

Mr Adams denied he had been too dogmatic in his musical preferences. 'We did play some modern pieces. We did one called "Love Changes Everything" or something like that.'

None of the rebels could be contacted yesterday, but the band's chairman expressed regret at the outcome. 'Some members wanted to play modern up-tempo music and Mr Adams did not, which is understandable for someone of his age, but he was stopping the rest of the band from doing so.'

He said they had tried to reach a compromise that would allow the band to play up-to-date pieces while Mr Adams would continue to conduct the older ones. 'In the end there seemed to be no compromise available and he was asked to resign. No one wants to chuck out someone who has served the band for 62 years and we very much regret what has happened.' •

18 July 1997

Jon Henley

Mystery bogey exorcised at last

Summer colds do not come much heavier than Goran Rudolfsson's. For four weeks the retired teacher had sneezed his way around the town of Hoverberg on Sweden's west coast with sinuses blocked and head buzzing. Until one day last week, when he spent half an hour pulling a yard-long strip of wadding out of his head.

'I was getting desperate,' Mr Rudolfsson said yesterday. 'It was miserable. It wasn't normal; I'd tried nasal sprays and decongestants and everything. Then on Friday I was blowing my nose again, and I felt something move.' An exploratory finger up the left nostril revealed the cause of the trouble. 'I thought, well, that's a bit odd,' he said. 'I tugged, and some came out. I tugged more, and some more came out. So I went to the bathroom, and tugged and tugged, and it took about 30 minutes but eventually it all came out. Amazing, really.'

The wadding – 31 inches long and an inch wide – had been left in Mr Rudolfsson's head by an absent-minded brain surgeon during a tumour operation he underwent in June. A spokeswoman at Umeaa University Hospital, where the operation had taken place, said such oversights were rare.

'Fortunately no harm seems to have been done,' she said. 'We have apologised to Mr Rudolfsson and thanked him for returning the cloth to us. He had washed and ironed it.'

The senior surgeon, Goran Algers, told *Lanstidningen* newspaper that the incident was 'clearly unacceptable, by any standards'.

But Mr Rudolfsson was delighted: 'The operation was successful, and I could sort the other problem out myself. You can't really blame the doctors — it was only a small mistake. They could have lopped off the wrong leg, or an ear.' •

30 January 1997

Martin Wainwright

And, in the name of work experience, I thee wed

Britain's army of teenagers on work experience – already responsible for stitching up hospital wounds and reporting on murder trials – has broken yet more controversial new ground. Acting on the 'Go for it' guidelines of career officers, an 18-year-old theological student stepped in to conduct a young couple's wedding, when a muddle over timing led to the vicar arriving an hour late.

Although the fresh-faced amateur priest did a technically excellent job, slipping Rodney Earnshaw's ring on to Shirley Wilson's correct finger and cruising through the responses, his initiative ended in disaster.

'We're terribly sorry,' said a Wakefield diocesan voice on the phone to the Earnshaws a week after the £8,000 ceremony in Golcar, near Huddersfield. 'But the lad wasn't ordained; in fact he'd only just got his A-levels. You're not husband and wife in the eyes of either God or the law.'

Rodney and Shirley are suing for the cost of a new wedding, but yesterday expressed grudging admiration for the unnamed student who was doing work experience as a server, or church assistant.

Rodney, a night-shift worker aged 25, said, 'I thought the lad was a bit young but he was incredibly believable and we had no reason to doubt him.'

The vicar, the Reverend Robin Townsend, arrived at St John the Evangelist's church at the end of the ceremony, after the teenager, who had stepped in out of a sense of Christian duty, had confidently asked more than 100 guests if they knew of any just cause or impediment to the proceedings.

The Reverend Townsend, standing in for St John's incumbent Reverend Martin Crompton, who was away, said he had not been informed of a time change and had watched the final moments at the altar aghast.

'To say that I was surprised that the wedding had gone ahead is an understatement – I was shocked and horrified,' he said. 'I haven't a clue who the lad is. The whole thing is very unfortunate and I am very sorry for the couple.'

The Bishop of Wakefield, the Right Reverend Nigel McCullough, said he was distressed by the turn of events, but could not elaborate because legal proceedings were expected. The church has offered to waive the fee for a second wedding, but the couple's solicitor, John Bodnar, said that without compensation they could not afford the dress, flowers, reception and photographer which had made the original ceremony memorable.

Shirley, who works for a make-up company and is also 25, said the day had indeed been memorable. 'It's not something you would ever consider to happen. The biggest day of our lives was totally shattered.' Mr Earnshaw agreed, but added, 'Everything was a blur at the wedding. I've really no idea who married us.' •

The long goodbye

....

25 January 1997

Michael White

An old roué rides to the rescue

Safely ensconced behind the Norman walls of Saltwood Castle again after a week's nocturnal canvassing in London, the new Conservative candidate for Kensington and Chelsea is purring like one of his expensive motor cars. But not as discreetly.

'The very first congratulations I got on my answering machine was from Alastair,' he chortles.

That was jolly nice of the Government Chief Whip, I venture. 'No, not Alastair Goodlad, Alastair Campbell,' says Alan Clark, politician and diarist, Thatcherite and philanderer.

It is that kind of detail which makes Alan Clark such an interesting candidate, the very thought of his trouble-making return to Westminster enough to cheer some MPs of all parties as much as it will alarm and depress others. The journalist in Tony Blair's press secretary must have seen the sheer fun of it.

But the press secretary in the journalist will also have made Mr Campbell see the possibilities. Excalibur, Labour's rebuttal computer, will be working overtime this weekend to dredge up all those cuttings about Bongo Bongo Land, the 'coven' of seduced Harkness women, his 'economy with the *actualité*' over arms sales to Iraq. All that and those *Diaries* – which he is still keeping!

At 68, Mr Clark is five years older than Sir Nicholas Scott, the sitting (indeed falling) MP he was picked to succeed at Thursday night's meeting of 1,000 or so members of the richest, safest Tory association in England.

The very thought that the Government, the party machine or the whips' office would welcome his selection sets him off again. He has good reason to believe they were keen to stop him. But he is used to that.

'I've done 200 party speaking engagements, God knows how many TV things. I write all the time. Don't they realise there is an asset that might be useful here? There were 1,200 Conservatives present. They know everything about me. They listened and they voted. It reminds me of my first selection in Plymouth in 1974,' he says. 'I said then "I owe my entire political career to Ted Heath."' It seems that the then prime minister wrote to the local agent, saying, 'In no circumstances must Alan Clark enter the House of Commons.' The agent showed it to the constituency president, says Mr Clark, 'and Open Sesame'.

How had he pulled off Kensington and Chelsea?

'It was masterly,' he admits. The last to speak among Thursday's four finalists, he had modestly told them, 'It's very good of you to wait', and then launched into a digression about why politicians kiss babies. 'To improve their ratings. If any of you saw me rush across and kiss a baby it was my own baby grandson, 15 months old and probably the youngest member of the association.'

Yuk? Yes, but less so from a man whose *Diaries* make Pepys sound monogamous. When Simon Hoggart reviewed them for the *Observer*, he noted that Clark appeared to be a faithless man obsessed with his wife, Jane, whom he wooed and wed at 16, when he was 30. Sure enough: 'I then introduced Jane, who said a few words. She played it brilliantly. Without her I'd be done – so sweet, so pretty, so fresh, a counterbalance to [pause] my slightly roué image.'

He was, he insists, 'the candidate for the left. You'd never expect that, would you?' By that he means he wooed members of the left-leaning Scott camp, who wanted some panache and style, as well as Euro-sceptic weirdos who had been trying to bring Sir Nick down for years, before he did it unaided in a Bournemouth gutter.

Having lost the Sevenoaks nomination and Tunbridge Wells, he'd led all the way this time. The vote went to a third ballot only because he had to get 50 per cent.

Yes, Alan, but why you? 'They want candour, they want a new look at the way the party works, the way voluntary activists can get their feelings through to MPs.'

That was why Chelsea ignored advice – too rich, self-confident and powerful to take any nonsense, Chelsea's new man says. His task is to 'heal the divisions'.

'It was an extraordinary coup. The candidate with the so-called drawbacks was selected for the strongest Conservative division in the country. I've been on animal rights picket lines, I've been abusive to the police, I'm a recognised green eccentric.'

What will John Major think? Mr Clark was a passionate Thatcherite whose letter of support to Mr Major in the 1990 campaign was mislaid by a drunken reporter. By his standards he has been loyal since.

'Some people say he hates me. I don't know whom he hates or loves. I like him, I like everyone.'

The campaign has cost him half a stone, lost appetite and sleep. The man is 68 after all. Had he asked his doctor's permission? 'He checks my blood pressure once a year. "A man of 50 would love a print-out like this," he told me. I've got three uncles over 90 still alive and I can read the price/earnings ratio in the *Wall Street Journal* without glasses.'

And the election? Can the Tories win? 'I could win it.' Pause, and a note of hesitation. You sense he thinks it's too late, but will not say so. The statesman's mood will pass quickly enough at Saltwood.

He is not a man to spot a tempting groin without wanting to kick or caress it. •

....

27 January 1997

Larry Elliott

Back to the future

I t was raining on Budget night in March 1988, but the City gents packed into a taxi edging its way up the Strand did not care. They were swilling champagne and puffing on six-inch Havanas to celebrate Nigel Lawson's decision to cut the top rate of tax to 40p in the pound.

Lawson's 1988 Budget was the high point of the decade that began on 2 April 1982 with General Galtieri's troops invading the Falklands. Coming at the end of the 1980–81 slump, the war against Argentina coincided with a period of sustained economic growth that spawned two landslide Conservative victories.

The decade's close can also be precisely measured. By the time Saddam Hussein's troops annexed Kuwait in August 1990, the economy was heading into recession, precipitated by a ferocious, two-year monetary squeeze.

For the right, this eight-year period was the time that revolutionised Britain, making industry more competitive and individuals more prosperous. Despite the misjudgements of the Lawson boom, it encompassed all the main structural reforms of the Thatcher era – privatisation, the abolition of the GLC and trade-union curbs.

The left has always been wary of these claims. It rejected the idea that much had changed, claiming the 1980s were a time of wasteful unemployment, growing inequality, underinvestment and de-industrialisation. Even more virulent was the battle over the 1980s' zeitgeist, the mix of materialistic individualism and social Darwinism that underpinned the Thatcherite credo. Madonna, a singer of modest talent but plenty of marketing aptitude, appropriately summed up the decade's glittery shallowness.

For much of the 1990s, the anti-1980s tendency was in the ascendant. But over the past year or so, 1980s supporters have been biting back. Viewed in an international context, British economic performance looks pretty good. With the French and Germans starting to embrace deregulation, the conclusion has been that we got it right and they got it wrong.

Revisionism has been under way on the left, as well. Tony Blair said last week, 'There are things the 1980s got right. But we need to change what the 1980s failed to do or made worse.'

Broadly, the debate about the economy in the 1980s should focus on three areas – macro-economic policy, the supply side and the spirit of the age. Macro-economic policy was supposed to kill off inflation. But it did not work out that way. Nigel Lawson admits that the most serious policy mistake of his time as Chancellor was the failure to spot the way in which financial deregulation would lead to an explosion in credit-based consumption. But of course the impact of this error was accentuated by the legacy of the slump of the early 1980s, when Mr Lawson was the lieutenant to Margaret

Thatcher in her crazed monetarist period.

As any economics student could have foreseen, chopping back the supply side of the economy and then boosting demand through financial deregulation could have only one consequence: inflation. And so it proved.

Lawson's boom in turn spawned the monetarist overkill at the end of the 1980s, crowned by the biggest cock-up of all, the decision to join the ERM in 1990. As a result, the Conservatives have been responsible for a most extraordinary bust-boom-bust cycle.

So, if 1980s macro-economic policy stands condemned, what about the supply side? Britain's investment deficit with other industrial nations – which predates Mrs Thatcher by decades – has persisted into the 1990s. No analysis of 'what needs to be done' is complete without the assertion that the UK has under-invested in capacity, both physical and human, has spent too little on research and development, and has a lengthy tail of under-achieving individuals and companies.

Yet the link between investment rates and growth does not appear to be so strong. Britain's rate of investment rose steadily through the 1950s, 1960s and early 1970s, without any appreciable impact on the trend rate of growth, which has remained stubbornly at around 2 per cent since time immemorial. Business investment is much the same as amongst competitors, and what marks us out is lower capital expenditure on housing and the public sector.

These are not inconsiderable handicaps, particularly the woeful neglect of public sector investment, the price of long-term unemployment and tax cuts. But it is arguable that the macro-economic roller-coaster of the 1980s and 1990s, coupled with the high cost of capital, has made companies adept at getting the most out of the capital they have.

Finally, there is the assertion that the 1980s were a time of unrelieved selfishness in which collaboration and co-operation were driven out by rampant individualism. But if this was the intention of the Thatcherite revolution, there is not much evidence to suggest that yuppie culture had much of an impact, apart from in the City. The same proportion of people continued to give money to charity, the number of blood donors continued to rise. Certainly, cinema attendances climbed, more people ate out and travelled abroad than ever before. Far from being an introverted, self-obsessed decade, there is a case for saying that the 1980s were gregarious, extrovert and bourgeois, with more people owning their homes and indulging a taste for wine and exotic foods.

What's more, for all the talk of moral decline, Britain became a less sexist, racist and homophobic country in the 1980s. Many of these changes were, of course, not unique to Britain. It could also be argued that it was not for the want of trying by Mrs Thatcher and her ministers that Britain remained immune to the sort of philosophy being peddled. The fact remains, however, that if you had a job and the chance of promotion in the 1980s, you were OK, at least in material terms. Although unions were battered by unemployment, lost strikes and industrial legislation, employers still acted as if they were powerful, pushing up real wages by 4–5 per cent a year in the middle of the decade.

It was only the second Conservative decade that changed the culture into one where firms downsized at will and workers were grateful to stay in a job. Mrs Thatcher's Faustian bargain was that people could enjoy the fruits of a consumer society but had to accept they were on their own when things got rough. In the 1980s, independence was a breeze. In the 1990s, it turned into existential fear. •

10 March 1997

Decca Aitkenhead
Election — what election?

Samantha Jameson is sitting in Burger King with her best friend, Donna Saunders, who is 17, and Donna's 10-month-old baby. Donna's boyfriend has just run off to Milton Keynes with his new 15-year-old girlfriend, so she has spent the afternoon with social services, trying to find somewhere to live. All they gave her was some phone numbers, so she is sleeping on Sam's floor. Sam, 22, lives in a hostel ('A right shithole; it's damp and it stinks') with her two small kids; she moved out of her boyfriend's after a fight. She holds up her hand, to show where two fingers were almost severed when she tried to stab him.

Donna and Sam are brimming with opinions. They think tax on fags is a disgrace, the Child Support Agency is a joke, Tampax should be free, weed should be legalised, abortion should be banned and the idea that girls get pregnant to jump the housing queue is bloody stupid. They think there should be special centres for mums in prison, so their kids can visit them. And if they saw Margaret Thatcher, they wouldn't waste spit on her, they'd give her a good slap. They think we are turning into America. They want me to put this all

John Robertson

Courtship in Northampton

down.

'Oi!' they call to a man at the bar. 'What do you think about politics?'

'Load of bollocks,' he shouts back.

'See?' they beam, triumphant. 'Men – they can't talk about anything.'

So, Donna and Sam will be voting in the election? You must be joking.

'The Government,' Donna declares, 'means nothing to me.'

Actually, the Government means everything to Donna. She and Sam's entire lives are dictated by what social services can or will do for them, what the Home Office feels about single mothers – and, in particular, about sending them to prison. Donna is up in court soon on serious charges. She gets £75 a fortnight, survives by shoplifting, and would benefit more than anyone from a sympathetic government.

But Donna and Sam, like every other youngster in Northampton, are convinced that 'politicians are all the same'. How, you wonder, could they know? They have only ever lived under one government. But that, it dawns, is precisely the problem; because they have all seen elections come and go, but never seen power change hands, some have mistaken a change of cabinet for a change of government. Others have mistaken the whole process for the show elections which dictatorships like to act out.

Donna and Sam don't see voting as their chance to get the Government out, but as an act of endorsing it. Which, if you were Donna or Sam, would be the last thing in the world you felt like doing.

Who, then, is actually going to turn out to vote on election day? Anyone with any bloody sense in their heads, according to a middle-aged Tory businessman in a smoky, stained pub off the square. 'The Tories have completely fucked up these last five years.' A Conservative since the age of 18, he now thinks the 'whole thing's been a con' and will vote Labour. He can't explain exactly what he means by a 'con', though. •

•••

13 February 1997

David Ward
Clarke's beanfeast for voters

Kenneth Clarke seemed as uncertain about what was in his shopping basket as a virgin might be about the contents of her new husband's pyjama trousers on her wedding night.

'As it happens, there is hardly anything in this basket that I would normally eat except a pineapple,' said the puzzled Chancellor during a baffling photo-opportunity outside an Asda supermarket yesterday.

Two baskets, one clutched by Mr Clarke, the other by Les Byrom, Tory candidate in the Wirral South by-election, were supposed to show what a family could buy with

The long goodbye

Andrew Price

Ken Clarke with candidate Les Byrom and foodstuffs costing the amount gained by families since 1992, according to the Tories

the £21 it had gained since 1992 as a result of the Government's management of the economy. But the media wanted answers to the big questions. 'Are you a regular consumer of Bran Flakes?' shouted one political analyst. No answer. 'What's the price of baked beans?' yelled another.

Mr Clarke had been stung. 'Do I look like a man who eats baked beans?' he snorted. Suddenly millions of C2 votes were heard sliding towards Labour's HQ in a former KwikSave down the road (where Jack Cunningham was opening a briefcase stuffed with £2,120 in £5-notes to show what 'the average, industrious, hard-working family in Wirral South has had to pay since the last election because of Conservative tax betrayals').

'Do you ever go shopping?' came a cry from the back of the Asda scrum.

The Chancellor replied, 'I do go with the missus to the supermarket.'

Missus? Would the retiring Mrs Clarke be waiting for him with a rolling pin last night?

Suddenly a five-foot dog-end hove into view, concealing Carol, wife of Tony Samuelson, who plans to stand in the election on a platform described as 'against Conservatives poncing on tobacco companies'. He thinks the party should not accept money from such companies.

Mr Clarke headed into the store. Mr Samuelson followed with a banner ('Hands Off Our Children's Lungs') and security men threw him out. He tried to get back in and there was what might be called a scuffle but not a fracas.

'This is Nazi Germany!' cried Mr Samuelson, who returned to the shop and attempted to stand behind the Chancellor during a live TV interview, working on the principle that if a minister could stand in front of a pile of oranges, so could he.

The cereal debate continued in the car park and Janet Harrison spurned Bran Flakes. 'I have to live on Weetabix. I feed my kids properly but I cannot afford to eat properly. I'm caught in the poverty trap – I cannot afford to go out to work because of the benefits I will lose.' She was not impressed by Mr Clarke's flying visit. 'He's saying "Look at me – I'm mixing with the common people." But it doesn't work.'

But Ian St John, formerly of Liverpool FC and Saint and Greavesie, now of BSkyB, had been impressed. He lives in the constituency and met Mr Clarke at a nearby hotel. 'I'll probably be voting for Les,' he said. 'My mother always voted Conservative and we were one of the poorest families in Scotland.'

At the same event, Mr Clarke was presented with a bottle of 18-year-old malt whisky, which he seemed to cherish rather more than the own-brand cola which later fell into his shopping basket.

He then breezed up to one of many men in suits. 'What business are you in?' he asked.

'Insolvency,' came the reply. •

- -

1 March 1997

Leader

Major has had it — but where is the buzz for Blair?

For the record, it has to be repeated that nothing is certain in politics. But don't be misled. Such provisos are now mere superstition. The reality after the Wirral South by-election is that Britain will have a Labour government in a couple of months' time. In all probability Labour will have a comfortable, and perhaps even a landslide, majority, certainly enabling Tony Blair to govern for a full term. Wirral South is simply the latest piece of evidence in a long and unvaryingly consistent, not to say boringly predictable, pattern of Labour ascendancy and Conservative eclipse. There is not one single piece of counter-evidence anywhere, whether from by-elections or from opinion polls, to give any hope to the Conservatives. John Major has had it.

Compared with Christchurch in summer 1993, when the swing against the Conservatives was a record-breaking 35 per cent, with Dudley West in December 1994, when it was 29, or with Staffordshire South East in April last year, when it was 22, Wirral with its swing of 17 per cent may seem a more modest achievement. And so, in that relative sense, it is; anti-Conservative feeling has moderated slightly over the past two years. But in absolute terms, 17 per cent is still a prodigious swing, and in the context of the political situation of February 1997, it more than guarantees Labour's general election winning prospects this time round. Since Wirral South is probably the last by-election before the 1997 general election, the by-election result with which it best bears comparison is Langbaurgh, which Labour took from the Conservatives in November 1991 in the last English contest before the 1992 election. Labour's swing in Langbaurgh was 3 per cent, at a time when its national opinion poll lead over the Tories was 2 per cent; by the time of the general election, six months later, the swing back to the Conservatives nationally was 5 per cent and in Langbaurgh, which they recaptured, it was 3 per cent. Today, by contrast, Labour leads the Conservatives by 16 points in the national polls and by 19 points in Wirral South. And the general election is no more than two months away this time, not six. There simply is not enough time for the Tories to recover from such a deficit.

You don't believe it? Then consider these further facts. Fact one: for the first time in the twentieth century, a government has gone through an entire parliamentary term without winning a single by-election. Fact two: the Conservatives have not won a by-election at all since Richmond in 1989, an amazing 38 contests ago. Fact three: Labour's swing in Wirral South exceeded its swing in all but one of the by-elections in the 1987–92 parliament. Fact four: Labour's opinion poll lead has been in double figures for 39 consecutive months, whereas before the last general election it had been in double figures only once in the final 16 months of the parliament. Of course it is prudent to assume that the result of the general election will not replicate the by-election result in Wirral South. It won't (or if it did, Labour would have an overall majority in the Commons of more than 160). But the prospects of Labour holding on to Wirral South in a couple of months' time are statistically and politically good, contrary to Conservative Central Office claims yesterday that it will automatically revert to its previous allegiance. In fact, the second worst piece of news for the Conservatives on Thursday was that the Liberal Democrat vote in Wirral South held up quite well in the face of a ferocious two-party squeeze. Putting it all together, this week's by-election points to a Labour Commons majority of around 70 on 1 May.

There is, however, a cautious downside to the Wirral result all the same. Labour's victory was a triumph of brilliant organisation. The party spent heavily, worked hard and fought a focused and disciplined campaign against a vulnerable opponent. It was a microcosm of the organisational superiority which Labour will deploy when the general election begins. There is every reason for confidence that Labour, with some assistance from the Liberal Democrats, is in a position to oust the Conservatives at last. But where is the enthusiasm and buzz for what Mr Blair is offering instead? If Labour are honest, they must recognise that the national mood is more about a determination to get rid of the Tories – and why not? – than it is about enthusing over the Labour alternative. •

··

27 February 1997

Roy Hattersley
Ideas from the grave

Crosland's Future: Opportunity and Outcome, David Reisman, 237pp,
Macmillan, £45
Anthony Crosland: The Mixed Economy, David Reisman, 248pp, Macmillan,
£45

I n the high summer of 1940, Anthony Crosland – scholar of Trinity College – left Oxford for what he hoped was to be a temporary interruption of his studies. German invasion seemed imminent and most undergraduates who were leaving academe for the army were gloomy about the future. But Crosland, by nature optimistic, felt able to write to his friend Philip Williams with news about his plans for after the war. 'I am engaged on a great revision of Marxism and will certainly emerge as the modern Bernstein.' At 21, he intended to become the political philosopher of the libertarian left – an ambition shared by few young men today.

Political philosophy (particularly radical political philosophy) has gone out of fashion. Discussion of the theory of socialism still revolves around what Crosland wrote 40 years ago. Crosland, like the German thinker Eduard Bernstein, found Marx's analysis interesting but his conclusions outdated. *The Future of Socialism*, published in 1956, was denounced as unacceptably reactionary because it insisted that the pattern of ownership was less important than the organisation of society in a way which achieved 'the highest practicable degree of social and economic equality combined with practical democracy'. *Tribune*'s review was headed 'Socialism? How Does He Dare Use the Word?'

Most members of the modern Tribune Group regard Crosland as a dangerous extremist. For as David Reisman makes clear in *Crosland's Future: Opportunity and Outcome*, the last of the socialist philosophers did not believe that 'equality of opportunity' was enough. 'The more equal start must be accompanied by the more equal finish.'

Crosland's Future is essential reading for any member of the shadow cabinet who regards it as important to have a framework of ethical belief on which the individual policies (and for that matter soundbites) can be hung. It makes the common mistake of insisting that Crosland believed that economic growth is essential for socialism to succeed, when in fact he described expansion as creating the conditions in which socialism was most readily acceptable and most easily implemented – a quite different judgement. But it leaves no doubt in the objective reader's mind that had not the Labour Party lost confidence in its own ideas, it could have developed a philosophy that combined social justice with material well-being in a way which would have made its conversion to benign capitalism unnecessary.

Parts of Professor Reisman's companion volume, *Anthony Crosland: The Mixed Economy*, read like a textbook of archaeology. Believe it or not, Tony Crosland wanted to nationalise the machine tool industry. If his 'revisionist' advice had been taken, we might still have one to argue about. Crosland's view – owing as much to Tawney as to Bernstein – was that decisions about public ownership should be taken on a case-by-case analysis, not a sweeping assertion that the end of private property was synonymous with the beginnings of a socialist society. It would be comforting to ask, who today does not believe that the merits of public ownership should be examined industry by industry? The answer is, apostles of the notion that the free market provides the best redistribution of resources and guarantees the greatest efficiency. Unfortunately, most of the shadow cabinet number amongst them.

So the lesson to be learned from *Anthony Crosland: The Mixed Economy* is simultaneously sad and encouraging – sad because so much obvious truth has been rejected, but encouraging because of what it demonstrates about the power of thought.

The enduring ideas about socialism – which may one day rise again from the grave – are the thoughts of a man who, since he had the sense to accept the limitations imposed by reality, understood that the social revolution would not be easily achieved.

His plans to bring that revolution about were called reactionary, though genuine revisionism was never that. Consider the undergraduate Crosland offering his views on who ought to succeed Clement Attlee. 'Aneurin Bevan not only will be, but ought to be, the next Labour leader. If only he could lose his imbecile wife, he would have Crosland solidly behind him.' But then Hugh Gaitskell, another genuine radical, came along. However, life at the Department of Education must have been interesting when Tony Crosland was Secretary of State and Jennie Lee (Mrs Aneurin Bevan) was his junior minister. •

5 March 1997

Simon Hoggart
Major reaches end of wiggly line

John Major arrived for Prime Minister's Questions looking quite improbably cheerful. He marched briskly into the chamber, sat down, then swivelled round to Michael Heseltine and shared a cheesy grin.

I had just come over the road from a conference on opinion polls run by *The House Magazine*, which is our main internal organ here at Westminster. All the pollsters had different ways of saying that the Tories – to use their precise psephological terminology – are screwed. Down the jacksy. Finished. Out of here. Sayonara, suckers.

All the graphs and bar charts and wiggly lines told the same story. Millions of Tories are switching straight to Labour. In the Wirral, nearly four Liberals in 10 voted Labour. Labour are well ahead on every policy which the voters deem important, except for crime, where they're more or less level. (Possibly Jack Straw's new policy of stringing up 10-year-olds for littering may even be thought too harsh by a wimpish minority.) If the pollsters have got this one wrong, they really are finished.

No wonder there was an elegiac tone to much of what the Prime Minister had to say. Nicholas Budgen, the right-wing Tory who sits for Enoch Powell's old seat in Wolverhampton, asked a question about 'primary purpose' and arranged marriages. This is code for keeping immigrants out, and Mr Budgen's neighbour, the Labour MP Ken Purchase, bellowed 'racist' at him. Then Mr Major said the same thing in more elliptical fashion. 'In the last 18 years we have seen the most extraordinary changes and improvements in race relations in this country, and I am not going to lend my voice to any policy which might damage that improvement.'

So Mr Blair said the Prime Minister deserved credit for his answer. No doubt he does, and no doubt he meant what he said. But there was a bittersweet, farewell edge to his words, as if he has acknowledged that the battle is over and he has only his reputation to save.

Mr Blair again raised the topic of the mysterious Stephen Dorrell, the alleged Cabinet minister who is on every BBC news bulletin, often several times, in spite of the fact that nobody has any idea who he is. Mr Major said he had been an 'outstanding' minister. 'I shall congratulate him on his superlative work, just as soon as I find out what he looks like!' (I made that up.)

Mr Blair said it was time ministers stopped playing with the Tory leadership and showed national leadership. Mr Major replied that over the past five years 'as we have tackled the real problems the country faces, we have had nothing but opposition from the Labour Party'.

But opposing is their job. That's what they're paid for. The Prime Minister might just as easily have shouted at his cook, 'For five years we have been tackling real problems,

The long goodbye

while all you have done is cook things!'

Paddy Ashdown asked the best question. After the Wirral by-election, the PM had said that the fightback should start immediately. So Norman Tebbit had attacked Michael Heseltine, Lord McAlpine had duffed up the PM and Stephen Dorrell took on the whole cabinet. Shouldn't they be in secure accommodation and electronically tagged?

As the laughter died down, Mr Major did one of his long pauses, like a comedian with faultless timing waiting for the perfect moment for a punch line. Of course there wasn't one. 'I'm pleased to see that on some matters you are in agreement with us!'

Then Ben Chapman, the Labour victor of Wirral, arrived to take the oath. He stuck a hand at Mr Major, who shook it warmly. Bafflingly, Brian Mawhinney steered Mr Chapman behind the Speaker's Chair, perhaps to be kneecapped in time for the general election. •

Sleaze I: the evidence

20 March 1997

Simon Hoggart
Prorogued by a roguish pro

My colleagues and I are constantly accused of being too cynical about politicians. We always look on the worst side, they tell us. We invariably assume the most venal motives. We may spend our lives in the gutter but we should sometimes follow Oscar Wilde's advice and look up towards the stars. Yet MPs are more cynical about themselves. It may be hard for you, the voters, to comprehend, but there are some who doubt John Major's motives for announcing the longest election campaign since 1918.

Now, it happens there are those among us who have long suspected that Mr Major's reputation as a fellow of rock-like integrity is not entirely deserved. We wonder whether, far from being a decent, upright, Rotarian sort of chap, someone so law-abiding he would report a neighbour for peeing in the shower, he is actually a slippery customer whom you should trust no further than you could throw Nicholas Soames. Indeed, we think that with his big honest eyes, his nervous grin, diffident manner and baggy sweaters, he could do well selling 10-quid Rolexes in Oxford Street. But that's the sort of cheap, reach-me-down cynicism you'd expect from a hack.

So you'll realise how shocked I was to discover that there are MPs who share my sordid doubts. They actually suspect that Mr Major has arranged for Parliament to be prorogued tomorrow in order to make certain that Sir Gordon Downey's report on sleaze is kept secret until well after polling day. They even said so in the House yesterday. Of course, it would never do to put it too baldly. After all, Sir Gordon's report may assert that all Members of Parliament are blameless. 'When Mr Al Fayed arranged for envelopes stuffed with cash to be given to MPs, he made it quite clear that this money was to be passed straightaway to the Parliamentary Greasers' Widows and Orphans Benevolent Fund.'

Or, 'The lengthy stays at the Paris Ritz were arranged purely as part of a parliamentary investigation into alternatives to homelessness. The honourable member has told us, and we accept his word, that his only wish was to make certain that the luxury of the facilities would not be overwhelming to someone who had spent the previous six months in a cardboard box.'

If, as is quite possible, Sir Gordon exonerates all MPs, then it would reflect badly on any of their colleagues who had jumped to outrageous conclusions. Simon Hughes, for example, a Liberal, yesterday said he wanted the report to be published 'so that the interests of all members can be protected, whether or not they are mentioned' – in other words, I am inquiring for the guiltless rather than against the culpable.

Tony Benn went into the Land of Oz, a mythic place where he is happiest. 'Madam Speaker, the prorogation of Parliament is for the Crown and the Prime Minister . . .

the House continues to sit until 8 April. During that period Sir Gordon, and the clerk, and the editor of *Hansard* remain officers of the House . . . we can instruct them to make available information gained at the behest of the House even if the House is prorogued . . .'

When Mr Benn is in march-of-our-great-constitution mode, you feel that his words shouldn't be spoken so much as stitched into a tapestry.

Bernard Jenkin, a Tory, suggested that publishing the rap sheet would be unfair. We were dealing with MPs' livelihoods. They were looking for a dispassionate and fair appraisal. (I read this to mean, in my horrid, sceptical way, 'Anyone who gets fingered might lose their seat, whereas if they get re-elected in time they might just be able to ride it out.')

In any event, Betty said that nothing could be done and we learned that the Queen has signed the prorogation order. So much for us cynics. •

20 March 1997

Leader
The whiff of a cover-up

Back in October it seemed fleetingly as if the Prime Minister had developed some understanding of the widespread public disquiet in this country about standards in public life. He urged Sir Gordon Downey to report as quickly as possible on the allegations surrounding Neil Hamilton and other MPs – 'well this side of a general election'. It was in Parliament's interests that it happened, he said, as well as in the interests of natural justice.

So what's changed? Why the dismissive shrug from Mr Major when the subject was raised yesterday? Why the curt and misleading statement that it was up to Sir Gordon and the Select Committee on Standards and Privileges and nothing to do with him?

Sir Gordon is apparently only days away from delivering a report into the most serious allegations about the conduct of MPs in 30 years. He was working on the assumption that – in accordance with usual practice – Parliament would be prorogued at the same time as it was dissolved: on 8 April. Too late, he has discovered that Parliament shuts up shop tomorrow. For reasons that no one has bothered to explain, Mr Major has abandoned precedent and prorogued Parliament 18 days before dissolving it. The singular effect of this action is that no one will be around to consider Sir Gordon's findings, which are destined to sit in a safe until such time as a new committee is convened. That is a disgrace.

It is said that Mr Major 'wants a long campaign'. Fine. Then adjourn Parliament tomorrow and prorogue it on 8 April. Such an action would not affect a single piece of parliamentary business other than Sir Gordon's report. It is difficult to avoid the conclusion that the reason the Government has acted in the way it has is precisely in order to avoid the risk of unsavoury disclosures of corruption and dishonesty in the immediate run-up to a general election. So much for the interests of Parliament and of natural justice.

No one has bothered to explain to the confused voters of Tatton or Beaconsfield why they are not allowed to know whether their candidates are straight, mildly dishonest or blatantly corrupt. All we are promised – at the eleventh hour – is a hurriedly prepared 'interim report' which is unlikely to deal with either the substantive issues or the major culprits.

Last night, the situation threatened to degenerate into farce, with *The Times* leaking part of the evidence to Downey and Mr Hamilton threatening to publish his own testimony to the committee and continuing to blacken the name of this newspaper at every opportunity. This leaves the *Guardian*, apparently bound by parliamentary privilege, in an invidious position.

Democracy depends on the electors having access to the information on which they can make reasonable choices. It is difficult to think of a greater mockery of the democratic processes than to lock up a report on the alleged corruption of MPs at the start of a general election campaign on the pretext of a parliamentary technicality.

The Queen signed the prorogation papers yesterday. But one of the advantages of the British constitution – as Mr Major has nimbly demonstrated in this matter – is that you can make much of it up as you go along. It would be a simple matter for Mr Major to delay prorogation until 8 April. If he is truly interested in the interests of parliamentary democracy and in natural justice, he can still make the necessary arrangements to allow the committee time to consider and publish the report. If he continues to oppose such a move then voters will be entitled to conclude that his primary concern is, after all, the obvious one: saving his own skin. •

* *

21 March 1997

Staff reporters
Sleaze: the evidence

One of the Tory ministers at the heart of the cash-for-questions scandal was made a Government minister despite having confessed to his Chief Whip that he had taken between £18,000 and £25,000 in undeclared cash payments from Mohamed Al Fayed.

Tim Smith was also allowed to remain as Northern Ireland minister after John Major had been told that he had confessed to taking £25,000 in cash while asking questions on behalf of Mr Al Fayed in Parliament.

His confession to Sir Gordon Downey, the Parliamentary Commissioner, is one of a number of facts about MPs seeking re-election that the *Guardian* reveals today and which would otherwise remain locked up in a safe until well after polling day. They will eventually be published as an appendix to Sir Gordon's report, which may remain secret for two months.

The Prime Minister yesterday refused to allow the Standards and Privileges Committee more time to consider Sir Gordon's report, due to be completed by next Tuesday. This is despite the fact that many of the 10 MPs whose behaviour is still to be reported on are submitting themselves for re-election on 1 May.

Transcripts of evidence taken behind closed doors in the past two months show that Mr Smith admitted taking the money in envelopes containing £50 notes without any invoices or receipts and without declaring the payments specifically for tax.

Mr Major, who was told of the allegations in September 1994, allowed him to remain a minister in one of the Government's most sensitive jobs, despite confirmation on 17 October that Mr Smith had taken the money. He was required to resign only after the *Guardian* published its original cash-for-questions story.

Mr Smith, who was also made treasurer of the Conservative Party after admitting taking the money, was, in the opinion of leading criminal lawyers, guilty of accepting bribes. But while Mr Major asked the Director of Public Prosecutions to investigate Mr Al Fayed for possible blackmail charges, he did not refer Mr Smith either to the DPP or the privileges committee. Mr Smith was never investigated by any committee of the House and the following year he was appointed to the Public Accounts Committee, charged with overseeing probity in public spending. He is standing for re-election in Beaconsfield, where he is defending a majority of nearly 24,000.

Transcripts of evidence presented to Sir Gordon's private hearings also reveal that:

• Neil Hamilton and his wife asked for – and enjoyed – a second free stay at the Ritz Hotel in Paris, owned by Mohamed Al Fayed, in 1990. This was after the leaking of the DTI report which said Mr Al Fayed was a liar.

• Mr Hamilton, a tax barrister, took an undeclared free air fare worth £1,500 to New Orleans and Aspen, Colorado. Not only did he not declare it, but he dishonestly claimed £1,500 tax relief as a business expense.

• Mr Hamilton did not declare £10,000 'commissions' to the tax authorities for nine years – until after the collapse of his libel case.

• In the same week Michael Brown, MP, sent a £1,500 cheque to the Inland Revenue to cover unpaid tax on another undeclared £6,000 'commission' seven years after he received it.

• Mr Hamilton and Mr Brown now admit lobbying ministers without declaring their financial interests – either to the ministers or in the Register of Members' Interests.

• Mr Hamilton admits he deliberately lied to the Deputy Prime Minister about £10,000 he received from the lobbyist Ian Greer in order to buy time for himself.

• Sir Michael Grylls, MP, and Ian Greer both admit giving false evidence to the

Members' Interests Committee. Sir Michael now admits that he had twice as many payments from Mr Greer as he told MPs.

- Sir Andrew Bowden, MP, admitted under cross-examination telling a number of contradictory stories about Mr Greer's donation of £5,319, largely from Al Fayed money to the 'Andrew Bowden Fighting Fund', which he never declared in any form.
- Sir Michael Grylls received more than £86,000 in secret payments from Ian Greer and his clients for parliamentary activities.
- Three witnesses gave unshaken evidence that they had seen envelopes being stuffed with cash for Mr Hamilton and had arranged delivery to him.

Mr Hamilton, who is defending a majority of more than 15,000 in the coming election, has made repeated TV appearances in recent days claiming the report will prove him innocent – despite confessing in private to the inquiry that he had cheated the Revenue as well as failing to make disclosures required by Parliament.

He has promised to publish his own transcripts of evidence given to the committee before the election and has quoted from other witnesses' evidence in interviews.

Sir Andrew Bowden is defending a majority of 10,000 in Brighton Kemptown. Michael Brown is defending a majority of 6,400 in Cleethorpes. Sir Michael Grylls is retiring from Parliament. •

21 March 1997

Leader

A people betrayed by Parliament

Because we believe in elections fought in the light, not in the dark, we are publishing today a summary of evidence submitted to Sir Gordon Downey on the cash-for-questions scandal. This is an issue which goes to the heart of parliamentary democracy. The facts the report reveals are, in short, that a number of MPs now offering themselves for re-election have secretly confessed to, or are plainly guilty of, criminal offences of bribery, corruption and cheating the Inland Revenue. Secret confessions, we now know, have been made to flagrant breaches of the parliamentary law on declaration of interests, and some of the evidence given to a parliamentary select committee has been shown to be lies.

Had things been handled differently, Sir Gordon's full report could have been published by Parliament itself. We would have much preferred that to happen. But yesterday it was clear that in spite of the forces anxious for publication – not just the opposition parties, but Sir Gordon himself, his masters, the Committee on Standards and Privileges, and even Conservative MPs who figure in the investigation – John Major and his Government remained obdurate, wholly indifferent to the public's right to know.

This affair began with concealment – concealment from Parliament and the public of the secret and squalid motives which led MPs to table their questions: the cash which companies and their lobbyists were ready so freely to put in their pockets. Now it culminates in a further concealment. John Major – honest John, as he used to be advertised, who began so well, setting up the Nolan committee, backing Sir Gordon's appointment, declaring on television that his report must be available before the election – has now decided instead on an election fought in the dark. For reasons which – insultingly – he has never even attempted to justify, he fixed the timetable for the election in such a way that Sir Gordon's report, which he himself had demanded, could not be published before the nation went to the polls. Since then he has sneeringly resisted every attempt to rewrite these arrangements.

Whose rights are infringed by this concealment? Most immediately, those of voters in those constituencies where MPs at the heart of Sir Gordon's investigations are offering themselves to the voters. The whole basis of the British electoral system cannot work if voters are denied essential information about those who aspire to represent them. The interim report published yesterday fulfils that requirement in the case of 15 named MPs – 11 Conservative, three Labour and one Liberal Democrat – whom Sir Gordon exonerates. The failure to arrange publication of the rest of his findings denies that essential safeguard in 10 other constituencies.

In eight cases the MPs involved (though some are not standing again) have been identified; in two cases, they have not. What are the voters to make of it? Either way, someone is wronged. Where these MPs are innocent, they have to fight the suspicion that they may be guilty. Where they are guilty, the concealment may save them from the retribution they deserve at the hands of electors. The electoral process is thereby frustrated: and needlessly frustrated, since but for John Major's obduracy, none of this need have occurred.

The injustice done to the rest of us is less specific, but it is real. Part of the context of the Government over the past few years has been sleaze. But without the Downey report, the electorate cannot judge how grave that offence has been. Either way, someone is wronged. The Prime Minister's failure to use the options before him to let the public see the report has fed the suspicion that the findings looked bad for his party. And the details we give today confirm that they do. John Major sought to dismiss the whole affair yesterday as an 'opposition stunt'. That is not how most voters are likely to see it.

It is already clear that the procedures the House instituted when seized by shame and remorse over earlier allegations will need substantial amendment. They need to reflect the comfort of members less and the rights of the public much more. Parliament, as for a while it seemed to accept, is on trial in this matter: its attachment to self-regulation will stand or fall by its resolution. For ourselves, we remain convinced that an independent commission against corruption, safe from interruption – or in this case disruption – by parliamentary prorogations or committees with in-built Government majorities can alone provide the safeguards required in an honest democracy; can alone ensure that issues like these are resolved in the light, not the dark.

We believe that Parliament holds its privileges not for itself but on trust for the people who are represented there. In this matter the Prime Minister and Parliament itself have singularly failed to protect the essential rights of the voter. It is because we believe that this balance needs to be redressed that we today publish the essence of Sir Gordon Downey's investigation. •

21 March 1997

David Leigh, David Pallister, Jamie Wilson, Richard Norton-Taylor, Ed Vulliamy and David Hencke

Lies, a failed libel case, gifts galore

First extract from Downey inquiry evidence

THE EVIDENCE

Neil Hamilton testified to Sir Gordon Downey and the inquiry's counsel, Nigel Pleming, QC, on 20 February.

Mr Hamilton's solicitor, Rupert Grey, gave his client's explanation of why he had suddenly dropped his libel case against the *Guardian*.

Mr Grey said, 'The accountants reported the existence of accounts showing that Sir Michael Grylls had received payments from Mr Greer which were substantially greater ... than had been previously described by Ian Greer in his evidence to the Select Committee in 1990. His credibility as a witness and plaintiff was thus seriously undermined.'

Nigel Pleming asked Mr Hamilton about his lie to Michael Heseltine when the allegations first emerged in 1994. He quoted a Cabinet Office memo: 'Mr Hamilton has given him an absolute assurance that he had no financial relationship with Mr Greer, and the president [of the Board of Trade, then Mr Heseltine] has accepted this.'

Q: That ... on its face, in the light of the information we have received, looks to be incorrect, that you did have a financial relationship, and that is obvious.

A: I did not mention the commission payments when I spoke to Mr Heseltine ... Pol-

David Gadd

Neil Hamilton

Graham Whitby

Tim Smith

itics is a rough game ... I knew that if there were to be another cause for adverse media comment against me ... it could be used as a very big stick with which to beat me and to cause my resignation to take place.

Q: Mr Hamilton ... what you are saying to me is that you deliberately decided to keep back that which you had remembered ... Here you were deliberately misleading the President of the Board of Trade. You explained why you did it; that there was the risk of further damage to you . . . this would be a very damaging document to you in the libel proceedings ... That would have put you in a pretty difficult light before a jury in a libel action.

A: Yes, it certainly would have been a difficulty. There is no disguising that.

The inquiry asked about new evidence of a second stay at the Ritz in 1990.

Q: Those three extra pages in the message book ... 'Guest apartment at the Ritz 5 July – 9 July ... '

A: A friend of mine was getting married not far from Paris so I telephoned to ask whether there was any chance, as we were going to Paris, of staying at the Ritz. I had completely forgotten about this.

Q: Do you recall what Mr Al Fayed said to you at the time?

A: He said, 'No, I do not think you can stay at the Ritz but I will talk to my son and see if his apartment is free.' He did so and he said why not spend the two nights at his flat and so we did.

The inquiry asked why he had taken payments of paintings, furniture and plane tickets from Greer, as well as a cheque.

A: Because the valuation for Revenue purposes of such a payment would be lower than if I received the payment in cash.

Q: Could you also look at your filed income tax returns for the year ending 5 April 1989, when you claimed against your consultancy fees, travel and subsistence overseas, £1,430 of which was travel overseas to New Orleans to develop business contacts. From what you told me a few moments ago, the flight was paid for you by Ian Greer, but here you are claiming almost the entire air fare against a business expense in the following year.

A: My accountant . . . presents it to the Revenue. He is the one who conducts these negotiations on my behalf with the Revenue. I tell him what I have done during the course of the year and he argues the toss with the Revenue.

Q: What it looks like, Mr Hamilton, is that by this method of payment in kind you were deliberately concealing what you were receiving from Ian Greer from the risk of registration as an interest in Parliament and also from the risk of it being taxed. The advice you are given by your accountant is to declare – 'declare', note – as ex-gratia payment. Did you declare it?

A: He prepares my tax return . . .

THE *GUARDIAN* CASE

Mr Hamilton lied to the Deputy Prime Minister, the Chief Whip and the Cabinet Secretary. He has admitted dishonesty over tax and to receiving £10,000 in undeclared 'commissions'. He has admitted accepting a second stay at the Ritz after the damning DTI verdict on Mr Al Fayed. Three witnesses gave unshaken evidence to Sir Gordon saying they saw cash being prepared and delivered to Mr Hamilton. He is not fit to be an MP.

• •

Second extract from Downey inquiry evidence

THE EVIDENCE

Tim Smith appeared before Sir Gordon Downey on 12 February 1997 and was questioned by Nigel Pleming, QC.

Mr Pleming at first quotes a letter from the lobbyist Ian Greer to Mr Al Fayed in early 1987: 'Tim is extremely sympathetic to you and your position and has promised to do everything he can to help . . . I think it is unlikely that he will accept the position of paid adviser to the House of Fraser before the general election is over.'

Q: Do you have any recollection of a discussion of paid adviser?

A: No.

Q: How does the question of money come up?

A: Well, I went to this meeting with Mr Al Fayed – I am pretty sure it was in May 1987 – to discuss these matters. Greatly to my surprise, he offered me this money.

Q: Do you recall how much was involved on the first payment?

A: I think it was £5,000.

Q: Would that have been in two paper-bound bundles of £50s?

A: No, it was in one envelope.

Q: But mainly £50 notes, would that be so?

A: I do not remember but that is likely though.

Q: This is one of the methods of potential payment. If we could go through – there are three possible methods – and see if they apply to you. One is the handing over of money in an envelope with, no doubt, an Al Fayed beaming smile as he hands it over.

A: Correct . . . I think I was handed money by him face to face and I think on one or two occasions money was couriered to me.

Q: That would be to your home address, not the House?

A: Yes, that is right.

Q: Do you recall approximately how many meetings there were when the money was handed over?

A: Oh, I think it was seven or eight.

Q: I can assume fairly safely that the money, when handed to you, went then into a bank?

A: Yes . . . it did not always go into the same account but I paid the money in.

Q: It did not burn a hole in your back pocket? Again that is very badly put.

A: I paid it into an account of one kind or another . . .

Q: What I wanted to ask you is your reaction to cash. This is not the usual way, I trust, that Members of Parliament get paid for consultancy work. Cheques would be paid in the normal way. Cash would be very unusual. Again, I hope that is right.

A: Yes.

Mr Smith is then asked to explain the discrepancy between his own admitted figure of £18,000 and the £25,000 mentioned in his interview with Sir Robin Butler.

Q: Is your £18,000 a precisely mathematically calculated figure?

A: No, it is not.

Q: Is it any more or less reliable than £25,000?

A: I have given it some thought and I think it is more reliable. I think I received £5,000 initially and then subsequently six or seven payments of £2,000, and I am afraid that is the best I can do.

THE *GUARDIAN* CASE

Mr Smith is not a fit and proper person to be a Member of Parliament as he corruptly took bribes to advance the case of Mr Al Fayed in the Commons and failed to declare his interest. He did not resign when he was caught out. His lack of records about tax or a detailed breakdown of the payments suggest he received more than he has admitted. •

22 March 1997

David Hencke and Michael White
Act now to end this betrayal of trust

John Major was under intense pressure last night to explain his failure to sack Tim Smith, the former minister who admitted accepting up to £ 25,000 from Harrods owner Mohamed Al Fayed. Mr Smith resigned only when the *Guardian* broke the story.

The embattled Prime Minister attempted to dismiss the detailed publication in the *Guardian* yesterday of evidence to the cash-for-questions inquiry as 'complete junk'. But Labour stepped up the pressure to get Parliamentary Commissioner Sir Gordon Downey's report into the affair published before the election, even if it means a brief recall of Parliament next week. Otherwise, senior party figures said, the election campaign would be marred by 'fundamental cynicism about Parliament's ability to investigate charges of the most fundamental character'.

Robin Cook, Donald Dewar and Ann Taylor argued that natural justice for the accused MPs and Parliament itself would best be served if Sir Gordon's report were completed and issued.

'The public will simply not understand if in the light of today's revelations this investigation was closed down by the early prorogation of the House,' Mr Dewar, Labour's Chief Whip, said. 'We believe a failure to act would be an abdication of responsibility and a betrayal of trust.' He added that the *Guardian*'s report 'contains an account of events which strike not just at the honour of individual MPs but at the integrity of the Prime Minister and his Government and the reputation of Parliament itself. 'It would be inconceivable if these matters were now left in a state of suspension.'

In the wake of the *Guardian*'s fresh revelations about Tory MP Tim Smith, Mr Cook repeatedly stressed how extraordinary it was that Mr Major had not acted against the minister until his hand was forced by the newspaper's initial revelations in October 1994.

Mr Cook said, 'What we now know is that the Government, and presumably the Prime Minister, were aware for 10 days that Tim Smith had received very substantial sums in £50 notes from Mohamed Al Fayed, and that no action was taken against him through those 10 days. Action was taken only when the matter became public in a newspaper. I find it quite extraordinary that a prime minister knew that a minister of the Crown had been receiving those payments previously and took no action till his hand was forced by a press report.'

A Downing Street spokesman yesterday said it was merely 'a coincidence' that Mr Smith resigned on the same day that the *Guardian* published allegations on cash for questions.

In a rare move, Mr Major later employed his Downing Street press secretary, Jonathan Haslem, to brief lobby journalists. Mr Haslem released details of the Prime Minister's diaries over four days in 1994, from 17 October – when, it was claimed, Mr Major was first informed that Mr Smith had taken cash – to 20 October, when the *Guardian* exposed the cash-for-questions scandal.

Downing Street insisted Mr Major had not known about Mr Smith's confession to Cabinet Secretary Sir Robin Butler on 10 October that he had taken the cash – even though Sir Robin's report shows the interviews took place at the same Tory party conference attended by both Tim Smith and John Major.

Nor was Downing Street able to throw any light on Mr Smith's claim – repeated twice yesterday – that he had originally registered his interest in 1989 on the advice of David Waddington, chief whip to Margaret Thatcher's Government.

Lord Waddington, now Governor of Bermuda, said yesterday he had no recollection of the meeting. 'I have no specific recollection of a meeting with Mr Smith and, after all this time, have no records to refer to. But I can say positively that if he had come to me and said that he had not declared a certain interest, namely his employment as a consultant or adviser, I would have told him to get on and declare it,' he said in a statement.

Earlier yesterday, Mr Smith said the *Guardian*'s claim that he was made a minister in spite of having confessed to his Chief Whip that he had taken £18,000–£25,000 was 'absolutely not true'.

He said, 'I can understand how the *Guardian* has come to that conclusion from the evidence but it is simply not true. In fact, after I told Sir Robin Butler the details of all this, I resigned about 10 days later as a minister.'

Both Mr Smith and Neil Hamilton, defending two of the safest Tory seats in the country, won confidence votes at their respective annual general meetings last night in Beaconsfield and Tatton, despite a minority of dissenting Tory voices.

The *Guardian* and *The Times* came under strong criticism from Sir Gordon for publishing part of the evidence to his inquiry. He issued a statement declaring: 'I deplore the action of certain newspapers and others in selectively leaking parts of the evidence to my inquiry.' •

27 March 1997

David Hencke
The Dishonourable Member

Tim Smith, the disgraced former minister who confessed to taking £25,000 in used £50 notes from Harrods owner Mohamed Al Fayed, yesterday buckled under intense pressure and resigned as MP for Beaconsfield, the third-safest Tory seat in the country. The MP – who only last week had enjoyed the full support of John Major, Michael Heseltine and Michael Portillo – was pressed to bow out of politics as leading figures in his own association and fellow parliamentary colleagues turned against him.

Last night it emerged that Mr Smith resigned within hours of being told of the existence of a letter, signed by 50 members of his local party, due to be delivered to Conservative Party headquarters. The letter would have forced an extraordinary general meeting of the association to debate his future.

Mr Smith's decision to quit put fresh pressure on Neil Hamilton, the other former minister at the centre of the cash-for-questions scandal. Mr Hamilton is accused of taking tens of thousands of pounds in brown envelopes from the Harrods boss. In a statement issued before Mr Smith had announced his resignation, Alan Barnes, chairman of Mr Hamilton's constituency Conservative association in Tatton, said, 'The resignation of Tim Smith as Conservative candidate for Beaconsfield is irrelevant to the situation in Tatton . . . The two cases are totally different. Mr Smith admitted from the beginning he had accepted money. Neil Hamilton has consistently denied accepting cash for questions from Mr Fayed or anyone else. When the full details are known, and the transcripts of evidence presented to Sir Gordon Downey are published, it will be clear that Neil Hamilton is innocent.'

But cracks in local support for Mr Hamilton began to emerge last night. Frank Keegan, treasurer of the Alderley Edge branch in Tatton, told BBC's *Newsnight*, 'It is difficult to find someone who actually supports the candidate in Alderley Edge. Many people want to support the Conservative Party, but on 1 May they may have difficulty voting for Neil Hamilton, and that could have a big impact on who wins the seat.'

Paddy Ashdown, the Liberal Democrat leader, said: 'Mr Smith, who appears to have done the honourable thing, is the first casualty of Mr Major's indecision and inept handling of the whole cash-for-questions affair. Sleaze is the issue the Tory party just cannot shake off.'

Gordon Brown, the shadow Chancellor, said: 'The pressure is now on John Major to step in, show some leadership and put his party in order. If he does not, this issue will run on until polling day.'

One Tory MP said Mr Smith's decision to resign had 'lanced the boil'. He added, 'Now we must wait for Hamilton to do the decent thing.' But Brian Mawhinney, Conservative

Party chairman, defended Mr Hamilton's position after describing Mr Smith's resignation as an 'honourable and right decision'. He said, 'There is a total difference between the two cases. Mr Smith openly admitted he took some money. Mr Hamilton strenuously denies that he did.'

While senior Tory sources praised the 'good grace and dignity' Mr Smith had shown, officials in Mr Hamilton's constituency said their man had no intention of following suit. In an interview with his local paper, the *Knutsford Guardian*, Mr Hamilton admitted he had been 'unwise' to accept payments totalling £10,000 from the former lobbyist, Ian Greer, for two other clients, and that it would have been better if he had declared them in the Register of Members' Interests. He firmly denied taking any cash from Mr Al Fayed – even though Mr Fayed's description of the system of cash payments had been independently backed by three witnesses and admitted by his colleague, Tim Smith.

In a statement, Mr Smith said yesterday, 'I now believe that it is in the best interests of this association and the Conservative Party if I withdraw my candidature from the general election on 1 May.' He went on, 'I very much regret that the action of the *Guardian* newspaper in support of the Labour Party has made my course of action inevitable with its complete disregard for both parliamentary privilege and natural justice.' •

• •

27 March 1997

Leader
A weak and dishonest man

A weak and dishonest man departed from public life yesterday. He left with ill grace and to a deafening silence from the men who had spent the weekend supporting his right to fight the coming election as a Conservative candidate: specifically, the Prime Minister and the Deputy Prime Minister. Had he not resigned, and had not the *Guardian* published extracts from his admissions to Sir Gordon Downey's inquiry, a fraud would have been perpetrated on the electorate on polling day. His departure from political life is thus cause for modest celebration.

But the story of Tim Smith's last eight years as a Conservative MP is also a dismal lesson in the denials and evasions at the heart of the last Government and of the privileges that Parliament claims to itself. Here is a man who should have left public life eight years ago, immediately after confessing his dishonesty to the Government's Chief Whip in 1989 (since the Conservative chairman, Brian Mawhinney, has made so much of his 'honourable' action, we should note that Mr Smith's admission was motivated not by 'honour' but by the knowledge that Tiny Rowland had discovered his acceptance of bribes and might have exposed him).

The Government Chief Whip seems to have been remarkably unimpressed by Mr Smith's confession. He seems not to have questioned him about any specifics. He did not inform any law officers about an apparent act of an MP accepting bribes. He did not inform the Privileges Committee. He seems to have kept no note of the encounter. Such, in 1989, were the concerns for standards in public life among those at the centre of the Conservative Government.

Far from being censured, Mr Smith subsequently thrived. He was shortly thereafter made a vice-chairman of the Conservative Party, as well as party treasurer. It was only when the *Guardian* first exposed his dishonesty in October 1994 that he was demoted. Again, there was no reference to law officers or to the Privileges Committee by Mr Major. Had Mr Smith not done the 'honourable thing'? So honourable, he was soon thereafter nominated to serve on the influential Public Accounts Committee, the body that oversees probity in public spending.

His case, then, is not one (as Dr Mawhinney would have us believe) of a rogue MP about whom all his colleagues were in the dark; his case is of a politician whose greedy and dishonest behaviour was well known and who nevertheless continued to prosper. That is the damning charge and it is not something that Mr Major should easily be able to shrug off.

The announcement of Mr Smith's 'honourable' departure was notable for two remarks. The first was Mr Smith's assertion that he had only ever been motivated by the interests of his constituents and his country. He is surely forgetting the interests of Mr Al Fayed, which he represented so resolutely as long as the brown envelopes filled with £50 notes kept coming his way. The second was his attempt to blame this newspaper for hounding him out in breach of parliamentary privilege. If it is a breach of parliamentary privilege to ensure that voters are saved from electing a dishonest MP, we suggest it is time that Parliament looked to its own privileges.

Parliamentary privilege means that MPs enjoy effective immunity from prosecution for dishonesty in relation to their work. Privilege means they can set up their own tribunal to judge themselves. Privilege means they can suspend that tribunal if the business of getting themselves elected intervenes. Privilege means they can appoint to that tribunal MPs who have announced their verdict before considering the evidence. Privilege means MPs can now – see Neil Hamilton – waive their privileges when it suits them. Privilege means MPs can also – see Tim Smith – refuse to waive their privileges when it does not suit them, even if that act becomes an impediment to the court's attempt at seeking truth and justice. Privilege means MPs can decree that the tribunal cannot sit. Privilege means Parliament can insist on no one writing about any of that if MPs so dictate. To breach such a muddled and self-serving set of conventions when they are pleaded in order to conceal iniquity may be thought a duty; for Mr Smith to blame 'a breach of privilege' for his downfall is simply contemptible.

What now for Mr Hamilton and the other admitted recipients of undeclared amounts of money? Will Mr Heseltine still gladly canvass for them? Will he and Mr

Coming soon to a Conservative-held constituency near you...

If you have voted for the Tory NOW WASH YOUR HANDS

REPRESENTATION OF THE PEOPLE ACT...

Major continue to parrot the line that Mr Hamilton is innocent until proved guilty? This notwithstanding his admitted lies to Mr Heseltine and his other confession to Sir Gordon Downey. This, notwithstanding the fact that he ducked his legal opportunity to prove his innocence in a trial in which the accuser, not Mr Hamilton, would have been considered guilty until proved innocent? Mr Hamilton has now told his local newspaper that Mr Major dismissed him as a minister in October 1994: no 'honourable' resignation for him. If Mr Major thought he was an unacceptable figure to serve as a minister, he must now say why he considers him an acceptable figure to serve as an MP.

This is an issue that unless resolved will justifiably continue to dog the Prime Minister until polling day. The simplest way out would, even now, be for him simply to publish Sir Gordon's report, a course of action for which Lord Nolan seems to have allowed. That will contain transcripts of all the evidence presented to Sir Gordon, together with his conclusions. Voters in the remaining nine constituencies where a doubt is still cast over their Conservative candidate would thus be able to vote in the light and not in the dark. That would be a bold and open thing to do, if somewhat belated. Does Mr Major have it in him? •

The Queen fires the starting gun for the election campaign

The quiet tide

'... It may be possible to misread the situation. Perhaps the polls are right ... and a
quiet tide is set to sweep Labour in with a massive majority.'

Mark Seddon

···

18 March 1997

Michael White

Fear is the key

J ohn Major and Tony Blair yesterday set a frantic pace for the longest election campaign in modern British history when they traded blows on the hustings of Middle England within hours of the Prime Minister's ritual trip to Buckingham Palace.

By the time Mr Major returned from informing the Queen of his intention to dispatch MPs to their constituencies as early as Friday – for a six-week campaign lasting until 1 May – the Labour leader was already canvassing his theme of the week, education, in a south London primary school.

After bringing his soapbox, talisman of his unexpected win in 1992, back to face hecklers again in highly marginal Luton yesterday, Mr Major issued a statement warning voters that their choice was safety first with the Tories – or 'a leap in the dark with a party you don't know and which doesn't want you to know what its policies are'.

Twenty points behind in most polls, Mr Major knows that fear is his best, slender hope of snatching a fifth Tory term. Labour strategists are equally aware that the election is theirs to lose by a slip or careless word. There will be no 1992-style triumphalist rallies as shadow ministers gently seek to reassure crossover voters that they are right to switch loyalties.

Before heading for a public meeting in Tory-held Gloucester, Mr Blair mocked Mr Major's claim to represent the real 'party of change' after 18 years in power. The Labour leader said, 'We have effectively been in an election campaign for a year. I welcome the chance to put our policies across.'

Labour claimed to be delighted at the spectacle of Mr Major 'scurrying off to Tory-held Luton', where both seats look set to become Labour for the first time since 1979. Given the divisions in the Conservative ranks and the looming leadership contest, campaign spokesman Brian Wilson even predicted that 'a long campaign is a potential disaster for the Tories'. That is the reverse of thinking at Conservative Central Office, which believes the longest of the 25 elections this century will allow Labour time to stumble.

Determined not to be squeezed out by his larger opposition rival, the Liberal Democrat leader, Paddy Ashdown, also welcomed the long-awaited announcement, confirmed by Mr Major on the Downing Street doorstep at 12.34 p.m. Mr Ashdown, speaking in his Yeovil constituency, condemned years of 'broken promises, incompetence and division' while promising – like Mr Blair – a positive campaign.

Apart from announcing that elections are 'also a lot of fun', Mr Major's campaign themes were laid out twice yesterday. Since 1979 'there's been a revolution in choice, in opportunity and in living standards', he said outside No. 10. 'At the general election there's a choice between the party that has brought that revolution about and the two parties that have opposed almost every single aspect of those changes.' It would be ironical if the opponents of change were given the chance to carry them forward.

Mr Blair mocked Tory claims to be the best bet for Britain. Cashing in on the 'time-for-a-change' mood detected around the country, he said, 'I say we can do better than this. We can have better schools, better hospitals and less violence on our streets.'

Mr Major, implicitly admitting how dire his political situation had become even before last night's defection by the *Sun*, said, 'A general election is not a gigantic opinion poll that will change nothing . . . or a TV talk show. It will affect the price of goods in the shops.'

Labour has increased its lead to 28 points, according to a Gallup poll for today's *Daily Telegraph*. No party has ever been so far ahead at the start of an election campaign. Translated into seats on 1 May, it would give Labour almost 500, reducing the Conservatives to a rump of about 150. •

18 March 1997

Martin Kettle

Strike first, fast and forget most voters

This is not merely the longest-anticipated election of modern times. It is also, though partly for that same reason, the most thoroughly prepared by those who will fight it. More thought, more planning and, in all probability, more money has been invested in the events of the next six weeks than in any other political confrontation in our history. No general staff went to war better prepared for the fray than Britain's political parties.

But there is nothing old-fashioned about the campaign to which we are about to be exposed. Election campaigns these days have been revolutionised in the same way as military planning. High-tech has replaced the poor bloody infantry long ago. Elections are no longer won, the strategists say, by supporters knocking on doors and by canvassers discussing political programmes on doorsteps throughout the land. Even old rituals like envelope-stuffing and election meetings (remember them?) are things of the past. Elections are won by preparation, resources and discipline. And in the words of the American general, these days it's about being firstest with mostest.

Try as you may, you do not get far in any discussion with politicians about the election without resorting to this language of warfare. This is, as the Trotskyists used to say, no accident. For the first time in our history, Britain is living in the era of the permanent campaign. Politicians no longer spend most of their time thinking or arguing, let alone governing. They spend it campaigning, and campaigning is a form of warfare by another name.

But who is the enemy? Those who came into politics for a cause could be forgiven for missing their aim here. For this is not any longer warfare between social classes or even primarily between political parties. In British politics, campaigning is primarily a war against and through the media, in which the press are not seen as a necessary evil or even – perish the thought – a necessary good.

The press are the end and not the means. We are the target in this campaign. They think that if they can capture us then they can capture you. This war will not be fought so much for policy advantage as for commanding influence. Capture Mount Brunson and Oakley Ridge, or even the Rusbridger Heights and (topically) the *Sun*-lit uplands, and the voters will lie before you undefended and vulnerable. To that end, all these efforts are now bent.

In fact there will be two elections taking place over the next six weeks, not one. The first election is the election that most people think is about to take place, an election conducted largely according to modernised versions of fairly conventional and traditional rules. In this election, the nation will become a giant forum in which the parties will parade their own virtues and attack their opponents' vices, and the voters, sitting in their front rooms by their televisions or reading their papers over the lunch break, will arbitrate between them.

Dream on. This platonic version of the fair election open to all may have lingered on in some vestigial respects until quite recently, but it no longer exists at all in the minds of the parties. This is because the parties are fighting the real election, the one that counts, and unless you are a swing voter in a marginal constituency, you are not part of it at all.

The parties do not like to go public about their lists of key seats or about the means that they employ to get at the voters who can swing these key seats one way or another. But this is where the election will be won and lost and where the parties long ago dug themselves in. The seats at issue and the voters who are deemed to matter are easy to identify. All you need is one of the volumes of electoral facts that are now widely available (not surprisingly, I commend for this purpose the *Guardian*'s own *Election Guide*) and which list the attainable seats in order of marginality. Then, having identified the seats, all you need is to hone the message to suit the voters who may change their minds.

It is to these voters that all political blandishments are now tailored. For months they have been the objects of clandestine reconnaissance and focused flattery. If you are such a voter, then nothing is too good for you. Your views are repeatedly solicited on the issues of the day. Your anxieties and your prejudices are treated with deference and respect. If it is possible to focus a policy to your needs, then rest assured that it will be done. If you are a core voter in a safe seat, on the other hand, forget it. The politicians are counting on you, but you no longer count.

In one sense, nothing could be more logical than this. In the first-past-the-post constituency system, all that matters in an election is to win more seats than the other lot. The seats in question are obvious, as are the relatively small proportion of voters who have an uncertain allegiance. The parties are therefore acting absolutely sensibly in focusing their efforts at this small sliver of the population. Yet the problem is that, in doing it this way, the whole election, and the ideal of the first election in particular, is irrevocably slewed. Like everyone else, swing voters in key seats get most of their information from television. Like most other people, they mould their sense of a party from brief but repeated exposure to the customised images of the party leaders. As a result, everything on the airwaves is aimed primarily at these voters alone and not at the generality of voters.

That, above all, is why you are frustrated (assuming that you are) with the images and messages orchestrated by Labour's massively disciplined and competent planners. It's because they aren't aimed at you in the first place.

Swing voters are, by definition, those who used to vote Conservative and who now contemplate voting Labour. Their views are, by definition, to the right of Labour's. Their preoccupations, it now emerges from the focus group surveys on which (in one sense rightly) the parties depend, are unusually self-interested. They are, it appears, still mourning the loss of Margaret Thatcher and remain besotted with the conceit of strong leadership which she encouraged and which Tony Blair therefore seeks to emulate.

The one thing they aren't, though, is typical. And yet they dictate the terms of the election on which we are now embarked. It is a bizarre irony that the high-minded campaign to secure a progressive majority is so heavily dependent upon a ruthless battle for the support of this so often feckless and selfish minority. ●

18 March 1997

Leader
Rising to the occasion

When did the first pundit first propose 1 May as the date of the 1997 election? It was, if collective memory serves, at least a year ago, and it is more than likely than John Major has also had this resonant springtime date ringed in his diary at least since the humiliating setback of the Staffordshire South-East by-election last spring. By last summer, 1 May was certainly the fashionable tip in all parties for election day, predicated on the Conservatives' continuing weak showing in the polls and supported by a chain of other reasoning which has grown no less compelling with the passage of time. May Day or not May Day may still have been the question that chatterers eagerly asked other chatterers whenever the subject of the election came round, but the reality was that the election date was always almost certain to be 1 May. The date was determined not only by the miserable drip-drip descant of the opinion polls but by such arcane questions as the new electoral register, the end of the tax year, the complication of an early Easter and, most important of all, the unavoidability of the local elections which will now take place, as they did in 1979, on the same day as the general election. What John Major announced yesterday morning in Downing Street (having first trailed the event in the Sunday papers) was therefore the worst-kept secret in the British political calendar.

Nevertheless, there is no denying that yesterday's announcement brings much general relief. 'At last' was the universal reaction, though it takes many differing forms. At last we know, say those who worry about not knowing. At last we can plan, say those who need to plan. At last we can have the long-awaited contest, say the protagonists. At last we can get rid of them, say the long-frustrated majority who never voted for them in the first place. Finally, and this in all too many minds for civic comfort, at last we can get the whole damn thing over and get back to ordinary life without all this politics. Those who are daily engaged in the political debate need to recognise this last reflex. For every person who is excited by the prospect of the election, there are many more who are already bored by it and who are largely indifferent to its long-expected outcome.

These alienated millions are unlikely to undergo any kind of conversion in the overlong weeks which stretch ahead between now and 1 May. This is already the longest-drawn-out British election campaign in living memory and the announcement, more than six weeks before the due date, is all of a piece with that. We live in the era of the permanent campaign. There is no doubt that Britain is suffering a more massive dose of electoral Americanisation this time round than at any time before. Mr Major may think that a long campaign will somehow rouse the sleeping giant of public opinion to slay the Labour dragon, but in this, as in so much else, he misreads the public. The public sleeps not from complacency but from boredom. The long campaign threatens rather than inspires.

Let us hope, nevertheless, for a campaign which rises to the occasion. For be in no doubt that this is a historic moment for our country. It is an opportunity to redraw the agenda of British history after a cripplingly long period of counter-revolution against some of the most fundamental values in our society. Whether the opposition parties will fully meet the challenge of giving the nation the alternative vision, based on different values and priorities, remains to be seen. But that our country urgently needs another way of doing things is beyond serious doubt. •

2 April 1997

Dame Barbara Cartland, talking to Alex Bellos
Why I vote Conservative

I will be voting for John Major. He is getting better and better every year. He is very, very good. He now speaks far better than he did. He's a brilliant speaker.

He is learning to be a real leader. He really does speak out. Look around and who else is like the old leaders like Winston?

I knew Winston when he was a little boy. He gradually got stronger and stronger. John Major came to lunch with me when he got in. He asked me what he should be doing. I said take England back to what it was.

We really want to be led, and John Major is leading as he has never before. I don't want to go in with Europe, and I am hoping the Conservatives don't join it. Every single bank, telephone and shop will have to be changed. Why do we want to alter things? It's appalling and crazy. Who is going to pay? We are. It is the ordinary person who pays.

What we want is a government that will make England what it always was when I was young. It was very, very strong. All people used to copy us abroad. Now no one does. They think we are silly fools. If we join Europe, we will find ourselves joined to other countries we have beaten.

The world has moved on, but badly. We need to go back to the days when everyone wanted to be a gentleman.

Sleaze? What's that? I have never heard of sleaze. My grandfather probably had affairs but he kept them to himself. Sex is nobody's business. My books sell all over the world. They don't sell very well in England because I won't write about sex.

The Labour Party are going to bring in a law that means you can go everywhere you want in the country. I have checked this with two people and they both said it was true. People will be able to walk into your garden and pick your flowers. It is absurd. My garden is a blaze of flowers. I don't want anyone in there. •

5 April 1997

Tony Brignull
A clear loser in Brochureland

This week all three would-be premiers chose to begin their campaigns in Brochureland. Here, where everything is scrubbed and deodorised, bright with promise and rich with good intentions, they launched their manifestos.

You will know Brochureland well. It is that fabulous country where cars shine eternally on roads free of jams and cones; where schoolchildren, untainted by sex, drugs or bullying, learn the recorder and pursue healthy outdoor activities. But it is political leaders who feel most at home in Brochureland; it is the one place where they have absolute control. Here there are no hecklers, no adulterers, no biased interviewers, no backbench bastards, no sleaze.

So what can we learn from the manifestos about the three main parties that their words alone do not divulge? If the Conservative manifesto were a house, it would be a sort of mock-Tudor pile, put up in a hurry. With cliché piled on cliché, there is not an original photograph in it apart from the charming but out-of-focus snap of John Major on page three. Peter Higgins, managing director of Lowe-Bell, who compiled the manifesto, testily admits he 'knows nothing of architecture and advertising' – and it shows. Words and pictures fight each other. The effect is old and tired.

Labour's manifesto is safely modern, like one of Wates's executive homes. They too have relied heavily on the stock photographs – smiling families, busy doctors and a fair sprinkling of VDUs – but their design is far cleaner. Someone has put discipline into this and no page deviates from its one-third visual/two-thirds text layout. You get the feeling this party knows where it's going, even if it's not very far in design terms.

By contrast, the Liberal Democrats have employed an architect and given him free rein too. With less cash they achieve more. Whereas the other two parties use full colour, the LibDems use only yellow. To compensate they have eschewed stock photographs and shot some very good portraits. In each case, the person poses a question, which the text answers. The effect is modern, stylish and clean.

Yesterday afternoon I tried to speak to the designers of all three manifestos. None was available. Strung out, I should think, fed up to the back teeth with politicians and last-minute revisions. I can't imagine any of them will vote on 1 May. •

. . . .

3 April 1997

Larry Elliott
Tax break comes at a price

John Major was feeling awfully pleased with himself yesterday. After the two weeks of purgatory he has endured since the start of the election campaign, he obviously saw his plan to give a tax break to married couples as the beginning of the Conservatives' long-awaited recovery.

Whether giving £18 a week to a parent who gives up work to look after the children or elderly relatives is a political masterstroke remains to be seen. What is certain is that it is terrible economics. Put simply, the political calculus behind the tax proposal is that it will play well with the swing voters in the Tory marginals that need to be won if the Conservatives are to win a fifth term. But while Basildon man and Worcester woman might appreciate an extra £900 a year from the Inland Revenue, they are unlikely to be impressed by the inevitable price of their tax cut: higher mortgage rates.

With only around 2 million couples set to gain from the plan, this may not be seen as a price worth paying. The cost of home loans is currently lower than it has been for a generation, but the economy has been prevented from lapsing into a traditional British boom-bust cycle by the tough fiscal measures adopted by the Government over the past four and a half years.

This trade-off was effectively forced on Mr Major once the economy was liberated from the Exchange Rate Mechanism in September 1992. By a stroke of good fortune, Mr Major stumbled upon a policy that ensured recovery from a deep, long and self-inflicted recession; sterling depreciated by 15 per cent, base rates came down from 10 per cent to 6 per cent.

But the political cost of this easing of monetary policy was that fiscal policy had to be tightened aggressively. The two Budgets in 1993 raised taxes by £17 billion, helping both to reduce the deficit accumulated during the recession and to prevent lower base rates leading to an explosion in consumer spending.

The Treasury was almost beside itself with glee at the way the recovery developed. Confounding the pundits, Britain experienced a spell of non-inflationary growth in which unemployment came down without triggering the customary rise in earnings. The UK's performance has not been nearly so spectacular as the Conservative propagandists would have us believe, but the economy is nevertheless in reasonably good shape.

Kenneth Clarke knew that this mix of monetary and fiscal policy was right, particularly for a country like Britain which has a propensity to consume more than it can afford. That is why the Chancellor persisted with it right up until the start of the election campaign. Expectations were high that the Chancellor would come up with extravagant tax cuts in both the 1995 and 1996 Budgets. On both occasions Mr Clarke came up with packages that were – given the size of the Government's opinion poll deficit – almost models of Gladstonian fiscal rectitude.

Now, with four weeks to go until polling day, it appears that the Government has had a change of heart. With high-street spending rising rapidly, the housing market buoyant, consumer credit increasing by a record amount last month and the Government's finances still deeply in the red, Mr Major has decided that the time is right to relax fiscal policy.

Whatever the eventual size of the tax break, one thing is certain. It will all be spent by hard-pressed families rather than saved. The prospect of tax cuts to come will boost consumer spending, creating additional upward pressure on demand at a time when the economy is already starting to run up against shortages of capacity.

The governor of the Bank of England, Eddie George, is already baying for higher interest rates to damp down the economy; the more exuberant consumers become, the larger the increase in borrowing costs will have to be. This would be unwelcome news for individuals, but it would also be the wrong recipe for the economy as a whole.

Last night the pound's value was almost back to the levels it was at on Black Wednesday, and industry is starting to once again suffer from an over-valued exchange rate. The sensible course would be to tighten fiscal policy by raising taxes. That would have the effect of cooling down the economy, taking the pressure off the authorities to raise interest rates. Market expectations that borrowing costs were not about to go up would, in turn, lead to a weaker pound, thereby helping exports.

At a micro-economic level, Labour was right to argue that the move would do nothing to improve the finances of the 20 per cent of households where none of the occupants of working age have a job. There could be a slightly beneficial impact on work incentives for workless households – because take-home pay would rise as a result of the transferable tax allowance – but independent analysis has shown that 70 per cent of the gain would be swallowed up by the loss of state benefits.

For the time being, these sorts of considerations play second fiddle to the need to regain the political initiative. Yet the fact remains that Mr Major's tax and spending proposals can be afforded only if the economy grows by at least 2.75 per cent a year for the next five years, compared with an average of under 2 per cent since 1979.

This is the Nigel Lawson theory of public finances – where unsustainable growth rates are used to justify tax cuts. Most of us can remember where that led. •

Sean Smith

Blair arrives in Milton Keynes

8 April 1997

Kamal Ahmed
Smile . . . wave . . . ignore

Dee Sullivan, one of Labour's press officers, checks the town centre plan one last time. On it are scribbled drawings of the stalls and passageways of Northampton fruit and flower market. Between the stalls, around the bric-à-brac and the bedding plants, runs a dotted line in blue ballpoint pen. That is precisely where Tony Blair will walk.

Control. At South Cleveland hospital in County Durham metal barriers arrive to keep the press away from the canteen. The nurses who sit there nervously drinking their coffee and waiting for him to arrive had been invited the night before. By the Labour Party.

Control. The meeting at the Victoria Hall in Kidsgrove, Staffordshire, was billed as a chance for Blair to meet sceptical Conservative voters. As he walked into the hall the audience clapped and cheered, rosettes bouncing up and down on the lapels of the party faithful. And not a Tory in sight.

Control. Tony Blair has 23 days to go in the surreal world of the election battle-bus, where stepping off the dotted line is not an option. Even his coach has mirrored windows, so that nobody can see in.

The script is simple. Smile, handshake, wave, ignore. Are you going to privatise anything, Mr Blair? 'Lovely to see you, what a great place. Hi there, hello.' Mr Blair, about those devolution plans? 'Who do you think is going to win the football match? Hi, is this your child? Great.' The unions? 'No promises, trust me, no immediate revolution. OK, time to go. Bye-bye.' There must be a little voice going around and around inside the Labour leader's head. 'Stay on message,' it says incessantly. 'Stay on message.'

Yesterday was his sixth day on the road since the battle-buses were unveiled in London on Tuesday. It was spent in London, convincing the City and the public that the party does not have a 'black hole' in its government finance plans.

The Conservative chicken turned up again, brandishing a banner saying, 'What are you going to privatise, Tony?' The chicken was bundled off by a phalanx of press officers, pausing only while a motorcycle courier made yet another attempt at tearing its head off.

'Hello, Northampton.' Blair's first words of his tour last week set the tone for the campaign. Bright and breezy, he will smile incessantly for Mr and Mrs Public, in stark contrast to his stern and composed look for the press conferences every morning.

Northampton, Derby, Bayswater, Stirling, Glasgow, Kidsgrove, Trimdon, Durham. To see Blair at each of these occasions produces a weird sense of seeing events rerunning continually before your eyes. He is like Bill Murray in the film *Groundhog Day*, where every day is a snowy one in the middle of February. Every day for Blair is a sunny one in a small town in Britain.

'I am not here to tell you that vote for the Labour Party on 1 May and by 2 May everything will be wonderful,' he told those gathered on a warm day in Northampton market square. He said the same thing in an old school hall in Glasgow and at the Victoria Hall in Kidsgrove.

He would have said the same thing in Stirling had it not been for the shower of hailstones, giving everything an increased 'Hello, bye-bye' urgency.

Until Scotland everything ran smoothly. In Northampton only Maggie De'Ath, who runs a jewellery stall just off the dotted-line route, sounded a note of caution. 'I'm not convinced by any of them,' she said. 'Anybody who rises to the top of a political party does not do it because of altruism but because they want power,' she said. 'That does not make them particularly attractive as people, however much they smile.'

Later that same afternoon it was to Derby and a question and answer session with invited business people. Here was the first evidence of what makes Alastair Campbell, Blair's press secretary, growl – the Conservative plant. 'Why do you refuse to debate the issues with the Prime Minister on the television, Mr Blair?' one local businessman asked. 'Are you running chicken?' Blair answered with the broad brush he employs when the questions are not to his liking, blaming the Conservatives for changing the terms of the debate. A local journalist whispered that the questioner had used the same form of words faxed to his newsroom that morning from the local Conservative office.

Before the question and answer session Blair gave a speech on Europe. This is not for local digestion but is for Westminster's delectation. Each day has a central message – Europe, Scotland, health – that is aimed at London. The most prominent spots are given to those areas, last week Europe and Scotland, where Blair feels the New Labour message has yet to penetrate the public mind. His advisers call it 'tackling the areas of misunderstanding'. 'We discovered that most people did not know that there will be a referendum on a single currency under a Labour government,' one official said as the coach bounced along towards Derby.

Wednesday was a battle-bus day off, with Blair being kept in the background due to the Conservative manifesto launch. He spent the day checking and rechecking his briefings on the following day's Labour manifesto launch, while Mr Campbell mused on how he could get Blair on the front pages alongside Mr Major. And then came the release of Blair's handwritten covenant with the people. Mission accomplished for Mr Campbell.

On the surface at least, the stumble came in Scotland, another area where Blair feels there may be a problem. Given that Labour had promised to legislate for a devolved Scottish parliament with tax-raising powers, how could he give the assurance that taxes would not increase under Labour?

At 35,000 feet in an ageing BAC 1-11 aeroplane Labour has hired for the campaign, Blair started to prepare the ground. John Penman, the *Scotsman*'s political editor, was called from the economy seats at the back of the plane to join the Labour leader at the front. Before his interview Mr Penman was told by Mr Campbell, 'No theological discussions on the minutiae of the constitution, eh?' Mr Penman ignored the plea.

He was told that Labour had absolutely no plans to raise taxes in Scotland, whatever the powers conferred on a devolved parliament. And then came that quote: 'It's like any local authority, powers which are constitutionally there, they can be used. It's like the smallest English parish council, it's got the right to exercise it.'

Gaffe it was not. Mr Blair, George Robertson, the shadow Scottish secretary, and Pat McFadden, the Labour leader's key adviser, who will be travelling with him throughout the campaign, had met earlier to agree the Scottish message.

Neither was it a mistake that Blair refused to answer a question put to him 11 times during the next day's bad-tempered press conference. Would he veto any future plans of a devolved parliament to raise taxes?

'The key is getting the message across,' a Labour source said. 'And Tony was not going to be deflected from that. It may look a bit awkward at the time and the headlines may not be quite what we want but the result is the right one. Tony got his message across that there will be no tax rises in either England or Scotland and that sovereignty remains at Westminster.'

It was the first time during the election campaign that the Labour leader had been under pressure. At the previous day's British manifesto launch he had asked for questions from the people he feels comfortable with, the television political heavyweights like ITV's Michael Brunson and BBC's John Sergeant, who pat him big-issue questions which he can bat back with calming words about 'trust' and 'reassurance'.

But in Scotland there is no friendly soft ball. Mr Blair does not have the advantage of knowing who all the journalists are and was reduced to asking for questions from 'the beard on the left', the *Sun*'s Andy Collier, and 'the beard on the right', the *Dundee Courier*'s Andy Nicoll. They kept asking him the same question, and he kept refusing to answer it. Joe Klein, the man revealed as the author of *Primary Colors*, the 'fictionalised' account of the 1992 presidential election campaign, had one simple piece of advice for Blair the next day. 'Change the message,' said the man who will be travelling with the Labour team throughout the campaign in preparation for a 10,000-word article in the *New Yorker* magazine. And so the next day we had health, solid Labour ground.

It is difficult to over-estimate the degree of scrutiny Blair is under. Officials at Conservative Central Office pored over video footage of his London manifesto launch performance after being told that he had an earpiece which gave him a direct link with Mr Campbell, supposedly advising him on how to answer tricky questions. The *Sunday Telegraph* photographer was told to check all of his pictures for evidence of the same link. He couldn't find one because it does not exist.

Such pressure does affect him. Blair's manner in front of the press is twitchy, dealing with every question as if it is an attempt to catch him out and make him look stupid.

At his adoption meeting in Trimdon, County Durham, Blair's father, Leo, was led to the stage to embrace his son, who, he said, made him 'very proud'. But even here, among real friends, the Labour machine keeps operating. 'No, he doesn't want to say anything,' said Anji Hunter, Blair's personal assistant, referring to requests to speak to Mr Blair senior. Can we ask him? 'No, he doesn't want to talk. I'll talk to him and give you some quotes.' It would only take a minute. 'No. Look, he has not been very well.' Control. •

....

9 April 1997

David Ward and Matthew Engel

A great night out for the Christian ladies of Tatton

Conservative activists in Tatton defied the party leadership last night by adopting Neil Hamilton, the former minister at the centre of the cash-for-questions affair, amid angry and chaotic scenes. At an acrimonious meeting, 182 members voted for his adoption, 35 against, four put their hands up as abstentions and 61 did not vote. The outcome ensures that the sleaze issue will haunt the Conservatives for the remainder of the election campaign.

Disgruntled Conservatives emerged from the extraordinary general meeting at the Dixon Arms, Chelford, to describe it as a disgrace, both because an opportunity had not

Christopher Thomond

Neil Hamilton in a wilderness of Martin Bell posters

been given to make the case against Mr Hamilton and because calls for a secret ballot had been rejected.

It was one of the great nights in the history of barmy British media scrums, so it was certainly a great night for the Dixon Arms and the members of the Tatton Conservative Association. They stood in the car park dressed as if they were about to be interviewed for the telly, which most of them were, several times. Some of the women looked as though they had spent weeks doing their make-up; the men were in ties and suits or blazers, some of them wearing braces from the time before the time before the last time when braces were fashionable.

Most of the Tatton Tories, it emerged from the interviews, had only the fuzziest idea what Mr Hamilton is supposed to have done. They just kept repeating like a mantra, 'Innocent till proven guilty, innocent till proven guilty.'

They are very big on this idea in Cheshire. Outsiders may not realise this. 'Isn't it shocking about the IRA, Edna?' 'No, Maud, they're innocent till proven guilty.' 'That's what I mean. Yet everyone rushes to condemn them, that's what's so shocking.'

There was no question of the media infiltrating last night's meeting, but though thick red blackout curtains had been erected at the windows, they were not entirely sound-proof. It did seem to be the older ones – and that means pretty old – who were most vociferously in favour of Mr Hamilton. 'I really thought we might have some Christians among Conservatives,' said one of his supporters from the Forgiveness for All faction. 'It's all got up to sell newspapers,' another barked.

But they still love the idea of being on telly. And so do the Hamiltons. They arrived like an A-list celebrity couple attending the Oscar ceremony. When Mr Hamilton was asked if he thought he was about to face the music, his wife posed theatrically and quoted, 'Let's face the music and . . . dance.'

A group of 12-year-olds had been hanging around all night, smoking the odd dropped dog-end, as thrilled as everyone else about the chance of getting on telly. 'Can we have a skate park in Chelford, Mr Hamilton?' shouted one. It was probably the best question of the night. 'Yeah,' said his mate. 'You've got enough money. Open your piggy bank.'

The kids were, unfortunately, barred from the after-match press conference when, for the first time yesterday, Mr Hamilton was forced on to the defensive. He did not like being asked about the absence of a secret ballot and what appeared to be his slightly stretched account of his encounter with Mr Bell.

Christine Hamilton stood by his side, grin fixed. She is a remarkable woman, maybe more remarkable than her husband. 'Infirm of purpose,' you can imagine her saying. 'Give me the microphone.' Pressmen were speculating about the possibility of a Mrs Hamilton candidacy – as an Independent Conservative. And a pro-skate park candidate. There is no need for the Natural Law Party; Mr Hamilton is already levitating. •

. . . .

19 April 1997

Smallweed

Rag-sorter's Disease and Derbyshire Neck

A Gloucestershire reader writes, 'Is Martin Bell the only candidate in this election to have a disease named after him? I believe there is something called Martin Bell Syndrome, also known, appropriately some may think, as Fragile X.' Smallweed wearily replies, What an impossible question! Do you know how many candidates are standing in this election? Am I supposed to plough through the lot? I suppose I cannot quote Parkinsonism or Wilson's Disease, since neither is standing, but some of the conditions disclosed in my medical dictionary clearly refer to protagonists in this election. Derbyshire Neck, for instance, is named after Edwina Currie. I dare say the term Rag-sorter's Disease (an alternative name for anthrax) derives from Alastair Campbell. And the term 'idioglossia', here defined as 'the continued utterance of meaningless sounds, the afflicted person "speaking" language intelligible to no one', plainly derives from observation of politicians. •

23 April 1997

Mark Seddon
The quiet tide

My colleague Bryan Rostron, an old *Mirror* hand and veteran anti-apartheid campaigner, turned to me last week as we were walking through the wasteland that is King's Cross and asked why, as the Tory years end, there didn't appear to be an enthusiasm amongst Labour people similar to that amongst ANC supporters in South Africa as apartheid crumbled? Perhaps the difference is that the ANC won the first general election that it was able to contest, while poor old Labour has lost four in a row. And yet, talking to Labour activists and candidates in rock-solid Labour areas, the reports are disturbingly similar.

'I have never known apathy like this in 25 years,' one North-east MP told me, while another in Scotland believed that 'boredom was trailing Labour into second place'.

A number of Labour candidates have found it difficult to motivate as many activists as they did back in 1992. But then we know where New Labour's best efforts are being targeted, amongst swing voters in marginal constituencies – most of whom have been voting Conservative.

Elsewhere, Labour voters are expected to turn out as usual – I hope that they do. Of course it may be possible to misread the situation. Perhaps the polls are right – and ICM's today is wrong – and a quiet tide is set to sweep Labour in with a massive majority.

There could be another reason for the apathy factor. The ANC's election platform was radical, it promised great change. New Labour on the other hand does not. It promises better management within existing resources. Its great fortune has been that the Conservatives have made themselves unelectable. I have no doubt that the architects of New Labour would shake their heads at Nelson Mandela for raising expectations too high amongst his supporters, only to see them dashed later.

I expect that Labour will win on 1 May, yet somehow the election campaign has not taken off. While New Labour is organisationally light years away from the Penny Farthing machine of yesteryear, it is politically as well. So much so that even leading lights from the old SDP, such as Baroness Williams, berate its conservatism. So too do many of the leading intellectual lights of the Left.

From Fitz the English bulldog (thank the heavens it wasn't called Fritz) to deep purple instead of blood red, New Labour gives every impression of wanting to divorce itself from a past that at its worst was indifferent and at its best was very good indeed.

How was it, for instance, that in 1945 a Labour government was able to embark on a massive housebuilding programme and create a welfare state so popular that successive Conservative governments felt obliged to support it? All this at a time when Britain had just emerged from a devastating war and was only a third as wealthy as it is now.

'Don't worry,' a veteran psephologist told me the other day, 'Labour is aiming for two terms. You will see the radicalism after the next election.'

Comforting words, but what I want to know is why it is that Labour has left it to the churches to speak up for the victims of the blessed Margaret? Few expected that the election of a Labour government would immediately usher in the new socialist dawn, but is it going to make a start? Can we have any socialism at all? Will we have to await proportional representation for the mould to break?

Despite the best intentions of some of those who will be in the next Labour government, by accepting the Government's spending plans, new ministers will shortly be forced to choose between increasing taxation or cutting public expenditure still further. Increasing taxation for the better-off has foolishly been ruled out, and relying on economic growth and a one-off windfall tax may not increase revenue by any great shakes. This is before anyone even starts to think about monetary union.

Across a whole front Labour has retreated just as the public has finally revolted against Thatcherism. And yet there are still plenty of reasons for voting Labour. Tony Blair may have stepped back from restoring the earnings link to pensions, but the Tories are proposing to privatise them. Labour is promising to bring in a minimum wage, devolution and skills training. The health service is safer in Mr Blair's hands, as are the schools. The pledges are thin, but they can be built on. I expect that they will.

There are those, such as the *Guardian*'s Catherine Bennett, who have had enough. She cites Peter Mandelson as the final straw, for coming to 'embody the party in his own lovely person'. But since Tony Blair has said that his project will be complete 'when the Labour Party learns to love Peter Mandelson', it never will – for it will be impossible to corral every party member down the Ministry of Truth's dismal corridors into Room 101.

Bennett is brave, but I think that she is wrong. What happens after the election is far too important to be left to a few super-activists at the top. Walking away is the counsel of despair. Which is why I hope that all Labour supporters will make one final effort to get the Tory bastards out. We can deal with our own, afterwards. •

• •

29 April 1997

Leader
Change is imperative

A former Conservative minister said in private recently that if his party won the 1997 general election, he would conclude that no change of government could be obtained in this country in the foreseeable future other than by armed popular revolt. Let us hope that his prediction proves unnecessary, even though the mere thought of a fifth Tory term underscores the importance of the decision which the voters must take this week. Without the defeat of the Conservative Party on Thursday there can be no progressive option in Britain of any kind.

Underpants inferno at Westminster

The principal reason why the Conservatives should be defeated on Thursday is that over 18 years they have imposed a redistribution of wealth to the rich, power to the powerful and opportunity to the privileged which now urgently needs to be undone. For 18 years, Britain has been the world's laboratory for an experimental counter-revolution. It has been driven by a dogma that says a nation's goods and services should be transferred from public to private hands. The result has been a new version of national failure. An economy which could have been blessed by windfall gains from North Sea oil has grown unremarkably and its fruits, in a grotesque maldistribution, have gone mainly to those who had most already.

In 1979, launching the counter-revolution, Margaret Thatcher hoped that 'where there is discord, may we bring harmony'. In 1990, her chosen successor, John Major, spoke of creating 'a country that is at ease with itself'. Both remarks seem absurd today in communities where so many households have no breadwinner, where public education has been undermined by the flight into private schools, where the redistribution of health care makes little sense, and where estates and town centres are too often out of bounds as public spaces. Violence and incivility to fellow citizens have increased. Environmental quality has been squandered. Instead of harmony and ease, the characteristics of the last two decades are insecurity and stress. For more than a generation, the Conservatives have driven their vision through the institutions of one of the most successful and socially cohesive nations in the world.

Change to this system and culture is now imperative, which is why the defeat of the Conservatives is important not merely for policy reasons but for the health of our culture and institutions. But we can undo the Conservatives' work only if we recognise the full seriousness of what they have inflicted. Thatcherism should not be rewarded with praise it does not deserve and its leader should not be made into a role model for the prime minister who must take Mr Major's place. Both a new government and a new form of government are needed. •

2 May 1997

Joanna Coles

Bubbly galore but good-timers weaseled out

C harles Moore had ordered 50 cases of champagne, which worked out at precisely three bottles per expected guest. Even if the editor of the *Daily Telegraph* had been expecting a Tory landslide, this might have been deemed a trifle excessive, but someone had to do it. You can't have a funeral without a wake, and no one else had offered. Where else were Lady Thatcher, Sir Charles Powell, Michael Portillo, John Redwood, Bruce Anderson and Paul Johnson expected to go? The traditional good-time Tories had weaseled out. Lord McAlpine had cried off, even Lord Archer didn't have the heart to proffer his customary shepherd's pie and Krug.

It started at 11 p.m. The champagne and crab cakes did the rounds as Jonathan Dimbleby chuntered in the corner on TV. For a while the starched upper lips stayed firm. By midnight ('Possibly a recount in Torbay . . . Crosby has fallen to the Labour Party. . . ') they had begun to tremble. By 1 a.m. ('There's Tony Blair at the Trimdon Labour Club and the celebration party has already begun') they were pursed white, and by 2 a.m. they were wrapped around the bottles.

'I've just filed a "Blair Wins" leader, so I want them to win now,' giggled Moore improbably. Behind him Bernard Levin put up token resistance to a glass of Pommery and then succumbed.

Resplendent in a peach suit, Pat Dessoy, the Prime Minister's older sister, was sitting upstairs quietly weeping. 'Hay fever,' she muttered unconvincingly. Did she know what her brother was going to do next? 'I don't like the *Guardian*,' she hissed. Yes, yes, but what about her brother? 'Some say he's going to work for a Swiss bank, others tell me he's going to work for the European Parliament. I don't know.' She shrugged, helplessly reaching for another handkerchief.

Around her, the guests shuffled awkwardly, but they've come to bury Major not to praise him, pallbearers to the coffin of Tory hopes. These were Thatcher's children not Major's men. Even the eulogies were nostalgic, groping back for the Thatcher glory years and the time of Tory triumph.

'Great day this is for Britain,' snorted Simon Heffer, Major's fiercest right-wing critic. Swaying gently as he balanced two bubbling glasses and Dimbleby announced another Tory loss, he remarked cheerfully, 'The British people are just showing their essential moral decency.'

It was the end of the party. 'A deserved disaster,' barked David Twiston Davies, the *Telegraph* letters editor. 'It will be a day of grief in the letters page tomorrow.' •

2 May 1997
Michael White
Until the bitter end

J ohn Major kept smiling to the bitter end and, like most rejected prime ministers, bitter will be the word for some weeks to come. But the combative gleam of the man with a love of campaigning went out of his eyes some days ago. He knew he was a goner.

Given the barely suppressed state of civil war within his party, Mr Major is unlikely to get a second chance. In any case, an unbroken six years five months in Downing Street is pretty good by any standard. In this century only Thatcher, Asquith and (narrowly) Harold Macmillan have done better.

But how will history judge him? And what will Mr Major do now? Yesterday he ducked the second question, knowing all too well that potential successors to the leadership are already plotting. What is certain is that he will do his best to hang on as long as suits him to deliver the job to a candidate he respects.

Then, who knows? He is only 54 and could go back to the City to make some money. Or he could 'do an Alec Douglas-Home' and remain available to serve as Foreign Secretary under a successor as Lord Home did under Ted Heath. It is a job which Mr Major briefly held before.

As for how history will judge him, on the BBC's *Election Call* on Wednesday the outgoing premier chose to highlight his government's 'strangling' of inflation as his most lasting achievement. If so, the British economy paid a fearful price: a deep recession, higher taxes (not enough) and borrowing (too much). It also lost £2 billion defending Mr Major's commitment to the European Union's Exchange Rate Mechanism before ignominious collapse on Black Wednesday, 16 September 1992. That may have been the day which doomed his government. Yet five years on John Major seems genuinely proud of low inflation, better growth than across the Channel and falling unemployment. Tony Blair will reap the harvest of recovery.

Aides also pointed to Mr Major's creation of the National Lottery as a lasting change in public life, or, as he put it, 'the most serious attempt ever properly to fund sport, arts and our cultural heritage'. Some people, Lady Thatcher included, unless she has changed her mind since she vetoed a lottery in her day, regard it as a terminal admission that Britain's governing élite has lost its way and its self-confidence: opting instead for surrogate taxation. Mr Major will have none of it.

He would also cite rising educational standards, a subject near to the heart of a grammar school dropout who, legend has it, lost a competition for a bus conductor's job to a cheerful West Indian woman who had better maths.

Even that list of achievements would be disputed by his enemies. They would say he wasted Margaret Thatcher's legacy and broke up the dominant coalition she created of aspirational, patriotic C1s. They redefected with the *Sun*. But she also left him the huge problems of a savage recession, Europe and the poll tax. Mr Major protected the Thatcher legacy from Neil Kinnock in 1992 and kept the show on the road before succumbing to Blairite modernisers on the centre-left. He helped force Labour further right.

Mr Major was always a tactician with no clear 'big picture' vision, not a strategist. His majority was small and falling after 1992, but he was unwilling or unable to impose proper discipline upon his party at Westminster. The result was highly damaging. Euroscepticism grew like Russian vine. So did sleaze, or at least the perception of it. Mr Major set up both the Nolan (sleaze) and Scott (arms to Iraq) inquiries, something Lady Thatcher might not have done. He implemented some reforms urged by Lord Nolan, albeit ham-fistedly. With Albert Reynolds in Dublin, Major took real risks in launching the 1993 Northern Ireland peace initiative, but history may say that he should have taken greater chances. Most damagingly, he stands accused of pandering to Unionism in January 1996 when he appeared to set aside the 'Mitchell six principles' on all-party talks, insisting instead on elections in the province and on prior decommissioning of paramilitary weapons. He must know this was the great prize that eluded him.

Ever the natural underdog, he fought and lost his last underdog's campaign with more public grace than he often conducted himself in office. When loyal staff cheered him out of party headquarters on Wednesday most of them probably meant it: nice guy, but time to start again. •

⋯⋯⋯⋯⋯⋯⋯⋯⋯⋯⋯⋯⋯⋯⋯⋯⋯⋯⋯⋯⋯⋯⋯⋯⋯⋯⋯⋯⋯⋯⋯⋯⋯⋯⋯⋯

2 May 1997

Leader
A political earthquake

'Few now sang "England, Arise", but England had risen all the same.'

So wrote A. J. P. Taylor of the 1945 election in which the Labour Party first claimed a working majority in the House of Commons. Fifty-two years on, Edward Carpenter's socialist song is even less often sung now than it was then. 'England, Arise' would not get past first base as a New Labour anthem. And yet its words – 'the long long night is over' – express our first feelings this morning. For England arose again yesterday, and without a change in the heart of England there can never be a change of government. Scotland arose too, for whom the wait has been grimmer and the possibilities this morning correspondingly brighter. Wales too is once more a waking dragon today. Northern Ireland? That's another matter. But 1997 now joins 1945 and 1906 as the third great progressive electoral landslide of the twentieth century.

What Hazlitt once wrote of the Bourbons – 'When a government, like an old-fashioned building, has become crazy and rotten, it stops the way of improvement, and only serves to collect diseases and corruption' – also reads like an almost perfect description of the condition of the Conservatives. Their government had to go because it was a bad government proposing obnoxious policies and because it was in the grip of an increasingly hysterical rage against Europe in all its forms. But it also had to go because it had governed too long and too loosely for the good of democracy and of politics. It was essential that the Conservatives were defeated and, after the longest period of continuous single-party rule since the 1832 Reform Act, at last they have been.

That said, this is not a moment for emphasising the problems which lie ahead. This is a moment for celebrating the fact that a degenerate Conservative Party has been dispatched into opposition, and for marking the first Labour election victory for almost a quarter of a century. We greet Labour's election with a congratulation, a cheer and a surge of hope that it can live up to the expectations which so many millions have placed in it. •

---

2 May 1997

Nancy Banks-Smith
Fatal flaws in chaos theory

'**A** landslide?' said Professor Tony King witheringly on *Election 97* (BBC1). 'It is an asteroid hitting the planet and destroying practically all life on earth.' This was terrible news for Peter Snow. He had a nice new landslide computer graphic all ready. He hadn't anticipated an asteroid. Well, you don't, do you?

In Snow's landslide 12 politicians, hurtfully called the Dicey Dozen, stood under a cliff. 'Look at that!' cried Snow and they were all buried alive. Except Michael Howard, who made no visible effort to dig his colleagues out. As an encore Snow, who in another age would have filled the stage with flags, also buried several prime ministers and Mr Portillo.

Early in the evening Jeremy Paxman had asked Mr Portillo, 'Are you ready to drink hemlock yet?' Much later, soundly thrashed by a Twigg, Portillo no longer had to be patient with Paxman. 'Oh, Jeremy, do stop this nonsense! I'm now a man outside the Commons. I don't have to bother with questions like that.'

Being hit with a cliff is a great test of character. Portillo went with as much dignity as a man can who has admitted before a late-night crowd ('Oo!') that he was christened Denzil Xavier.

David Mellor was hauled away yelling 'Get off back to Mexico!' at Sir James Goldsmith.

Mellor said it was not so much a landslide as a sea wall collapsing all round you. This was a blow to Snow, who hadn't got a sea wall either. Snow did have a computer game in which Tony 'Top Gun' Blair went round shooting up blue tower blocks. 'Angela Rumbold's seat is quite an easy one to hit!' Dame Angela, rather a spare sort of woman, has every cause for complaint.

It was a night like a bullfight. As the carcasses were hauled away, the new intake looked young and fresh and milky as veal calves.

Unlike the TV presenters, touched up by Sharon in make-up, veteran politicians at the count had faces as white as fish bellies. Dame Angela gave a sharp grimace. Michael Portillo chewed his cheek.

Martin Bell's face seemed clenched in pain, which was unusual as he was winning. He said, 'I expected 48 hours in politics and I've got five years.' That's the tariff for the crime. Five years.

At Stevenage, to celebrate Barbara Follett's election, her husband produced a jeroboam of champagne. A large lad with a ponytail struggled to shift the cork. A larger man with a moustache joined in. Ken Follett produced a purple New Labour towel for better purchase. As the night wore on, the battle of the bottle continued unabated. 'We will keep you abreast of Stevenage as the night goes on,' said Dimbleby.

Outside the Festival Hall the singing crowd were waving their arms like sea anemones. Tony Blair, who had just flown in, said, 'It's been a long journey, has it not?'

He tends to say 'Has it not?' and 'Is it not?' coaxing agreement. Dimbleby called it a tight-laced speech.

At Downing Street John Major was undoing his corsets and making the comfiest speech of his life ('So right. OK. We lost') to a few staff. It was punctuated with gusts of laughter as the telephone rang. No one answered it. •

2 May 1997

David Ward
Even the tellers cheered for the man in white

The people of Tatton this morning decisively rejected Neil Hamilton, the disgraced former minister at the centre of the cash-for-questions affair, in favour of a crumpled hero in an off-white suit.

Anti-corruption candidate and former BBC journalist Martin Bell romped home with a majority of 11,000 on a 76 per cent turnout, sensationally overturning the notional 22,000 headstart enjoyed by Mr Hamilton in one of the safest Conservative seats in the country. Mr Bell polled 29,354 votes to Mr Hamilton's 18,277.

Mr Bell, who said at the beginning of his three-and-a-half-week campaign that his political career could be the shortest on record, now faces a possible full five years at Westminster. When he turned up for the count, even the tellers cheered.

In his acceptance speech, Mr Bell said that it was not his victory, but a victory for the people of Tatton. 'This is a proud moment for the people of Tatton and a humbling one for me.' Pledging to remain independent, serve a single term and not take a party whip, he said he would 'shed light into some dark corners of the Mother of Parliaments. It is a strong signal to the rest of Parliament, which will be heeded . . . In the words of G. K. Chesterton, "Smile at us, pay us, pass us, but do not quite forget that we are the people of England, that never have spoken yet."

'You have spoken.'

Mr Hamilton, his voice shaking, said he was 'devastated' by the result. •

3 May 1997

Matthew Engel
The history man

This was our Velvet Revolution, and yesterday the population went wild, British-style. People were seen breaking into half-smiles in public while reading the papers; some thought about making eye contact in the Tube; others even considered talking to complete strangers, then remembered themselves and drew back. After all, almost one adult in five had missed the mood sufficiently to vote Conservative, and it was remotely possible that you could meet someone willing to admit it.

The quiet tide

The extent of Labour's landslide meant that comparisons with 1945 were inevitable. But there was no repetition of the remark attributed to the lady diner at the Savoy as news of Clement Attlee's triumph filtered through: 'But this is terrible. They have elected a Labour Government and the country will never stand for that.'

The Savoy seemed calm at lunchtime, and the expensively suited young men in the restaurant were probably all employed by the Labour Party anyway. Mr Attlee could never have entered Downing Street with one-hundredth of the studied triumphalism of Tony Blair, or one-thousandth of his *élan*.

The new Prime Minister did not quite go for the full Roman emperor's option. He omitted to drape himself in a purple toga, dragging the defeated general in chains behind his chariot. His symbolism experts must have lost their nerve on that one. Instead, the new Prime Minister progressed on foot from the Thatcher Memorial Gates to No. 10, working a cheering throng, who had all been given security clearances, flags and – in some cases – placards with suspiciously similar handwriting. The ones I spoke to had come from places as far afield as Millbank Tower and Walworth Road. Spontaneous enthusiasm works best if you leave nothing to chance.

This was the *pièce de résistance* of Labour's campaign show, the final celebratory burst of electoral fireworks. At least one hopes it is. There is a lingering suspicion that the next five years could be like this. It worked all right for Kennedy, Reagan and Clinton; and Blair is the first British leader charismatic enough to make the comparisons sensible. When he reached the podium he refrained from quoting Francis of Assisi like Mrs Thatcher and he certainly did not get spattered with paint like Mr Heath. He said he would lead 'a government of practical measures in pursuit of noble causes'. Then he said there had been enough talking. 'It is time now to do.'

But it wasn't. It was time for another photo-opportunity. The children posed charmingly, and Tony and Cherie hugged and waved, and hugged again. Finally, the door shut behind them, and the Prime Minister began that mystical process of governance of which he – until that moment – knew as little as the rest of us.

John Major once said he was told things the moment he went into No. 10 that he did not know even after being Chancellor and Foreign Secretary. Yesterday Mr Blair was let into whatever darkness lies at the heart of the state. The rest of us, meanwhile, tried to come to terms with the magnitude of what had occurred. It was not easy. At 1.47 a.m. Paddy Ashdown was saying it looked as though there was going to be a change of government. Five minutes earlier BBC1 had flashed up 'Lab gain Hove'.

'Sometimes,' says the Queen in *Alice Through the Looking Glass*, 'I've believed as many as six impossible things before breakfast.'

Yesterday we all had to believe dozens of impossible things before breakfast. I am convinced there was a moment when Ian Lang was about to say it was only a mid-term blip. But it really has happened. The long years of Toryism are history.

John Major was driven away from Downing Street in a Jaguar which appeared to be leaking oil rather alarmingly.

Outside Downing Street, London looked as it always does on a warm spring day:

more frazzled than sunlit. The West End was clogged with traffic, and there were beggars in the Strand.

You can't blame the Government. Not yet. Reality will intrude soon enough: everyone knows that, the Prime Minister better than anyone. But for one shining moment everything does seem bright and new again. Please God, don't let Labour ruin it. •

· ·

2 May 1997

Bel Littlejohn

I'm still waiting for that phone call, Tony

ejoice! That was the first word to come into my head when I realised, after 18 long, soul-destroying, Thatcherite years ground down by the weight of vested interests, that at long last New Labour was home and dry. Rejoice! But then disillusionment began to set in. As readers of this column will know, no one has supported Tony Blair and New Labour more than Bel Littlejohn. So it grieves me to say this, but the early indications suggest that Tony is reneging on some, if not all, of his election promises.

Let's begin at the beginning. I was with the lovely Barbara Follett in Stevenage last night when the news began filtering through that Tony had pulled off the big one. It had been a long, hard day, with Barbara going spare trying to decide what to wear for her live on-stage appearance with the Returning Officer for Stevenage. 'I don't want to overdo it, Bel, do I? I mean, Hervé Leger's running me up something fantastic for my maiden speech, but I think election nights call for something more solemn, more tentative. I want to show my solidarity with the working classes, if any. How about my blue Gaultier dungarees? Or might the Returning Officer also be in blue? I'd hate to show him up!'

The quiet tide

In the end, we settled for a lovely deep rich red, with lipstick and shoes to match. When the result came through, I had to restrain the super Ken from whipping out his Gibson Les Paul and treating the assembled crowds to a rendition of The Who's recent 'Won't Get Fooled Again'.

Then it was ta-ra to Stevenage, and thanx everyone for all the help, and back to their home in Cheyne Walk, just this side of Battersea, for the party of a lifetime. To celebrate, Barbara had given all the staff the evening off. Of course, this meant getting in new and largely untrained staff, but they coped magnificently with the sparkling wine (from the hard-working Bollinger co-operative).

It must have been 2 or 3 in the morning before the doubts started to seep in. Neither Tony nor a single member of his inner cabinet had taken the trouble to call Barbara or myself to offer us highly placed jobs on government committees. Barbara has every reason to believe herself ideally suited to a ministerial position – Junior Environment Minister with Special Responsibilities for Colour Co-ordination, or something along those lines – yet for the past five hours Tony Blair has maintained a resounding silence on the matter.

My God, I hope his new lofty position as Prime Minister hasn't gone to Tony's head. But so far – and, yes, I admit it's still early days – all the signs are that it has. A warning: if he continues to override the wishes of the people as he has done in these first five hours, his premiership will go on as it began: sluggish and self-satisfied. Make way for shattered dreams. •

Tony Blair invites Mrs Thatcher to Downing Street for counsel

The Velvet Revolution: early days

30 May 1997

Simon Hoggart
Smiling through

President Clinton arrived in Downing Street, hobbled out of the car and started smiling. Mrs Clinton smiled too. So did Tony and Cherie Blair. Goodness, how they smiled. They did not stop.

It must have been quite painful, smiling all the time. When they posed outside No. 10 they looked like participants in a mass Moonie wedding. Mr Clinton was very glad to be amongst us. No wonder, since it meant a full 24 hours more without anyone mentioning Paula Jones. So it was unkind of a photographer to shout, 'Could you get down on one knee, please?'

The other photographers laughed their heads off, but the Clintons and Blairs just kept on smiling. The President had a walking stick, calling to mind the old American joke: 'How does a Razorback [Arkansan] count to 20? Takes his boots off. And 21? Drops his pants.' Now President Clinton can count to 22.

They went inside. I checked out the limo. Just an ordinary armour-plated Cadillac Fleetwood Brougham runabout. In the back was a folder marked 'For the President: Information', which, if it's like other American guidebooks to London, may be highly misleading: 'Prime Minister Blair hates informality. Address him as "Your Sublime Excellency"... passengers on the Tube will love to see pictures of your grandchildren...'

There was also a black bag containing a jumble of used plastic bags, which was encouraging, because it looked just like the rubbish in the back of our car.

Inside, Mr Clinton swept into the Cabinet Room. Tony Blair, still smiling like a Teletubby, welcomed him. 'We are absolutely delighted to have you here. It is a very great day for us.' Then he said it again. This kind of brown-nosing is the small change of international diplomacy.

'The courage and strength of leadership you have shown have brought enormous benefits...'

The President addressed Mo Mowlam. 'I saw you on TV, being optimistic about Northern Ireland, which is an article of faith in my life and my household.'

Really? Is Chelsea taught optimism about Ulster over the cornflakes?

He made a little joke, about wanting to have a 179-seat majority. The Cabinet laughed sycophantically, and when he had finished they thumped the table. A colleague who was present described it as 'a dignified banging', which is something Mr Clinton knows all about.

The wives headed off to the Globe Theatre to see part of *Henry V*. Its famous line, 'Once more into the breeches, dear friends,' is also an important watchword in the Clinton household.

The husbands went to the White Room and smiled at each other. (This all made a few seconds of CBS TV at home, just before the weather forecast.) Mr Clinton said he had read the Labour manifesto. 'The future, not the past. For the many, not the few. Leadership, not drift.' He was getting the message. Verbs lose elections.

Later they appeared in the Rose Garden. Bees buzzed, sirens whined. Into the sleepy atmosphere, Mr Blair coined some exciting new clichés: 'We prefer reason to doctrine, we are strong on idealism, we resist ideology.' They are intolerant of intolerance, respectful of respect. 'New times, new challenges, a new political generation . . .' We might have 10 years of this.

Mr Clinton slightly spoiled the mood with a tribute to John Major ('I had a good and productive relationship with him') but not even that stopped Mr Blair smiling.

Then the President strained credulity one last time. He was so glad he had come in time to see Britain's 'unique and unspeakably beautiful spring'. But at that point, the only time he'd been outdoors was on his ride from the airport. Now I live near Hounslow. No one has ever called it unspeakably beautiful, even in nice weather. But this was a summit meeting and had nothing to do with reality. •

---

7 June 1997

Mark Lawson

Our never-ending love affair with Blair

The image of the 'honeymoon' for a leader's initial relationship with the electorate is familiar. But, in the case of Tony Blair, it scarcely tells the story. The voters of Britain, it seems, have rung down to the concierge to reserve the suite indefinitely, blissfully scribbled 'Definitely' on the 'Do Not Disturb' notice on the door and jumped back under the duvet.

A Gallup survey for the *Daily Telegraph* gives the new Prime Minister an 82 per cent approval rating after a month in office, the highest since records began, and double the figure achieved by Margaret Thatcher even before she had time to upset anyone in 1979. And – when respondents were questioned on 10 early New Labour pieces of proposed

The Velvet Revolution: early days

Labour legislation – eight policies showed clear majority support, including 90 per cent approval for the reinvestigation of Gulf War Syndrome, 89 per cent for the outlawing of land mines and 60 per cent for the ban on tobacco advertising.

To anyone who has followed British politics and sport during the last 20 years, this week has become increasingly surreal. Italy are humbled at football, Australia humiliated at cricket and a left-wingish prime minister apparently unites the country.

If the word Camelot had not come to stand in England for greedy and arrogant men who award themselves vast pay rises from money raised for charitable causes, we would know which historical comparison to reach for. Even traditionally hard heads will nod in recognition at these words from the historian Arthur Schlesinger on the first month of the Kennedy administration: 'The air had been stale and oppressive; now fresh winds were blowing. There was the excitement which comes from an injection of new men and new ideas, the release of energy which occurs when men with ideas have a chance to put them into practice.'

The Camelot comparison might seem absurdly flattering to Blair but, in fact, in one important sense it understates the improbability of his current popularity. The American reaction to Kennedy was partly a euphoria born of ignorance and deference. The President, we now know, had secrets sexual and medical (the renal condition, Addison's Disease) which were ignored as part of a general glamorisation of his character. Blair deserves credit for having achieved his own mood of national renewal – however ephemeral it proves to be – in the face of a much more revelatory press and sceptical general public.

A lasting ideological conversion of Britain remains the least likely explanation of these events. Blair is clearly the beneficiary of elation at the change of political scenery and also, perhaps, of a political version of hype. A media superstar – which the Prime Minister became with the amazing scale of his victory – wins many new fans in their first wave of fame, with people wanting to be part of the excitement. Music fans queue to purchase the Number One CD; voters now rush to buy Blair's record.

Cynicism and logic dictate that these eerie political conditions cannot last. The political classes understand that there must come a time when the Prime Minister's approval score is lower than his age and the Government's policies are mocked.

For a start, as with much of what New Labour has done, it is easy to see the early successes as a mere triumph of presentation. What Blair has so far done – and done brilliantly – is to create a genuine atmosphere of change and even radicalism with minimal state expenditure. But the bans on international and domestic weapons and cigarette sponsorship and the sympathy towards sick Gulf War veterans are low-tax humanitarian policies with such general support as to be almost apolitical. The liberation of the Bank of England and the creation of a City regulator were similarly cross-party initiatives.

Cunningly, Blair seems to have begun with a period of consensus government. Admittedly, there is some skill in guessing, for example, that a more independent Bank of England would be widely welcomed. In contrast, when the Major administration reached, in its final weeks, for a supposedly populist policy, it was in such a state of ideo-logical sclerosis that it tried to tempt a Britain edging towards republicanism with a new royal yacht.

Here, the image of the political honeymoon becomes double-edged. This time, not only the voters have observed the protocol of young marrieds but the Prime Minister as well. He has kept the conversation general, studiously avoided rows. Yet the issues which would produce a reassuring echo of 'yes' in a focus group are few and may already be exhausted. The worrying – or realistic – news for the Prime Minister in the Gallup survey is what happens to the figures when the questioning reaches the great affairs of state. Here, for the first time, the response is less than half positive: 48 per cent approval on the European Social Chapter, 40 per cent on meeting Sinn Fein without the precondition of ceasefire. At this point, the new maths of the first 30 days come up against the traditional arithmetic of politics. Here lies the reality of leadership.

And political statistics often lie, perhaps appropriately, even more than the average kind. George Bush lost the presidency less than 18 months after winning 92 per cent popular approval in the aftermath of the Gulf War. Even so, it is still remarkable for Blair to have generated such excitement with an election rather than a war victory (always a notorious rabble-rouser). The statistics of these two months – the May par-liamentary landslide, the June 82 per cent approval ratings – should stand, whatever now happens, as an important fact of British history: a weird period of national aspi-ration and happiness.

Perhaps, in mid-August, the England cricket captain will brandish the Ashes while the Prime Minister hosts, to universal acclaim, a press conference to celebrate his first 100 days. Common sense and history, however, suggest that such explosions of hope tend soon to be viewed retrospectively as small tragedies of unanswered yearning. •

3 July 1997

Leader
Mr Brown's *tour de force*

Economically, Labour's first Budget for 18 years is a *tour de force* even though there must be doubts whether enough has been done to puncture the consumer boom. Gordon Brown delivered it with unremitting gravitas, gathering together all the themes he has so consistently espoused in recent years, and more. Against the austere backdrop of a sharp fiscal tightening he managed to fire a salvo of micro-economic measures that delighted Labour MPs and lots of interest groups. It was a Budget for big and small business (lower corporation tax), for investment (tax write-offs), for film-makers, for training, for welfare to work, for single mothers, for savers and for housebuilding if not house owning. And – dropping unexpectedly out of the sky at the very end of the speech – an extra £1.2 billion for the health service and £1 billion for schools (plus another £1.3 billion phased over five years). No one on the Government benches seemed to worry about the disingenuousness of these last measures since, though funded from the contingency reserve, they clearly breach departmental ceilings on which Mr Brown had inadvisedly put a cap. Nor did anyone worry that the new 2.25 per cent rise in NHS spending next year is less than the 4 per cent rise the Conservatives had implemented during the last four years. When you are expecting nothing anything is welcome.

Mr Brown certainly intends to be an Iron Chancellor. He is raising taxes (including the one-off windfall on utilities) by £5.9 billion this year, £6.6 billion next year and £5.2 billion the year after. By the end of next year the Budget deficit will be down from £22.5 billion to only £5.5 billion. Of course, merely planning something doesn't make it happen. Remember, the first Medium Term Financial Strategy of the Conservatives promised something similar in 1981 but it didn't materialise. But that doesn't alter the courage with which the new Chancellor is tackling the excessive borrowing requirement he inherited. He is taking enough money out of the economy, the only question is whether he is taking it out of the right places. The £5.2 billion to be raised from utilities over two years and the startling £11.6 billion over three years from the abolition of tax credits for pension schemes is big money. It will affect all of us eventually through lower pensions and maybe higher prices. It will bring down the deficit but have minimal effect on spending in the high street, which is the most immediate economic problem. It's true some £730 million extra will be taken out in extra fuel duties this year, but this is small beer compared with the pace of the spending spree even before it is aggravated by the spending of the building society hand-outs (an unearned windfall that the Chancellor dared not touch). Higher stamp duty for more expensive houses, along with the cut in mortgage relief, will take some of the froth out of the housing revival but there is little to stem the consumer boom. If this is right, then the Bank of England will have to step in and correct the situation with higher interest rates, with all that that means for manufacturers battling against an over-valued pound. It's no use reducing corporation tax and increasing investment reliefs if industry sees its goods being priced out of the market.

The concessions to education, housing and health are unreservedly welcome, but they have to be seen against the two-year Tory spending plans which just did not add up. Labour MPs cheered as Mr Brown announced a £1.2 billion allocation of contingency-fund money for health spending next year, but ministers may yet have to raid this year's contingency fund if they want to avoid a health crisis this winter. The education service will be in better shape. The threat of rising class sizes and up to 12,000 teachers made redundant has been averted. A separate capital programme – £1.3 billion over five years – represents an extra £150 for every pupil in the school system.

Mr Brown has done well in dismal fiscal circumstances to start rebuilding the pillars of the welfare state from a position of ongoing erosion. The only qualification is whether he has done enough to dampen consumer spending. If the Government doesn't get the short term right, then its estimable emphasis on the long term could be jeopardised. •

3 July 1997

Alex Brummer
A touch of the New Deal

The rhetoric of Gordon Brown's maiden Budget, with its forceful talk of a modern route to economic strength and modernising the welfare state, was his precise way of telling the public that Labour is different from its predecessors. And it is. However, in the face of the downbeat assessment from the financial markets – which are obsessed by his failure to do something dramatic to restrain consumer spending – some of the radicalism of what Mr Brown is actually doing can be missed.

Sure, the perception that interest rates will have to rise and the impact this has already had on sterling are important. But that has been evident from the financial markets for months, which have been projecting sharply higher interest rates by year end.

The drama in Mr Brown's Budget is in what has been most predicted, the excess-profits tax on the utilities, which over two years will raise £5.2 billion from a wide range of companies stretching from the regional electricity firms, the hardest hit along with water, to multinationals like British Telecom and BAA, which escape relatively lightly.

But the other side of the excess-profits tax – a series of measures which will allow young people and the long-term unemployed to climb a ladder of opportunity – is uplifting. The Chancellor may not have quite found the elevating language to convey this and there is the risk, like so many training schemes of the past, it will be poorly executed. But the sheer scale of this exercise – which has the quality of Franklin D. Roosevelt's New Deal about it – could mean it will work. Nor should anyone be mean-spirited about the idea of lifting £1.3 billion out of the windfall receipts to repair the fabric of the nation's schools over the term of this Parliament.

Some spending on schools, however modest, is better than critics of the Government's decision to stick with Tory control totals for public spending could have hoped for.

The second mega change in this Budget is the one which for most people is least easy to understand. But the abolition of the advance corporation tax is at the heart of Mr Brown's Budget settlement. It raises huge amounts of cash: £2.3 billion in the current financial year, rising to £3.95 billion next year and £5.4 billion in 1999–2000, dwarfing the revenues from the windfall tax. The tax collected is the equivalent of a 5p increase in the basic rate of income tax.

The Velvet Revolution: early days

This is the tax bombshell which was waiting to be exposed during the election campaign but was never able to surface because of Labour's efficient spin-doctoring. This tax also ideally fits in with Labour's strategy of persuading industry to invest more. By removing a tax advantage to pay more in dividends, the Chancellor is clearly banking on corporate Britain investing more of its retained profits.

But the change on ACT will affect almost everyone in Britain in an occupational pension scheme. Over the short haul, with a few Band-aids, the well-funded established occupational schemes with defined benefits may be able to muddle through using surpluses, as the Chancellor indicated in his speech. But over the longer run it means additional costs of £500 billion for Britain's occupational schemes, or a radical change in pensions provision. When the United States took similar steps, disaster was also predicted for corporate America and Wall Street, but the effects were to establish the equivalent of money purchase schemes over which individual investors have been allowed greater control. The result has been a massive move into equities, which has helped to fuel the current share boom on Wall Street and raised the level of shareholder involvement.

The compensation to business for the ACT hit on pension funds and the utilities measure is the straight cut in corporation tax. It is by no means a cheap giveaway and will be worth almost £2.25 billion to the corporate and small-business sectors by the 1999–2000 tax year. The curiosity is that the CBI in effect is opposing the cut on the grounds that it fails to compensate for increased pension costs.

Certainly, for the moment there is nothing dramatic to rein in the current consumer boom. However, over a full year, if the duty, tax relief on mortgages and stamp-duty increases are taken into account, some £2 billion is being taken out of the consumer sector.

If necessary, Mr Brown still has the March Budget to impose increased taxes on consumption should the windfall boom not have worked out. Sure, interest rates may have to rise, but the scale of the post-Budget surge in sterling is unwarranted. •

Jonathan and Lolicia go to court

Sean Smith

Sleaze II: impaled on the sword of truth

··

21 June 1997

Luke Harding and David Pallister
He lied and lied and lied

The *Guardian* last night called on the Director of Public Prosecutions to prosecute Jonathan Aitken for perjury and conspiracy to pervert the course of justice after the dramatic collapse yesterday of his libel trial. Aitken, the former Cabinet minister, discontinued his libel action against the *Guardian* and Granada Television after new evidence proved he had lied to the High Court. He now faces public disgrace and a legal bill for £1.8 million.

Aitken, who lost his Thanet South seat at the election, failed to turn up for yesterday's two-minute hearing, in which his counsel, Charles Gray, QC, agreed Aitken would pay almost all of the defendants' legal bill.

Aitken's action collapsed after the *Guardian* produced new evidence in the High Court on Wednesday: British Airways flight coupons and Budget car hire documents showed the ex-MP committed perjury about the payment of a bill for his controversial stay at the Paris Ritz in September 1993. The documents proved that his wife, Lolicia, and his daughter Victoria, then 14, had flown directly to Geneva and had never visited Paris, as he had told the High Court. His wife had flown back from Geneva, while her daughter went on to boarding school. That meant Mrs Aitken could never – as he insisted – have paid the bill for the Ritz, where the then Minister for Defence Procurement spent time with Saudi businessmen. The *Guardian* said the bill had been paid by an Arab associate, in contravention of ministerial rules.

On Tuesday, Aitken had filed a signed witness statement from his daughter, now 17, in which she told how she had travelled to Paris that weekend by ferry and train. Her story backed up her father's version, but was exploded by the *Guardian*'s discovery of the BA documents. Aitken had intended to produce his daughter as a witness on Thursday, when, had she stuck by her statement, she would have been required to lie on oath. But because of the *Guardian*'s evidence, Mr Gray on Thursday asked Mr Justice Popplewell for an adjournment.

Aitken announced later that night that his marriage was over, and by then his lawyers had already negotiated the humiliating settlement. •

21 July 1997

Commentary

The amoral architect of his own ruin

J onathan Aitken's revisionist biography of Richard Nixon is a revealing text for those seeking clues to the extraordinary downfall of talented, complex but ultimately amoral men. Aitken aptly describes Watergate as a 'Shakespearean tragedy', a phrase which equally well captures the scale of his own terrible undoing. In the space of six weeks he has lost his political career, forfeited a fortune in legal costs and seen his 18-year marriage founder. He must now face the consequences of being caught out lying on oath in the High Court and of weaving a determined conspiracy to pervert the natural course of justice.

Aitken's life, like that of Nixon on the morning of Friday 9 August 1974, is in ruins. His epitaph for the former President could well stand as his own: 'Even the most generous explanations for his conduct do not bring him exculpation. In his frenzied efforts to fight his way out of the quicksand . . . he made himself guilty of many "crimes" – among them deceit, negligence, bad judgement, mendacity, amorality, concealment and a disastrous reluctance to face up to personal confrontations with the individuals who were creating the worst problems.'

Aitken's overall empathy with his subject is a matter best left to the psychologists. But it is extraordinary that any man could write a 600-page book on Richard Nixon and yet not learn the fundamental lesson of his tragedy: beware the cover-up. Aitken's own downfall was caused by a cover-up, a lie about a weekend in Paris in 1993. We still do not know why it was so vital that he should have lied so doggedly and consistently about that weekend, but it was emphatically the lie, not the trip, that finished him.

That initial lie ensnared not only him but his family, for it was vital to Aitken to be able to pretend that his wife paid his bill at the Ritz Hotel in Paris. In fact, as we were eventually able to prove, Mrs Aitken spent the weekend in Switzerland with their daughter Victoria. Thus was Aitken's 17-year-old child also sucked into an ever more desperate conspiracy. It would be inhuman not to feel sympathy for the Aitken family as they contemplate the wreckage of their lives. But it is hard to feel much compassion for a man who would send in his own daughter to tell lies on oath – a serious criminal offence which could even have cost her her liberty – to save his own skin. Such behaviour in any father, never mind a Privy Counsellor, is repulsive. That is why the police should send for the court papers with some urgency.

This is the fourth libel case the *Guardian* has been forced to fight in as many years in pursuit of what we modestly considered to be the public interest. In the absence of effective regulations governing the political process the media has found itself sucked into a vacuum. In the absence of the criminal law, the libel law has been used as a weapon both of disclosure and of control. The libel laws can indeed be effective in searching out the truth – though they should be reformed and never again should a defendant be denied the fundamental right to a jury. But they are a poor substitute for the thoroughgoing Corruption Act of the sort that is now promised, though long overdue.

As the evidence spilled out in Court 10 the impression grew ever stronger of the dismal complacency at the heart of a government which had already dealt feebly with a succession of revelations by this and other newspapers. As with Hamilton and Smith, the Aitken affair was treated as if it were a matter of footling consequence. It is painfully clear that Sir Robin Butler set about his inquiries into the *Guardian*'s initial allegations with all the ferocity of a spaniel. Once his case was closed, Jonathan moved on and up. Just as Tim Smith was promoted after admitting taking £25,000 from a company under investigation by the DTI, so Aitken was elevated to the Cabinet. Why on earth not? We had the least corrupt Parliament in the world, and anyone who said otherwise was a conspiracy freak or else simply out to undermine the Great Institutions of State.

In court Aitken was perfectly frank about his inclination, if not his right, to lie to journalists, notwithstanding his own distinguished former career as a reporter. Truth and openness – causes so important that famously he stood trial at the Old Bailey in their defence – were trifles to be jettisoned once on the other side of the fence. Mendacity and secrecy destroyed him. We take no pleasure in the ruin of a man with many talents and qualities. We did our best to avoid the anticipated outcome. But ultimately it was he who unsheathed the sword of truth and he who was inevitably impaled on it. •

••

21 June 1997

David Pallister and David Leigh
Three days quarrying in a deserted hotel basement

A record of Aitken's telephone calls from the Ritz showed that at 10.15 on the Sunday morning, 19 September 1993, he had telephoned the Hotel Bristol in the Swiss village of Villars, where Victoria was going to school. The call, it was assumed, could only have been to his wife, Lolicia. If that was right, then she could not have returned to Paris that morning to pay his bill.

Aitken realised the dilemma and in the course of his evidence he suddenly introduced his mother-in-law into the Hotel Bristol that morning. Lolicia's Yugoslav-born mother, Nada Azucki, who lived in Switzerland, had come to spend the night at the hotel, sharing the room with Lolicia, Aitken claimed. She remained in the hotel room, while Lolicia left early and came back to Paris. So the Sunday morning phone call was to his mother-in-law, Aitken told the court. It was an unlikely tale but the defendants could not disprove it. The Hotel Bristol had closed down since 1993.

It was *Guardian* reporter Owen Bowcott who found the crucial clue. While Aitken was still testifying, Bowcott flew to Switzerland and drove to the shuttered and abandoned Hotel Bristol in Villars. It was in the hands of receivers, but the caretaker told him there were boxes of old records in the basement. Bowcott waded through them for three days. Then he struck gold. He faxed back to the lawyers in London four-year-old print-outs of the guest lists, reservation dockets and bill payments for that weekend.

There was Lolicia's bill. She had taken a double room, which her daughter Victoria had shared the previous night. But on the crucial night in question, Lolicia's urge to get value for money had proved her undoing. The hotel dockets revealed that she had obtained a 80SF reduction on the room rate 'because of single occupancy'.

There had been no mother-in-law staying in the room. Aitken's story about the phone call was false. The documents were rushed back to London and Aitken was confronted with them in the witness box. •

....

4 July 1997

Leader

The Downey Report: a liar and a cheat — official

I t bears saying again: British public life is amongst the least corrupt in the world. We have no Bettino Craxi, Gianni de Michelis or Bernard Tapie here; no Mafia, no pork barrel. The sums involved in Westminster corruption make the Americans, the Spanish and even (see Mr Haughey) the Irish laugh. The great majority of MPs have always been honest, decent and hard-working. But this bears saying again, too: there was in the late 1980s the beginnings of a significant culture of corruption at Westminster. A small group of politicians began to get a sniff of the rich pickings that were dangled before them by the lobbying companies mushrooming all around. They liked what they smelled and began to take advantage of the muddled rules on registration to indulge themselves to an increasingly lavish extent. When even Ian Greer in his autobiography writes disapprovingly of the shamelessness of the greed-driven MPs he encountered during that period you get some measure of the climate of the times. It was not corruption on a vast scale, but it was not nothing either; and the complacent sneers of MPs and commentators as the villains were exposed over the past four years did no favours to the cause of honest politics in this country.

Now there is an official verdict, and that verdict is: guilty, as charged. Men who rose to hold the highest positions in British political life took secret sums of money to represent in Parliament a company under the threat of investigation by the DTI. They took gifts, holidays and cash. They did their best to cheat the Revenue. They charged their own constituents to represent them. They concealed their gifts, their holidays and their money from their own colleagues and from the voters. They lied to the press, they lied to their colleagues and lied to their superiors. When cornered Hamilton lied more elaborately and more viciously. Like Jonathan Aitken, he smeared his accusers and, repellently, sought to destroy careers. In this, he found willing accomplices in Parliament and even in some areas of the press. Taken as a whole, it is perhaps the most unedifying episode in political life since the war.

All this, and more, is chronicled in Sir Gordon Downey's doorstopping 896-page report, published yesterday. Lord Salmon, who chaired a Royal Commission on Standards of Conduct in Public Life in 1974, wrote, 'Corrupt dealings are secretive. Few, if any crimes, are harder to prove.' There can be no doubt that Sir Gordon has done just that in a meticulous work of great care and balance. Every scrap of evidence has been weighed and tested. In some cases Sir Gordon has even subjected disputed documents to forensic ESDA analysis. His conclusions are deliberate and compelling. Mr Hamilton has the right to protest, and protest he inevitably will. But it was he who chose Sir Gordon, having failed in the courts. Let him sulk around the studios for £75 a throw, but it is apparent to all that he is finished in public life, and it would be better for him quietly to come to terms with that finality.

Does self-regulation then work? Let it first be said unequivocally that this whole affair was the result of the failure of self-regulation. It was the work of the press and the press alone which led to the creation of Nolan and the subsequent reforms. Let it also be said that Sir Gordon's work would in all likelihood have been impossible without access to mountains of documents obtained on discovery through the courts; without the fruits of months of work by our reporters and without the *Guardian* spending tens of thousands of pounds in legal fees to assist him. That is a poor precedent for future complainants.

It is no disrespect to Sir Gordon to say that it would be better in future for cases of this complexity and size to be dealt with by a Tribunal of Inquiry. It is also right that future Hamiltons and Smiths should not be able to hide behind parliamentary privilege, but should be prosecuted in the criminal courts, just as local councillors are. In any event, the rules should be changed to allow Sir Gordon to publish his own report rather than depend on a nod from the Standards and Privileges Committee or to be frustrated by a prorogued Parliament. And one final thing: can we please reform the libel laws? •

4 July 1997

Peter Preston

Blusterers pay no penalty for subversion of Parliament

Almost four years ago, when this affair began, there was no Parliamentary Commissioner for Standards and no Nolan committee to recommend his appointment. There was only Commons self-regulation. It's more than a reward for those long years in the journalistic salt mines to find so vigorous and common-sensical a report – and know that a new government will make some of the things so miserably detailed here a matter for the criminal courts in future.

Trivial lies? Trivial hand-outs? Downey has the answer to that as he addresses Neil Hamilton's claim that 'the scale of the benefit is defined by the cost it represents to the giver'. Sir Gordon says magisterially, 'That is false. It is the value to the receiver which matters and the fact that this may be notional . . . makes no difference.' Downey, sleeves rolled up, is talking principles here. He has a view of what a career in public life ought to entail. He finds that Hamilton did not understand.

The Parliamentary Commissioner is not a judge in the High Court. His powers of cross-examination are limited. His resources are finite. But he also has the opportunity to act as jury as well as judge: to use his common cokum.

That he does to formidable effect. Ian Greer had constantly misled parliamentary committees. Why should he have stopped now? There may have been no one in the room taking pictures as Mohamed Al Fayed passed brown envelopes to Hamilton. But the totality of the evidence was – and is – compelling.

Sir Gordon and his advisers know when they were being strung along, battered with that peculiarly obsessive mass of detail Hamilton seems to specialise in. He could, and has, perceived the broader truth.

There may be a few attempts this morning to stress the number of MPs who emerge without any stain at all. Quite right; quite fair. That, however, is really a particular comment on the Downey remit and rules of procedure.

Sir Gordon runs a complaints body. To move, he needs a complaint. The *Guardian*, the bearer of so much information, is a newspaper which exists to print facts first and make complaints later, if at all. The complaints Sir Gordon was investigating were thus ultimately culled by him from the pages of the paper and from a later book. They include everything that could possibly have been an infringement, however small.

There is neither wonder nor disappointment that many of them were not out of order: only satisfaction that such payments to MPs' campaigns, however tiny, will come under stricter scrutiny in future.

The heart of the matter, from the start, was the exploration of a lobbying company,

The first story: October 1994

October 1994

Hamilton libel case collapses: 4 October 1996

A minister resigns: 26 March 1997

Downey Report finds MPs guilty: 4 July 1997

a former client who had turned Downey's evidence in disgust, and a small repertory company of Members of Parliament, most of them entangled with the Tory back-bench committee for trade and industry. It is the workings of that committee, under Sir Michael Grylls, which deserve extraordinary examination – and the pressure the committee could exert on ministers who could not know the secret reasons for their allegedly mass concern. That is not 'a small affair'. It was an orchestrated subversion of Parliament.

And the awful thing, the damning thing even up to the moment of their testimony to Downey, is that some of those involved thought they could bluster their way out. Sir Michael 'deliberately misled' the Select Committee on Members' Interests. He 'persistently failed' to declare his interests to ministers over the House of Fraser. His evidence to Downey itself was a genteel shambles.

The same words – 'deliberately and persistently' – apply to Tim Smith, with a 'disingenuous attempt at concealment' thrown in for good measure. And what of Hamilton? He misled Sir Robin Butler and almost everybody in sight, including the Deputy Prime Minister. He misled the Inland Revenue; he tried desperately to mislead Sir Gordon.

No doubt we shall hear of him protesting on and on to the full committee and then across the airwaves, offering his services as panel-show guest or culinary expert. But here, I think, there's greater food for thought. Sir Gordon merely polices those who are still members of the Westminster club. He has no sanction over those, like Sir Michael, who have left it voluntarily — or involuntarily in Hamilton's case.

Nothing will happen to those he criticised. •

Two years ago, this policeman issued a writ against the Guardian *alleging libel and claiming damages. Yesterday he was sent to prison for 10 years for drug offences (see page 120)*

Joanna Nathan-Ayres

Influential moments: campaigns, crimes and causes

23 May 1997

John Vidal
Evading a ring of besiegers

Pete the window cleaner, Lee and Jack the Dog lead us through the woods. We easily dodge two guards smoking on the ridge; we duck below the sight line of others and creep and slip through the rosebay willow herb and wild garlic. We're in for a bollocking and a very long walk home if caught.

In 45 minutes, after one river crossing by fallen log, we reach the razor-sharp perimeter fence. It's eight feet high, four miles long and surrounds and divides the 100 or so protesters holed up in tunnels or trees in five camps.

Last night the security guards extended it down to the River Bollin. The fields too are now full of guards. Every day the noose tightens. The camps are now split by the fence, though most are connected to each other by precarious aerial ropeways. Some are running low on food and alcohol. Most have personal eviction stashes but these are reserved for when the bailiffs arrive. In the meantime, each camp needs provisions.

I am carrying fresh fruit, veg and Chilean wine to share with the Cake Hole tunnellers at Flywood camp. Having left the protest site by the main gates without problem, the only way back in that does not involve criminal damage is by tree or river. The *Times* reporter takes to the branches, the *Guardian* to the water.

Paul is coming in with me. He is the head of a Derbyshire development charity and wants to see his daughter, Erin, whom he has barely seen in 10 years. We strip down and, under the eyes of the guards behind the fence, we plunge into the chest-high deep river. Immediately we regret it. Just upstream is one of Britain's leading chemical works.

Our 300-yard-long river walk is accompanied on both sides by jeering guards. Twice we stumble. Finally, soaked from head to toe, we reach River Rats camp, where there's tea, a fire and Erin to welcome her father with news that she has glandular fever. 'It means I can't snog dad,' she says. •

•••

25 May 1997

John Vidal

There are moments in my life I believe I'm influential

There's a scratching sound deep within the shaft; then a narrow beam of light and a tousled head pops through the trap door. Logic (Matt), the third Cake Holer, has been putting up shelves in his chamber – a hole dug to fit batteries and possessions. He passes up a sack of clay which, like 40 other tons of earth, has been chipped away with hammer and chisel by people lying upside-down. It joins the dam.

The three tunnellers sit staring into their hole. With their head-torches on, they look like young surgeons considering a difficult operation. They smell of woodsmoke, earth and garlic. The talk is of politics and development, the humour is at the gallows end of black. But their minds are on this week. As the eviction begins, the three have physically and mentally cut themselves off from those who remain above ground, like the tree people, 'pixies' (saboteurs), the brew crew, the media tarts and all the other protesters.

It is a variation of a condition known as 'tunnel fever', something which hits everyone who spends time digging below. The symptoms are not wanting to come up for air, losing all track of time and place, and spending whole days underground. 'It becomes your life. You find yourself digging 12 or 15 hours a day, dreaming of tunnels,' says Matt. 'You have meals sent down to you. It becomes impossible to come out, obsessional.'

By 2 a.m. on Sunday the wind has blown off the rain. There are howls from the woods where the occupants of Battle Star Galactica, a multi-storey tree-house, are in full song. In the distance there are screams as look-outs spot security guards or police in the undergrowth.

Denise goes to bed first. She is two months pregnant and just starting morning sickness. Her protest is at what she calls the naked profiteering of the airport and at the future of her unborn child. Denise will wriggle perhaps 90 feet to her chamber at the far end of the Cake Hole. Her journey involves twisting, several turns up– and downhill, some of which are easiest done backwards. It will take almost 10 minutes. In no place is the tunnel more than three feet by three feet. Almost all of it is well shored, but her chamber has much bare earth.

Her chamber is at the back of the tunnel, with only token wooden shoring. A sign at her door says, 'Hello, boys, don't forget to wipe your feet.' She has decorated her hole with stars and angels that her mother sent. She will leave behind an amethyst and has buried a crystal for protection.

Logic goes next. The former NHS auditor from Lancashire is 23, bright as a button and into gadgets, computers and high-tech. He started the tunnel six months ago and his chamber is eight feet long, 32 inches high and three foot wide. He has friends' pictures on the wall, and there's one of Swampy in Armani clothes which was published in the *Daily Express*. There's also a poem by Carol Batter that ends:

> *Even though I'm Mad*
> *And Even if I'm Mental*
> *There are moments in my life*
> *I believe I'm influential.*

He has copies of *The English Patient* and he has rigged up an amplifier. When the doors slam shut and the bailiffs pump in their own air supply, he'll use it to generate his own electric lights.

Muppet is next. His totally unshored chamber is a sanctuary with small shelves for precious possessions. He too has taken down stones to return to the earth. He has planted seeds which have germinated and are now eight inches high.

Last, I head down. I have slept behind the third metal door for the past week. I can neither sit nor crawl. Getting into a sleeping bag takes eight minutes; boots off four; having a drink two; a pee (into a bottle) six; turning over takes a minute; turning round involves backing down the corridor into another chamber and manoeuvring like a car. It takes 10 minutes.

Apart from planes and the thunder, the silence 15 feet below and 30 feet into the hillside is absolute, the darkness complete. Within 10 minutes there is no sense of time. Touch becomes vital, the earth is damp. It helps to hold the wooden shoring, but there is no claustrophobia. For the first two nights the air was full of dust and tasted as foul as any poison. It is much better now since Muppet and Logic have installed computer fans to suck air through plastic pipes leading outside.

Oxygen deprivation is the most serious hazard facing tunnellers – more even than fear of cave-in. As mountaineers know, it leads to hallucinations, wild dreams and asphyxiation. Before the new air-conditioning it could take 15 minutes to recover from the exertion needed to reach a chamber and half an hour to recover from a night's sleep. All have hallucinated below from lack of oxygen.

'Once I physically couldn't get out. I was seeing animals and strange lights. Another time we all came out like absolute zombies,' says Dave.

Candles regularly would not burn or matches light.

There are compensations. In this place of total stillness the acoustics are fabulous. Vaughan Williams's 'The Lark Ascending' becomes a poem of pure sound, oddly suitable for subterranean homesickness. Even Abba – one of Muppet's favourites – has quality. Only the jets shudder the harmonies. •

27 February 1997

David Fairhall
Ministers misled over Gulf War pesticide

Failure to provide defence ministers with correct advice on the use of dangerous pesticides during the Gulf War led to Parliament being misled for more than two years, an internal Ministry of Defence investigation has confirmed.

The military officers and civil servants responsible – identified to the House of Commons defence committee yesterday as likely to be in the Surgeon General's department – will now be subject to further investigation. They could face court martial or other disciplinary action.

The MoD inquiry was launched by its permanent secretary, Sir Richard Mottram, in December when the department admitted that organophosphate (OP) pesticides, similar to sheep dips and chemically related to nerve gas, were widely used by British troops and seemed to be one cause of the Gulf War Syndrome afflicting hundreds of veterans. A memorandum outlining the investigation, but withholding the names of those likely to be accused, was produced yesterday when members of the committee interrogated the armed forces minister, Nicholas Soames. It listed six main findings:

• the answers to six parliamentary questions in 1994 on the use of pesticides in the Gulf were incorrect;

• flawed advice to ministers concerning pesticides between July 1994 and September 1996 constituted 'a fundamental failure of the working practices adopted by service and Civil Service staff';

• confusion resulted in incomplete information being given to the defence committee;

• the MoD received a number of indications during 1995 that OP pesticides were bought locally in the Gulf, but they were not followed up;

• by June 1996, MoD staff knew that OPs had been used more extensively than previously reported but appropriate action was not taken;

• ministers did not hear the full facts until 25 September 1996, following which Mr Soames gave Parliament the information and apologised for misleading it.

The MoD memorandum quotes four *Guardian* reports between June and October 1994 which might have alerted officials to the problem much earlier. The first two of these pointed out the similarity between the symptoms of agricultural OP poisoning and those suffered by Gulf veterans. The second pair quoted MoD denials that OPs had ever been used and then produced evidence that at least one type – malathion – was used to delouse prisoners. In answer to a parliamentary question, Lord Henley, for the MoD, said malathion had been used without protective clothing only to delouse 50 Iraqi

Christopher Thomond

Richard Turnbull, Gulf War Syndrome victim

prisoners. The misleading answer was repeated by Mr Soames two days later, in answer to a question from Labour's shadow defence secretary, David Clark. The memorandum also identifies four occasions when ministers or their private offices received information about the local purchase of OPs or questioned the line being taken in Parliament, but 'on none of these occasions were ministers or their private offices told that a serious mistake had been made or that Parliament had been misled'.

Misleading cases
Parliament was misled by ministers on five occasions:

11 July 1994: 'No organophosphate (OP) insecticide or pesticide sprays were used by British forces' – Jeremy Hanley;

21 July 1994: Lord Henley issues list of 'insecticides' which makes no mention of OPs;

1 November 1994: Lord Henley admits that 'some 50 Iraqi prisoners of war' were treated for lice using a powder containing the OP malathion – thereby underestimating the number of prisoners treated;

3 November 1994: Nicholas Soames repeats Lord Henley's misleading answer;

3 November 1994: 'I am aware of only 10 British service personnel who would have been involved with organophosphorous pesticides used by the UK forces during the Gulf conflict' – Nicholas Soames. •

28 February 1997

Leader

For whom the buck stops

The possibility of a connection between the pesticides and the illnesses was raised in 1992 in the United States. In 1994, when concerns had begun to rise in this country, a number of newspaper reports (including four in the *Guardian*) drew detailed attention to possible links. The MoD adamantly resisted these allegations and continued to do so right up to autumn 1996, when ministers were finally informed of the possibility. This is not merely a failure of working practice. It is a failure of attitude. The MoD did not want to believe and therefore did not investigate as it should have done. •

12 May 1997

David Fairhall

Labour orders Gulf War Syndrome review

Gulf War veterans are to be invited to meet the Government's defence ministerial team to discuss fresh research into Gulf War Syndrome. Ministers are offering to extend the existing medical assessment programme, covering 1,000 veterans, and the limited research programme already agreed. This is expected to include a study of the combined effect of multiple vaccinations and anti-nerve gas tablets given to troops in the Gulf, often accompanied by dangerous insecticides, as well as the long-term statistical analysis recommended by the Medical Research Council. But there is still no promise of financial compensation unless the Ministry of Defence can be shown to have been negligent.

The Government's initiative was announced last night by the armed forces minister, John Reid. He promised an investigation into how decisions on medical treatments were made during the 1991 conflict and why ministers and the public were misled about the widespread use of organophosphate pesticides (OPs) – a point on which Dr Reid's predecessor, Nicholas Soames, was forced to apologise to the House of Commons last year.

The prospect of some direct research into the likely causes of the syndrome, instead of a three-year epidemiological study, will be welcomed by veterans' representatives. The MoD might have opted for this course earlier had it not been overruled by the Medical Research Council. But there will be disappointment that the Government has no plans to offer compensation other than war disability pensions.

To obtain more, veterans must prove illnesses came from Gulf service and the MoD was negligent in its medical treatment, although this was intended to protect against disease, or chemical and biological weapons attacks. •

....

1 January 1997

Kate Hine
Diary of an NHS defector

During my brother Tom's last days, I resigned from the National Health Service after 13 years as a physiotherapist. I felt I could no longer be a part of an unjust and grossly inadequate organisation.

Tom had everything to live for when, at the age of 28, he suffered a heart attack and died. He was single, a keen sportsman and was just setting up his own courier business. Only 12 weeks earlier, a similar attack caused massive internal damage, but the hospital had wrongly diagnosed it as bleeding ulcers and sent him home.

The gradual but steady fall in standards over the last five years had been bad enough, but Tom's experience took it all one step too far for me. He was such a brave man and never complained. Watching him die so slowly and painfully made me determined to do something.

Tom was right behind me when I made the decision to resign, and I promised him I would do everything I could to draw attention to the obscene shortcomings in the NHS. For years, I had been forced to deliver a substandard service. Now someone I loved was on the receiving end of it. We may never find the proof, but I'm convinced Tom's first heart attack was missed because he wasn't admitted for observation. The most likely reason for sending him home at 4 a.m. was because there were no beds available. My experiences from inside, as a member of staff, and Tom's from outside, as a patient, illustrate so clearly that the basic needs of very sick patients are being neglected.

I was 21 when I qualified as a junior physiotherapist in the early 1980s. It was a job I had wanted to do for as far back as I can remember. My mother had always worked in the health service in medical secretarial roles and we had this shared commitment to it, to the importance of sustaining and improving the good levels of care available to all people.

It was when I returned to work after having my second baby in 1990 that I noticed the beginnings of a gradual but steady decline in standards. There had always been concern about the length of waiting lists and some of the equipment was a bit out of date, but the day-to-day care of the patients was perfectly good. That was changing.

I remember one of the first signs. We had a patient with pneumonia on the orthopaedic ward. She was choking and I needed the suction equipment to clear her chest and throat. When I went to use it, the filter section was missing. I called out for help, but there was only one qualified nurse on a ward with 33 patients. The student nurses had no idea where the equipment was kept. I had no choice: I applied the pipe without the filter but ruined the equipment. I saw the nursing officer and made a statement, but the whole affair fizzled out.

In the months and years ahead I often had to neglect my duties as a physiotherapist to deal with nursing matters because there were fewer and fewer nurses available. Tension grew between the different disciplines working within the hospital as they all became overstretched.

Once I was called in from home to help with a patient having chest problems. The man needed to be ventilated and moved to an intensive treatment bed, but there wasn't one available. I stayed for two hours doing as much as I could, racing around looking for bits of equipment. Although I used a hand-operated bag to ventilate the man and stabilise his condition, there were no two ways about it: he needed to go into intensive treatment. But a bed didn't become available until the next day. The man died three days later.

What I loathed most about situations like that was that the man's family had no idea that his life was in danger because a bed couldn't be staffed. I couldn't let it go. I made a statement, but, as always, the whole affair just fizzled out.

In recent years, I stayed with the NHS because I believed things would improve. Then one day I realised that nothing was going to change. A patient was having difficulties breathing. When the doctor was asked about the next step, he said the patient was not for 'active treatment' – in other words, he should be allowed to die. The next morning he was suddenly put under the 'for active treatment' category. It is impossible to prove, but I know from my own experience that his status changed only because an intensive treatment bed became available.

These are tragic incidents that are going on in our hospitals every day. I believe people should know about them and I'm determined, for Tom's sake, to make sure they do. •

9 January 1997

Letter to the Editor

It is sad that such a dedicated worker as Kate Hine should feel as she does about the quality of medicine practised in so many of our hospitals. As a practising physician, I would support her – indeed, would suggest that the situation is much worse than she describes. The pressures on all grades of staff are enormous, leading to an unacceptable standard of medical practice.

It is for every responsible doctor in the health service to speak out and, through public information and education, bring more pressure on a Government which clearly does not care about what is happening in the health service.

Much discussion has taken place as to why there has been such an increase in the admission of acutely ill patients, leading to this fall in clinical standards. It is self-evident to those in practice that the majority of these patients are from poor and deprived backgrounds – rarely do I see my middle-class friends as ill as those on emergency duty. This is further evidence of how health-service deficiencies are aggravating the ill-health of those who are experiencing increasing deprivation as the wealth gap gets larger. •

(Prof) J. D. Ward, consultant physician,
Royal Hallamshire Hospital,
Glossop Road, Sheffield S10 2JF

8 February 1997

Alison Daniels
Guardian victory in landmark libel case

A High Court jury's decision to throw out a Police Federation-backed libel action by five Metropolitan Police officers against the *Guardian* was hailed last night as a victory for press freedom. The verdict leaves the federation facing costs of more than £500,000, in addition to paying a substantial part of the newspaper's costs. It is the organisation's first defeat in 96 legal actions.

The five officers – Reynold Bennett, Bernard Gillan, Paul Goscomb, Gerald Mapp and Robert Watton – had claimed that two articles published in the *Guardian* on 31 January 1992 suggested they were involved in planting and dealing drugs. This meaning was denied by the *Guardian*. The newspaper's crime correspondent Duncan Campbell reported that eight unnamed officers had been transferred from Stoke Newington police station in north London after allegations that an anti-corruption operation headed by a senior officer was under way.

The *Guardian*'s editor, Alan Rusbridger, said, 'This was an opportunistic action by a trade union which has systematically tried to shut down legitimate reporting in an important area of public life. I think the jury recognised that – and they saw for themselves that Duncan Campbell is a fine, decent and honest reporter. It's a good day for the press. It would be an even better day if the libel law were changed to give better protection to smaller papers who have been forced to cave in when threatened with the huge costs of fighting an action.'

Mr Campbell said the verdict was an important one for journalists who want to honestly report investigations into alleged corruption.

The editor of the London *Evening Standard*, Max Hastings, whose witness evidence was ruled inadmissible by the trial judge, Mr Justice French, said, 'I passionately believe that this case had an importance for the British press as a whole and that we should all be grateful to the *Guardian* for taking the enormous risks of fighting it against all the odds.'

Deputy general secretary of the National Union of Journalists, Jacob Ecclestone, said the verdict would encourage others to 'stand up to the federation bullies'.

One of the country's leading libel lawyers, Mark Stephens, of London firm Stephens Innocent, said, 'This decision will hopefully embolden newspapers which have effectively self-censored their reporting.'

A High Court jury took five and a half hours to reach a majority verdict in favour of the *Guardian* after a trial lasting more than two weeks. In court the *Guardian* strenuously denied that the allegations detailed in the articles identified the five plaintiffs to anyone outside a small circle of relatives and colleagues, implied guilt or prejudged an anti-corruption investigation, Operation Jackpot.

Defending the newspaper, George Carman, QC, told the jury the officers' action was strained and contrived and a wholly unjustified attempt to gain damages from a national newspaper. For the officers, Tom Shields, QC, had argued that the articles stigmatised the five officers.

In the course of the trial, the court was told by retired deputy assistant commissioner Michael Taylor that, if they proved true, the allegations had the makings of a major police scandal, while the chairman of the Police Complaints Authority, Peter Moorhouse, confirmed that the allegations were extremely serious.

As well as ruling against hearing evidence from Mr Rusbridger and Mr Hastings, Mr Justice French ruled that significant sections of statements made by other defence witnesses were inadmissible.

In the past 33 months, the Police Federation has fought and won 95 defamation actions, netting £1,567,000.

The Metropolitan Police paid out £500,000 between January 1992 and the end of 1996 in civil action settlements for claims of malicious prosecution and false arrest to people arrested by officers from Stoke Newington.

Yesterday's verdict was greeted with disappointment by Fred Broughton, chairman of the Police Federation. 'We are surprised that the jury did not share our view of the meaning of the article,' he said. •

....

8 February 1997

Alan Rusbridger
We're a half-free press

J ustice was done in the High Court yesterday. A jury backed an honest reporter doing the work a reporter should. We toasted those 12 men and women last night at the *Guardian*. Their instincts about the case were right and true. But there was no toast to the judge or the law. The trial – which could have cost the paper nearly £750,000 – should never have happened. It would never have happened in countries which do more than mouth platitudes about the freedom of the press.

If, at the end of a trial we won, we say that the case was an accident of justice, that is only partly a reflection on the judge, Mr Justice French, who presided (after a manner) over the trial. It is also a reflection on other judges before him who have seemed to care little about the press's role in a free society. It is a reflection on Parliament, which has tinkered with the law of libel but never reformed it. And it is a reflection on all in society who do little to nurture or protect the freedom of expression they affect to care about.

The immediate and most localised effect of yesterday's judgement in *Bennett and Others* v. *Guardian Newspapers Ltd* is that editors may be bolder in reporting on cases of suspected corruption in public life. In recent years one trade union – the Police Federation – has succeeded in shutting down much fair reporting and comment about a subject of vital concern.

During the 33 months to March 1996 (the latest figures available) the Police Federation fought – and won – 95 such actions for defamation, recovering £1,567,000 in damages. Small local papers and magazines routinely cave in, knowing that they cannot possibly afford the cost of going to trial. Yesterday's victory for the *Guardian* should change that climate a little. But that is entirely due to the jury. The signal from the courts remains the same: they will do little to protect you if you engage in robust investigations of people in public life. Do not come bleating to judges about the public's right to know or the public interest. They do not want to know.

The cause of the action dated back more than five years to two carefully researched articles about unnamed police officers who were being investigated for corruption in a troubled inner-city area of London. Duncan Campbell, an experienced and respected crime correspondent, had been investigating allegations of corruption at Stoke Newington police station since October 1991. He had spoken to convicted drug dealers, to local solicitors and to a former police officer, all of whom had either specific allegations or broad concerns about officers at the station. Campbell also met with the man heading the inquiry, Detective Superintendent Ian Russell. By the time of our articles, there was a major inquiry into the station, with five officers working under Russell. One detective constable had already been charged with theft and fraud.

On 28 January 1992, Scotland Yard issued a press statement saying that eight Stoke Newington officers had been transferred to other stations. That single act was virtually unprecedented in the Metropolitan Police, and the news spread like wildfire from station to station. Campbell wrote two pieces about the transfer of the – unnamed – officers, together with background material he had accumulated during his investigation. No officers complained about those articles at the time.

The inquiry went on to become one of the biggest inquiries into police corruption undertaken by the Police Complaints Authority. Sir Peter Imbert, then Metropolitan Police Commissioner, described them as 'the most serious allegations of police corruption for 20 years'.

In time, one of the *Guardian*'s main sources for the original pieces had her conviction quashed on appeal. Another source received a five-figure sum in damages, and 13 people convicted on the evidence of officers from the police station had their convictions overturned by the Court of Appeal. In a further 20 cases, the Crown Prosecution Service offered no evidence. In all, more than £500,000 in damages was paid by the Met as a result of civil actions taken against officers from Stoke Newington.

You might think that there could be little that was controversial about a serious newspaper reporting on events of this importance and scale, especially if the officers were not named. We have seen what has happened in inner-city areas where confidence in the police – and the regulation of the police – has broken down. Lord Scarman's report after the Brixton riots of 1981 makes much of this: 'Unless and until there is a system for judging complaints against the police which commands the support of the public, there will be no way in which the atmosphere of distrust and suspicion between the police and the community in places like Brixton can be dispelled.'

Unfortunately, the Police Federation has a different view of what should and should not be reported about the police. It has access to a huge fighting fund for legal actions of all sorts. In 1995, it spent no less than £5.2 million of its £7.7 million revenue on legal services. The libel actions by police are known in the force as 'garage actions', since the average damages are just enough to build a nice extension.

The tactics employed by the federation in this case were textbook stuff. They waited until two years and 51 weeks had passed – a week before the cut-off point for launching a libel action – before issuing writs on behalf of the eight officers who had been suspended and who still had never been named by the *Guardian*. Three officers did not pursue their actions, for reasons the court never heard. That left five, who by then had been cleared of any wrongdoing by the PCA.

The fact that the *Guardian* had not named these men counted for little in court. All submitted statements from relatives or colleagues saying that they had recognised to whom the articles referred. Out of a *Guardian* readership of more than a million, perhaps 300 readers knew their identity – and they would, of course, have been the very people most likely to have been in the know.

And so the slow and expensive wheels of libel were set in motion. The *Guardian* considered an important principle was at stake. We considered our reporter should be defended. He had reported the story fairly and accurately and had even tried to assist the original inquiry. Two senior policemen – Superintendent Russell and former Deputy Assistant Commissioner Michael Taylor – would give evidence on his, and the paper's, behalf. So would the Chairman of the PCA. Even though – after two false starts – the costs were already approaching half a million pounds, we thought we should fight.

It is at this point that the peculiarities of the English libel law began to bite. We had hoped to be able to argue qualified privilege: that is, that the community had an equal interest in receiving the information as we had in publishing it. If we had so succeeded, the policemen would have had to prove that Campbell was being malicious or reckless as to the truth of what he wrote.

Mr Justice French turned out not to be interested in whether or not it was in the interests of the public to know about allegations of police corruption or whether the *Guardian* had a duty or right to pass on the information. During the course of some somewhat rambling and error-strewn judgements he struck out that defence, together with much of our evidence. He went further. He ruled that the *Guardian* could make no mention of anything that happened after the articles were published. We could say nothing about the subsequent vindication of our main sources. To the jury, they may have simply looked like the malicious claims of convicted drug dealers. We could convey little idea of the scope of the police inquiry, or the damages the police finally paid out. There was no mention of the 13 cases overturned, nor of Sir Peter Imbert's concerns. We could not point out that one officer at the centre of the allegations, DC Roy Lewandowski, had been jailed for 18 months.

The judge's decision to exclude any evidence of events following the publication – with the exception of the plaintiffs' evidence that they had been cleared – was backed by the Court of Appeal. By the end of the trial, the jury could be forgiven for thinking that the *Guardian* had been making mischief out of very little and that there never had been any public disquiet about the station. The judge's summing-up would certainly have reinforced that impression. It dealt extensively with the policemen's case and made only nodding reference to the *Guardian*'s defence. Mr Justice French, who appeared to be having difficulty following some of the legal arguments in the case, managed to avoid mentioning any of the *Guardian*'s witnesses, save for a solitary sentence from Campbell in which he referred to the size of the *Guardian*'s readership.

In America and other countries with a more developed sense of the balance between free expression and individual dignity, the case would never have come to court. That is largely thanks to a Supreme Court ruling in 1964 which fundamentally changed the law of libel in order to allow the media to report on, and comment on, public life.

Influential moments: campaigns, crimes and causes

The ruling of Justice William J. Brennan in *New York Times* v. *Sullivan* was a ringing defence of the right – and duty – of a free press to be able freely to report on matters of public importance of a sort that it is hard to imagine coming from any English judge. As in the *Guardian* case, *Sullivan* concerned an unnamed police official. At the original trial, the man – Police Commissioner L. B. Sullivan of Montgomery, Kansas – collected $500,000 in damages from the *New York Times*. In upholding the *Times*'s appeal, Brennan revolutionised American libel law, even allowing newspapers to make false statements uttered in the heat of debate, provided they were not maliciously made.

Brenann said, amongst other things, 'Debate on public issues should be uninhibited, robust and wide open and . . . it may well include vehement, caustic and sometimes unpleasantly sharp attacks on government and public officials.' Newspapers faced with the possibility of huge libel damages might well succumb to a 'pall of fear and timidity' and tone down any criticism of public officials. The threat of massive costs 'dampens the vigour and limits the variety of public debate'.

Public officials would in future have to prove actual malice: i.e. the plaintiff would have to prove the reporter was reckless as to whether what he or she was writing was true or not. Subsequent rulings have made it clear that any police officers with the power to make arrests should be classed as 'public figures'.

The European Court of Human Rights has also gone much further than England in allowing criticism of public figures during political controversies. A test case, *Lingens* v. *Austria,* found that a libel award against a commentator was a breach of Article 10 of the European Convention on Human Rights because it would deter journalists from contributing to public discussion of issues affecting the life of a community.

Some jurists believe that *Sullivan* tilts the balance too far in favour of the press. They point to judgements in other countries which have managed to achieve a better equilibrium. But most lawyers are agreed that British libel laws are out of step with the trend in international law and are increasingly an inhibition on public debate.

To say all this is not to excuse the press, which must take its own share of blame for the current indifference to the vital role it has to play in the public life of this country. Too many papers have behaved in too cavalier a fashion, confusing the public interest with what interests the public. They have brought us to the brink of legislation which will further shackle an already half-free press. But our judges and politicians must wake up to the way in which the cost, the risk and the balance of the present state of the law all militate against honest reporting by responsible newspapers and broadcasting organisations.

Bennett and Others v. *Guardian Newspapers Ltd* could have been the case that helped push back the limitations on the press in this country. It hasn't done that. But the 12 men and women of the jury had a better sense of justice and freedom of speech than the lawyers. They recognised a good and decent reporter – known as such by police officers the length of the land – and protected him. For that small mercy, this paper's thanks. •

25 February 1997

Duncan Campbell and Lawrence Donegan

Bent copper gets 10 years

A serving Metropolitan Police officer from a station at the centre of corruption allegations was sentenced to 10 years' imprisonment yesterday after being found guilty of conspiring to smuggle cannabis worth millions of pounds into Britain. Ronald Palumbo, a detective constable formerly based at Stoke Newington police station, north London, was one of four men jailed for their part in a drug-running operation uncovered when Customs officers stopped a lorry returning from Spain in November 1995 and found cannabis worth over £2 million in a secret compartment.

The jury at Canterbury crown court was told that Customs believed the gang had carried out three other smuggling trips on the same scale. The prosecuting counsel, James Vine, told the 32-year-old police officer he was what was known as a 'bent copper'. Palumbo, of Chingford, Essex, had previously issued a writ against the *Guardian* seeking damages for alleged libel in connection with an article he claimed defamed him. He was jailed yesterday with his father-in-law, Kenneth Harris, 43, of Welling, Kent, David Ng, 37, of Higham Park, London, and Reginald Illingworth, 39, of Greenwich, London. All four had denied two drug-smuggling charges. Harris, described by the judge as the commander of the organisation, was jailed for 12 years, Ng 10 years and Illingworth nine.

During the 15-day trial, the jury heard that Customs at Dover uncovered the smuggling operation during a random search of a lorry carrying satsumas from Spain. They found the drugs 'expertly concealed' in the floor of the trailer. The vehicle was owned by Harris. Police then discovered that he had faked documents showing it had been carrying legitimate loads.

The jury was told that Palumbo had driven the lorry on the first trip and flew to Spain to act as a courier on the other three. He helped load the cannabis on to the lorry on the final trip, the prosecution said.

The detective was transferred from Stoke Newington police station in January 1992 as part of Operation Jackpot, an investigation into alleged corruption at the station. He was later suspended and charged with perjury and conspiracy to pervert the course of justice. He was acquitted at the Old Bailey in December 1995.

In a civil action brought by housing worker Rennie Kingsley against the Metropolitan Police in the same month, the court was told that Palumbo had planted a drug on Mr Kingsley and fabricated evidence against him. The officer was also involved in the arrests of other defendants who later alleged they had been the victims of fabricated evidence. The Met paid out a total of more than £500,000 in damages for false imprisonment and wrongful arrest to people arrested by officers from Stoke Newington. In all, 13 people had their convictions quashed by the Court of Appeal.

On 25 January 1995 Palumbo issued a writ against the *Guardian* through the Police Federation's solicitors, Russell, Jones and Walker, in which he claimed damages for libel in connection with an article published three years earlier. He also sought an injunction to restrain the *Guardian* from publishing 'any similar words defamatory to the plaintiff'.

The writ was never served and he was not part of the action which the *Guardian* successfully defended earlier this month against five other officers, all of whom had been cleared of all wrongdoing and whom the *Guardian* accepted were not involved in corruption in any way.

Palumbo is the second Stoke Newington officer to be jailed. Former Detective Constable Roy Lewandowski was jailed for 18 months in 1992 for stealing from a murder victim's house. •

....

25 February 1997

Duncan Campbell

'For long, lonely years we wept in despair . . . now we're free'

They came into the dock of Court Number Four to be met by the sort of affectionate applause that greets a favourite actor as he arrives on stage for a familiar play. The audience in the packed public gallery must have felt, as devoted audiences do, that they already knew what the conclusion of this particular morality play would be. The three who had stepped into court as convicted murderers under the watchful eye of Securicor were about to leave it as free men. The Bridgewater Three – Jim Robinson, Vincent Hickey and Michael Hickey – were yesterday granted unconditional bail in anticipation of a successful appeal which the Crown will not contest.

The 19-year-old drama, in which four men were wrongly convicted for the murder of the 13-year-old newspaper boy Carl Bridgewater, is almost over. Theresa Robinson, the actress who married Jimmy in the midst of his sentence, was sitting in the court with a bouquet of freesias, roses and carnations and a smile bright enough to light up every gloomy corridor in the Royal Courts of Justice.

Ann Whelan, who had campaigned with such resilience for her son Michael, was dabbing her eyes behind her glasses as she waited for the moment she must have pictured a thousand times in her imagination. Ann Skett, the mother of Vincent, who had visited him in what must have seemed like every prison in the land and had arrived in court still uncertain if the men were to be released, sat with her eyes fixed on the door through which they entered.

As the three came in, Vincent, shaven-headed now and dressed in a grey sweatshirt and blue trousers, ducked and weaved like a chirpy middleweight boxer and gave a thumbs-up to his family. Michael, with the slightly ethereal air of someone who would be more at home at Glastonbury than Gartree, smiled into the mass of welcoming faces. Jimmy, with his Bridgewater Three campaign T-shirt under his blue denim shirt, blinked back tears as he spotted Theresa and the enraptured children from his first marriage.

Three other men in the court had their own parts to play. Lord Justice Roch, Mr Justice Hidden

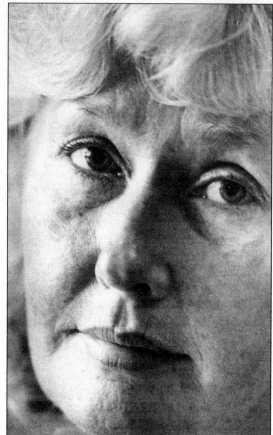

Don McPhee

Michael Hickey's mother, who campaigned tirelessly

and Mr Justice Mitchell, who graduated from Clare College, Cambridge, Emmanuel College, Cambridge, and Hertford College, Oxford, some years before the Hickeys and Robinson were completing their educations at Her Majesty's Pleasure, took their places in their high-backed chairs and gazed at the most crowded appeal court since the Birmingham Six were freed.

Lord Justice Roch said that he recognised that 'emotions are involved in this' but asked that the public gallery behave with 'dignity and restraint'. To their credit, they did, although as evidence of forgery and connivance and deceit emerged over the next two hours there must have been more than a few buttoned lips that would have loved to shout out some injudicious expletive.

A couple of years ago there had been a drama-documentary made of the case called *Bad Company*. Two of the actors, Susan Wooldridge, who played Ann Whelan, and George Irving, who played Jimmy Robinson, and who both joined the campaign to free the men, were in court. There were representatives too from the rolling confederacy of miscarriages of justice – the Birmingham Six, the Tottenham Three and others – happy to see others now centre stage.

And there was something hauntingly familiar about the eyes of a dashingly handsome young man with long dark hair and a Nehru jacket listening patiently to the litany of malpractice spelled out by Michael Mansfield, QC. Mr Mansfield was representing the young man's father, Pat Molloy, the fourth defendant, who had died in prison in 1981 after being browbeaten into a confession, as the court was told, which he later retracted. For Nick Molloy, who had grown up with the shadow of his father's conviction for killing a schoolboy, yesterday was also a moment of release.

The three Court of Appeal judges granted the men immediate and unconditional bail after they had heard Crown counsel, Jeremy Roberts, QC, accept that the case against them was 'flawed'.

Vincent Hickey's barrister, Alun Jones, QC, fired a warning shot at those members of the establishment who have already started a damage-limitation exercise, whispering behind their hands that the men are being released on a 'technicality'. 'I represent a man who has been waiting to have his day in court for 18 years,' he thundered.

The three appellants left the dock to collect their bagged prison belongings and their wits. As they departed, Michael Hickey gave the judges a cheery, clenched-fist salute. The lunchtime traffic in the Strand was brought to a standstill as the crowds gathered to see the men emerge on to the streets. A hundred lenses pointed at the group as they smiled and waved. The media had been their ally and their enemy in their years inside. 'You helped to convict us,' said Jim Robinson at the press conference that followed at St Bride's, Fleet Street, 'and you helped to get us out.'

When Gerard Conlon of the Guildford Four had emerged as a free man after his successful appeal in 1989, he had electrified the crowd outside the Old Bailey with his cry of 'I am an innocent man.' The three released yesterday had already proclaimed their innocence from the rooftops of the jails where they were held. Now a reporter asked what they most looked forward to doing.

For Jim Robinson, it was to be able to open a door by himself. Vincent Hickey, still a likely lad after all the years inside, suggested with a grin that the questioner 'think about it, mate'. Michael, rambling slightly in the glare of the television lights, said he most looked forward to walking in the rain.

That wish, unlike so many they have nursed over the years as they battled on with only their loyal lawyers and their faithful families and friends behind them, will surely be granted. •

21 February 1997

Paul Foot

Justice 18 years too late

J ubilation is the first emotion. As soon as I heard the news bulletin that the men accused of the murder of the newspaper boy were to be freed, I imagined them in Brixton revelling in the knowledge that this was their last night in jail: they had been inside since December 1978, when they were arrested and falsely accused of the murder.

I thought of the two women who in their very different ways have campaigned for their sons' freedom: Ann Skett, mother of Vincent Hickey, and Ann Whelan, mother of Michael.

But the jubilation swiftly turns to anger. Why has it taken so long for this grotesque injustice to be righted? The answer is that the judicial and police authorities are extremely reluctant to admit even the possibility that their system can go terribly wrong.

In December 1981, I sat with Ann Whelan and her husband, Fred, in the Court of Appeal listening to the astonishing new evidence in the case: that the first suspect for Carl Bridgewater's murder had committed another murder nearby. Lord Lane, Lord Chief Justice, contemptuously brushed the evidence aside and refused the men even leave to appeal.

The interests of justice were then left entirely to Ann Whelan. She approached witnesses, was reported to the police, hounded by people whose word she questioned. When at last the case was referred to the Court of Appeal in 1988 by the then Home Secretary, Douglas Hurd, she spent two and a half days in the witness box while the prosecution and the judges accused her of rigging evidence and interfering with the course of justice. When Ann Skett took some notes she was rudely reprimanded by Lord Justice Russell.

Throughout the nine-week hearing the central planks of the prosecution case were knocked out. All the new evidence favoured the men; none of it favoured the prosecution. Yet on 17 March 1989, the three judges clung to the rotten verdict. The whole affair stank of cover-up.

But this was before the dam burst on the great injustices of the 1970s. The following October the Guildford Four walked free, then came the Birmingham Six; Judy Ward; the Tottenham Three . . . Suddenly it was clear that the courts can make awful mistakes, and often do.

The bad fortune of Jimmy Robinson and the Hickeys was that their case came before the deluge, and so they rotted in prison for another nine years.

The new evidence which finally clears the men concerns the confession of Pat Molloy. The story of Molloy is a tragedy within a tragedy. He alone of the four arrested men had taken part in no burglaries or armed robberies in the weeks before the murder.

He was a skilful carpenter.

Molloy was arrested because he was a friend of Robinson's. He was taken to Wombourne police station, where he was held without access to friends or lawyers for 10 days. During those 10 days he signed the crucial Exhibit 54, a confession to being at Yew Tree Farm on the day the boy was shot, along with Robinson and the Hickeys. As soon as he was allowed to see a lawyer, Molloy denounced his confession and insisted he had never been to the farm and had been with Jimmy Robinson at his girlfriend's house on the afternoon of the murder.

Molloy was advised not to deny his confession at the trial, but to give no evidence and hope he would be convicted only of manslaughter – as he was. As soon as he was packed off to prison he was struck down with remorse. In a stream of letters to friends and family, he gave his story of what happened at Wombourne police station: he had been beaten across his face, his teeth had been broken, his food had been salted so he was forced to drink from the toilet bowl, he was bribed with beer and cigarettes, and eventually held tight from behind while the words of his confession were whispered into his ear.

All this has until now been declared by the authorities the fanciful ramblings of an Irish carpenter. Molloy died in 1981 and was never able to tell his full story in open court as he intended.

There will be talk in high society today about the men getting off on a technicality. It will be put about that they got off because a couple of coppers lied. Let us be completely clear. These men did not kill the newspaper boy. Someone else did. And instead of the standard sulking which we can now expect from the Staffordshire police, perhaps some senior officers from their ranks might take it on themselves to bring the real murderer to justice. •

14 January 1997

Luke Harding and Clare Dyer
'I'm sometimes afraid to go out'

Eleven-year-old Simon Bradford peers round the front door of his parents' first-floor council flat in east London. 'Do you like fishing?' he asks, before skipping down the hall and tucking into a bowl of chocolate ice-cream.

Ever since Simon moved into the block of flats in Tower Hamlets four years ago with his disabled mother Anita, aged 48, and father Raymond, 46, he has been the victim of bullying and intimidation. He has been hit with a cricket bat. As he cycled to school one day, a youth tried to knock him off his bike. There have been taunts and name-calling.

Most days Simon – an engaging hyperactive boy with spiky blond hair and outsize glasses – helps his mother with basic household chores. He cleans the kitchen and when she suffers an epileptic fit he runs her bath and fetches her clean clothes. He has done so since he was four.

In a ground-breaking ruling yesterday, the High Court ruled that Tower Hamlets was under a legal duty to consider accommodating Simon in a safer place. It was the culmination of the family's fight against a neighbourhood 'campaign of hatred' and means councils will now have to give much greater weight to children's needs when faced by requests for housing.

The Bradfords first made an urgent application for transfer in July 1995, after they came home to find 'white trash' bayoneted into their front door. Nine days after the family complained to Tower Hamlets council, a workman finally removed it.

Simon Bradford at home in east London: 'I'm sometimes afraid to go out'

Mrs Bradford, severely disabled since the age of three, has been beaten up twice and sexually assaulted once outside the flat. Her wedding ring has been stolen, excrement has been pushed through the letter box and her motability car has had its tyres slashed 18 times.

The first-floor flat is hardly suited to her needs. She has fallen down the front steps several times and broken a leg and her wrist. 'I'm just too scared to go out any more,' she said last night. 'We want to go to Kent, but the council refuses to move us.'

Mr Bradford, a former mercenary who says he looks after his wife '25 hours a day', has kept a regular log of the campaign of hate against his family. 'When we complained, we were told there was nowhere else for us to go. A woman from the council came to see Simon, but all she asked him was "What football team do you support?" and "Do your parents hit you?" They have taken no account of my wife's medical needs. They have suggested she goes into an old people's home, where she would receive round-the-clock care, but we do not want the family split up.'

Mr Justice Kay ruled that the London Borough of Tower Hamlets had acted unlawfully in failing to assess Simon's individual needs under the provisions of the 1989 Children Act and ordered the authority to carry out such an assessment 'as soon as reasonably practicable'. The judge said that the whole family faced a daily ordeal 'of very considerable harassment'. 'The family has been harassed within the home by abusive and hoax telephone calls. This campaign of hatred has culminated in attempted arson on their home and the daubing of phlegm and faeces over the door of their flat and their car.'

Simon's solicitor, Nicola Mackintosh, said after the case, 'This is an horrific story, but it is also an important case for the rights of children generally.'

Stephen Cragg, a barrister specialising in community care and judicial review, said, 'It will not be enough for councils to say "We've assessed the family's needs under the Housing Act and the National Assistance Act." They will then have to go on and do a separate assessment from the child's point of view. It's probably going to lead to a lot more work for local authorities . . . it will make accommodation decisions for families with children in need complex, and will require a degree of co-operation between housing and social services departments which sadly does not exist in many authorities at present.'

Simon, who attends a special school in Tower Hamlets for children with learning difficulties, was described by his head teacher as 'a sad little boy', said the judge. He was finishing his ice-cream as he tried to describe how he had coped. 'I've only got one friend at school who talks to me and I'm sometimes afraid to go out, so it is sometimes a bit difficult.' •

. . . .

18 March 1997

Ian Guard *
Rule of the mob

Ralph wept for the end of innocence, the darkness of man's heart, and the fall through the air of the true, wise friend called Piggy
Lord of the Flies

The schoolteacher who recently quit because of the furore caused by her allowing a young boy to rap the knuckles of six classmates who had allegedly been bullying him made me wonder what Sir William Golding, author of *Lord of the Flies*, would have made of the episode. Golding, a schoolteacher himself, knew about boys. He knew that the *Lord of the Flies* scenario plays itself out in every school. He knew also that such conflicts are not about right or wrong, or the issues at stake. They're about the individual opposing the mob, and the cost of standing out as different.

The schoolteacher, Brenda Davies, paid the penalty with her job. But I fear that the real cost will be paid by the young boy. He will grow up in the belief that he inadvertently cost Ms Davies her career, not the bullies. He will be left at the hands of his tormentors and will probably continue to endure such a position until the day he leaves school. When he then steps into the adult world, scarred by his experiences, will he be able to reinvent himself? Or will he find that he cannot change, and suffer further punishment as a consequence? At the end of *Lord of the Flies*, Ralph weeps for 'the end of innocence, the darkness of man's heart'. The young boy in Ms Davies's class will grow up very quickly. He will wonder not just why the bullies won, but why he was singled out in the first place. As Golding knew, there is no reason. He portrayed a group of schoolboys whose persecution of the individual stopped only at death, yet their hatred had no rational basis.

The law of the jungle dictates that difference stands out and is therefore prone to be attacked.

When the 1963 film version was released, adults were so horrified that children were forbidden to see it. They adopted the naive view that such persecution could only happen on a desert island. The reality is that the island was only significant in removing everything which might detract from presenting the naked aggression as vividly as possible. Is the real reason that bullying in schools does not end in death because such a thought horrifies the bullies? Or is it because they are more afraid that their cruelty will finally be found out? In Golding's novel, Ralph initially is one of the bullies, joining Jack in mocking Piggy and finding safety in numbers. Yet at the end, he mourns 'the true, wise friend called Piggy'. He has experienced life on both sides of the divide.

One wonders how Golding's schoolboys would have behaved upon returning to school. I suspect that Jack, having triumphed over Piggy, would have continued his wickedness. Yet when a teenager like Stephen Lawrence is murdered simply for being black, adults wonder where such savagery originates. The answer lies with the Jack in every school playground. At least Golding, as a schoolteacher 50 years ago, could have rapped Jack's knuckles without repercussions, and Jack would have learned a worthwhile lesson. Now, as Piggy would have asked, 'What would grown-ups say?' They'd probably be more concerned that Jack's parents might complain rather than considering his victims or the consequences of allowing the evil to continue. •

* From Cambridge University, in *Guardian Higher Education*

. . . .

31 January 1997

David Brindle
NHS spending fall 'correction'

The new edition of *Social Trends*, the official digest of social and economic statistics, was yesterday withdrawn from sale on its first day of publication in order to amend one chart showing a fall in real Government spending on the NHS.

The unprecedented move, which is highly embarrassing for Whitehall, came after Government statisticians accepted a Department of Health complaint that the chart was wrong. In a statement, the Office for National Statistics, which publishes *Social Trends*, said it had ordered 'a thorough review of quality control procedures'.

The chart is based on figures indicating that in real terms NHS spending fell by £1 billion over three years from 1992. That conflicts with ministers' assertions that the

Tories have awarded the NHS a real increase in funds in each year of office.

After the *Guardian* drew the department's attention to the chart ahead of publication, first it and then the ONS issued revised figures showing funds had risen annually.

ONS director Tim Holt, who yesterday said sales of *Social Trends* had been suspended, added, 'No further copies will be distributed by the Stationery Office until a correction slip has been printed.'

Social Trends, which last year sold more than 6,500 copies, is regarded as an unimpeachable source of data and is relied upon by academics and researchers in the public and private sectors. It is hoped the 248-page 1997 edition will go back on sale next week.

Dr Holt said his department accepted it had used incorrect figures to construct the chart. 'Cash spending on the NHS needs to be adjusted for inflation to allow real comparisons to be made over time. An error in the calculations was made which meant the figures were meaningless,' he said. His statement was stronger than comments by other statisticians, who have suggested that the figures may not have been what were intended – but they had validity.

The figures should simply have been adjusted to iron out inflation. In practice, they were also adjusted against the performance of the economy as a whole. The result was that NHS spending was shown to have fallen behind general economic growth. •

20 December 1996

Richard Norton-Taylor

Report denies Deputy PM's 'leak culture'

The *Guardian* has been disclosed as the leading recipient by far of Whitehall leaks over the past two years. A Cabinet Office paper, drawn up at the request of the Deputy Prime Minister, Michael Heseltine, shows that 24 of the 70 leaks were first published in this newspaper.

Mr Heseltine ordered the Cabinet Office – the source of many of the leaked documents – to produce a report after MPs asked him to back up his allegation that politically motivated Labour supporters were responsible for a 'leak culture' in the heart of Whitehall.

The Cabinet Office report has identified 430 Whitehall leaks – which it calls 'unauthorised appearances' – since 1980, but does not substantiate Mr Heseltine's claims. 'Civil servants are not the only people who have had the opportunity, or the motive, to have been responsible,' says the report, drawn up by civil servants. Although it says it is clear that one motive is to embarrass the Government and help the Opposition in criticising it, it makes no reference to Labour-supporting civil servants.

In a note to the Commons public service committee, Mr Heseltine has told it to 'disregard' claims he made last week that a Labour candidate leaked documents while she was in the Treasury – a mistake described by John Prescott, Labour's deputy leader, as a 'humiliating climb-down'.

Sir Robin Butler, the Cabinet Secretary and head of the Civil Service, told the committee that he condemned leaks – but refused to endorse Mr Heseltine's claims that they were all politically inspired. He pointed out that 70 per cent of the documents had been leaked directly to the media, without any Labour Party involvement.

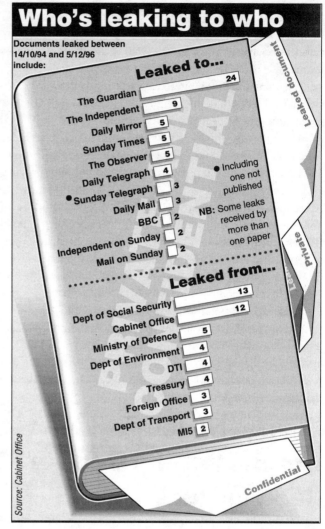

Who's leaking to who

Documents leaked between 14/10/94 and 5/12/96 include:

Source: Cabinet Office

Leaked to...

The Guardian	24
The Independent	9
Daily Mirror	5
Sunday Times	5
The Observer	5
Daily Telegraph	4
● Sunday Telegraph	3
Daily Mail	3
BBC	2
Independent on Sunday	2
Mail on Sunday	2

● Including one not published

NB: Some leaks received by more than one paper

Leaked from...

Dept of Social Security	13
Cabinet Office	12
Ministry of Defence	5
Dept of Environment	4
DTI	4
Treasury	4
Foreign Office	3
Dept of Transport	3
MI5	2

However, the leaks row took a new turn yesterday with Whitehall officials accusing Mr Heseltine, and Tory MEP Graham Mather, of a concerted attempt to smear the Civil Service after Mr Mather produced a report based on computerised searches of newspaper articles for the word 'leak', claiming civil servants had leaked 80 sensitive documents this year.

Jonathan Baume, general secretary-designate of the First Division Association, which represents top civil servants, called the exercise 'completely bogus'. While condemning leaks, the association said many could have come from ministers' special advisers or the growing number of private contractors with access to Whitehall documents.

Sir Robin, meanwhile, appealed for help in tracking down the leakers. 'It is an uphill task finding who is responsible,' he said. But he also remembered the old adage from television's *Yes, Minister*, where Hacker, the minister, tells Sir Humphrey, the permanent secretary, 'I give an authorised briefing; you leak; he's been prosecuted under the Official Secrets Act.' •

23 October 1996

Simon Jones
Howl of the open highway

They came in their hundreds: middle-class, mostly middle-aged, definitely middle-England. Not an eco-activist in sight. They gathered in a public hall in Kidlington, Oxfordshire, on an autumn evening.

Kidlington, a sort of exploded ribbon development, is notable because Richard Branson lives there and the A34 passes nearby. Branson is a big noise. The A34 is a deafening noise for the 20,000 people who live in the surrounding villages. In six years, they have heard traffic on Britain's loudest road triple to 57,000 vehicles per day. It is the main Euro-route from Glasgow to Madrid and resounds across the countryside with a continuous howl.

The meeting was angry. A white-haired gentleman stood up and declared: 'There is only one way we can get change, and that is to block the road.' Cheers and applause. How? someone asked. 'By driving slowly in convoy in both lanes.'

Would Andrew Leadbeater, the county council engineer who had addressed the meeting, back direct action? 'It's not on for someone in my position to condone breaking the law,' he said cautiously, but he sympathised. 'It's not breaking the law to drive slowly,' someone called out.

Government stubbornness has driven them to extremes. The Department of Transport has repeatedly ignored appeals for quieter porous asphalt (the noise is the result of a ribbed concrete surface) which would cost up to £7 million. The Government says it would be a poor use of taxpayers' money. John Watts, the roads minister, refused to come and hear the noise. People complained they could not sleep, or open windows on summer days. Sitting in the garden was a test of endurance.

'How many of you would be prepared to think about direct action?' the chairwoman, Betty Roberts, asked: 200 hands went up. 'How many would be prepared to help organise it?' Four hands went up.

But then John Gidney, from Oxford (they can hear the road there), stood up: 'We are losing faith in the democratic process, in the judicial process, in the parliamentary process – and now in the planning process. Unless we take direct action now, we will still be suffering from that terrible road in two years, in five years, in 20 years. Our children have only one childhood to play in the garden. Our old people have only one old age in which to enjoy peace and quiet. If you want change, you must seriously inconvenience those who use the road and those at the Transport Department. I am prepared to organise direct action, and take names and addresses of those who will join me.'

His oratory was stirring, and it worked. As the meeting ended, many queued to give their names and addresses. Two petitions – one to the European Parliament – collected hundreds of signatures.

Then the mild protesters of Oxfordshire – having declared war on the traffic which is wrecking their lives – trooped out and left. In their hundreds. In their cars. •

30 July 1997

Sarah Boseley

The roads programme: a dead-end street?

Joe Hetton's little front garden has been struggling against next door's thistled wilderness for three years. His immaculate brick and paintwork point up the empty starkness of the adjoining terrace with its boarded-up windows.

Joe lives on the edge of the man-made wilderness that runs for 1.5 miles alongside the A40 commuter route into west London. Endless green hoardings, liberally splattered with flyposters and graffiti, hide the trauma and sheer mess caused by the demolition of 200 homes to make way for a road widening that has just been scrapped in the Government's 'dirty dozen' review of transport schemes.

People like Joe cannot and do not believe it. Oh no. Not scrapped. On hold. They have lived with the ons and offs of this project for so long that they are certain it has to happen some day. So many people could not have been moved out and their homes knocked down for nothing.

Joe has lived at number 283 since 1956, when his mother and father moved in. His house would stare straight at the daily traffic jams were it not for a little path beyond his wall and a bank of foliage and flowers he and his family have tended for 40 years. 'My brother planted that 18 years ago,' he says of an evergreen bush. His house is blighted by the project. 'They are taking the wall and half the garden,' he said, indicating a couple of yards of earth and flowers that technically belong to the Highways Agency. 'They are going to knock the wall down, but it was in such a state I had to do it up.'

The next four houses are derelict behind the hoardings. Their owners took the option to sell to the Highways Agency, since their gardens were destined to disappear. Joe Hetton could have done the same. 'But I had been nursing my mother and she had just died and my brother died of a heart attack eight weeks earlier and I didn't want to go anywhere.'

Many of the older people in the pleasant, if noisy, suburban streets are philosophical. The extraordinary thing about the decision not to go ahead is that all the fuss was over. The project, launched in the early 1970s, had been approved, 200 houses had been compulsorily purchased at a cost of £19.1 million and the land had been cleared and cables and pipes laid for a further £5.9 million. Local people were no longer fighting the road. They were fighting the rats and the dirt let in by dereliction and demolition.

Vera Bondarenko has lived at the Acton end for 25 years in a substantial 1930s three-bedroom house. Her garden used to back on to houses lining the A40. Now instead of shrubs, there is wilderness and illicitly tipped rubbish. She is resigned to what has happened. 'I'm not cross but it's not nice. I had a lovely view out of my window because of other people with gardens. There were roses and other flowers. We used to say hello when we were out watering and they were too. Now it is just a reminder of something. It is just like a wasteland. What can the people say if the Government decides to build and then they don't? They ruined so many lovely houses and there is so little living space these days. We haven't got anything out of it. Just dirty windows and dust.'

So what will now replace the demolished houses and gardens? 'It is too early to say,' said a spokesman for the Highways Agency. 'We will be assessing the options, looking at what is best for the taxpayer and the local community.' Those people who were forced to leave will be pleased to hear that. ●

••

5 April 1997

Nick Davies and Eamon O'Connor
The boy business

I t is an ordinary flat. The camera pans around the room catching sight of a bookshelf full of paperbacks, a desk which is untidy with letters and files, a couple of paintings on the wall, a chair or two, and then the open doorway. As the camera waits, a man suddenly appears there. The only sound is the crackle of the video tape.

The man looks as ordinary as the flat. The camera carefully avoids his face, but his build suggests that he is in his twenties. He is casually dressed and his feet are bare. He is carrying something across his arms and, as he walks towards the camera, it becomes clear that it is a small boy, probably seven or eight years old, dressed in jeans and a T-shirt.

The boy is limp, his legs trailing over the side of the man's arm. His head lolls backwards over the crook of the other arm. But it is the boy's head which catches the camera's eye. It is hooded, and the boy's hands are tied.

The man walks across the room as the camera follows. He tips the boy with an awful gentleness into a wooden chair and pushes him into a sitting position. He takes the boy's wrists, lays them along the arms of the chair and straps them into place. Then he yanks off the hood and the camera closes in on the face of the boy.

This is the cinema of sexual abuse. The film is known as the 'Bjorn Tape' after the name used for the boy who is its central character and victim. It has been sold to paedophiles all over western Europe and it is the subject of an intense police inquiry.

It was made in Holland in March 1990. The man on the tape is British, although nothing is known about the man behind the camera. Neither they nor Bjorn have been identified. Stills from the tape have been released by Scotland Yard's Paedophilia Unit to ITV's *Network First* documentary, *The Boy Business*, to be shown on Tuesday.

The 'Bjorn Tape' is important, not only because of the crime which it reveals, but also because of what it discloses about the inner workings of a bizarre and cruel world. As the veils of ignorance have been removed from paedophilia over the last decade, it has become clear that paedophiles will operate not only as strangers, hovering around public places where children gather, not only as family members, abusing their own children, but also as entrepreneurs.

For the last two years, we have been investigating the activities of a group of British paedophiles who exploit children ruthlessly – as sex objects for their own pleasure and as a source of profit in the international sex industry. They have based themselves in Amsterdam, where they have taken advantage of Dutch tolerance to turn their obsession into a lucrative business, running brothels and escort agencies, and producing pornographic films. To do this, they have imported their 'raw material' from abroad – from the economic chaos of eastern Europe and from the poorest streets of the inner cities of Britain.

Working with police in Britain and Holland, we have identified some of these men and traced some of their victims. Most disturbing is evidence that up to five children have been abducted, tortured and then killed in front of the paedophiles' camera.

Three British men who lived in Amsterdam in the early 1990s have spoken quite independently of each other of their knowledge of paedophile 'snuff movies'. All agree that they were made in Amsterdam by British paedophiles. Two of them name the same individuals, though neither admits to his own involvement.

One has identified two houses where, he says, the films were made and has named two Dutch criminals who, he says, were involved in distributing the films. He has also given detailed descriptions of the boys in the films, described a club in Oslo where one of them was picked up and identified a lake where, he says, their bodies were thrown. His allegations have been taken seriously by Scotland Yard, who have interviewed him twice at length, and by the Dutch Ministry of Justice, which last month launched a formal inquiry.

The origins of this extraordinary story lie in a small incident which briefly disturbed the calm of the British Embassy in Amsterdam on the morning of 3 August 1993. The Dutch police called to say that, on the previous night, they had found a young British boy who needed help to get back home. The boy was telling a very odd tale. He said he had been held against his will in Amsterdam in some kind of brothel and that he had escaped by climbing out of a toilet window and running through the streets until he found a policeman. The British Embassy repatriated the boy and also alerted Scotland Yard.

The boy's name was Gary. He was 14 years old and had grown up on a rough estate in the North-east. He had never met his father and had already spent years dodging in and out of trouble with the law. He described how several months earlier he and his friend Peter, also then 14, had run away together and gone to London, sleeping rough in squats, begging and thieving for a living. Their main aim, he admitted, had been to 'get out of their heads' and so they had contacted a man whom Gary had met once in the street, a helpful man who had given Gary his pager number and said that he could always get Gary drugs. His name was Warwick Spinks.

Spinks told the two boys that he had got some LSD for them at his home in Hastings in Sussex. He paid for them to go there on the train with him and took them back to his flat, where suddenly he produced a kitchen knife and made them strip naked. The burly 30-year-old ordered them to have sex together while he took photographs.

When they failed to perform as he wished, he buggered both of them. Both the boys pleaded with him to stop, but Spinks told them he liked it best when they were scared. He kept them in the flat for two days and gave them LSD. Some of the time, Gary was weeping.

Back on the streets, the two boys reported nothing – they were no friends of the police – and they returned to scavenging for anything that would get them stoned. Towards the end of July 1993, Gary alone contacted Spinks again, in search of more drugs. Spinks met him in Hastings, gave him some LSD and some hours later, in a state of wild confusion, Gary found himself on board a Jetfoil *en route* from Dover to Ostend.

Spinks and another man were beside him. They had got him a false ID, pretending he was a 17-year-old called Michael Samuels. Gary guessed they must be going somewhere to get more drugs. He was wrong. They were going to central Amsterdam, to a club called the Blue Boy, where Spinks was going to sell him.

At first sight, the Blue Boy looks like an ordinary bar: loud music, low red lighting, a counter full of spirits along one wall. The clues to its real nature soon emerge. On the walls, there are collages of naked and semi-naked young men. On top of the bar there is an album – rather like a mail-order catalogue – in which there is page after page of advertisements for young men who are available to the Blue Boy's customers.

'We always have a wide choice of truly the best boys in town,' says a flyer lying on the bar. A young man walks on to the tiny stage at the far end of the bar, dances and strips. Other young men appear, wearing only brief underpants, inviting customers to come upstairs to the little bedrooms with the neat white towels on each bed, to the S and M room with the cage and the bed with straps at each corner. 'Indulge your wildest fantasies with the very best boys in town.' In Amsterdam, it is legal for males aged over 16 to work in the sex industry. But when Warwick Spinks sold him to the Blue Boy, Gary was only 14.

Gary says that in the club he was drugged and sexually abused. 'People could do what they wanted to you,' he says. The ownership of the club has since changed hands, but under the old management other young men who worked in the Blue Boy have complained bitterly that they were trapped, by threats of violence and by the removal of their passports. They say they were pressured to do as customers demanded, regardless of whether they consented.

On the evening of 2 August Gary scrambled out of the toilet window and found a policeman. The secret world of Warwick Spinks was about to collapse. Acting on Gary's evidence, Scotland Yard's Paedophilia Unit raided Spinks's flat in George Street, Hastings. There they found a collection of seven photographs, showing Gary and Peter locked in a naked and timid embrace; and a mugshot of Gary which had been used to produce the false ID in the name of Michael Samuels. They charged Spinks with abduction and buggery and, in March 1995, at Lewes Crown Court, Warwick Spinks was jailed for seven years.

The Spinks who was exposed in that trial was a deeply secretive figure. Outwardly, he was an ebullient, streetwise East Ender, nephew to the Olympic boxer Terry Spinks, a bit of a show-off who liked to boast that he could speak half a dozen languages, a loud-mouth who liked to hold court in the nightclubs of Amsterdam, Prague and Tenerife (where he owned flats which he rented out to tourists). Behind that façade, he was an obsessively promiscuous paedophile who loaned his flats to other paedophiles and crisscrossed Europe in search of young boys – 'chickens', as he called them – for his own purposes and for sale to others.

In the two years since that trial, we have entered Spinks's world, drawing on information gathered by both British and Dutch police in what they jointly called Operation Framework. The information includes tapes of Spinks which were secretly recorded by an undercover police officer in Holland and paperwork with recorded details of his paedophile deals. Some of his victims have also come forward, some anonymously, others openly.

The world of Warwick Spinks was based in Amsterdam, where scores of British paedophiles settled after a police crack-down in London in the late 1980s. In 1985, Dutch police reviewed their intelligence on child pornography and found almost nothing relating to Amsterdam: in four years, they had come across only three cases. Seven years later, after the arrival of Spinks and his friends, they repeated the exercise and found that nearly 250 people in Amsterdam were involved in the industry, most of them foreign; they seized 6,000 videos.

The paedophiles established their illegal life among the relaxed and lawful surroundings of the gay bars and brothels of Amsterdam. In the late 1980s, Spinks worked in one of these, the Gay Place, a brothel which no longer exists, where he sold alcohol and young men to tourists.

One of his customers was a gay man from Birmingham called 'Edward' (not his real name), who says that even then Spinks was operating as an entrepreneur, not only selling lawful sex with young male prostitutes, but also meeting a very specific demand in the sexual marketplace. 'People would approach him,' Edward says, 'being the sort of character he was, and say that they wanted to have sex with boys who were younger than the age allowed in the brothels, or to have rough sex, or extremely dangerous sex with under-age children.' According to Edward, Spinks was soon searching out suitable young boys all over Europe.

He always called them 'chickens' and he was soon finding them in Munich, Berlin, London and, after the collapse of the Soviet empire, in the Czech Republic. 'He would find their weak spot,' Edward says, 'so he was able to approach the boys and offer them something that they needed at the time, whether it was just a roof over their head or security or money or drugs or just two meals a day.'

Spinks made similar boasts to another man who befriended him in Holland but who was, unknown to Spinks, a police officer working undercover. Spinks told him, 'I am good at picking up stray chickens. I have been all over the world, I'm an international slut.' He described how he picked up boys in Dresden, in Bratislava in the Czech Republic and in Poland, where, he claimed, they cost only 10 pence.

'All those chickens with no money,' he chuckled.

In London, he said, he was particularly keen on the hamburger bars around Piccadilly Circus. And he was full of excitement about Hastings. 'The chickens down the coast are very bored. They have got no money, they are not streetwise like Londoners and they spend all of their time in arcades.'

Kenny Abbott was 17, homeless, penniless and drifting into drugs in November 1992, when Spinks befriended him at Victoria Station and gave him his phone number. By now, Spinks was living in Britain again and a few weeks later invited Kenny to come on a trip to Amsterdam. Kenny accepted. 'I didn't have many friends at the time and he seemed OK.' But on the first night in Amsterdam, Spinks took Kenny to a private club and showed him an album of photographs of naked boys, aged between nine and 13. 'Some of them looked scared. Some of them looked drugged up,' Kenny says. One of the pictures, showing a boy of about 10, was marked 'virgin'.

Spinks took Kenny on a tour of Amsterdam clubs, got him drunk and then raped him. Later, Spinks tried to insist that Kenny repay a debt by recruiting young boys for sex and for making films. He pointed to a group of 13-year-olds playing and told him he'd pay £200–£300 each for boys like that. Kenny remonstrated. 'I says, "What do you get out of it?" And he says he likes them to cry, he likes to see pain. I mean, that's what he does. He just enjoys it.'

The boys that Spinks found were an investment as well as a pleasure. He pimped them through his own escort agency. In his flat in Hastings, police found two lists marked Klantenlyst – Clients – and Jongenlyst – Boys. The boys were listed by age and sexual characteristics. The clients were listed by name, telephone number and sexual preference. Michael of Slough wanted light corporal punishment, Richard of Paddington wanted trios and was married, Mike from north London preferred his boys smooth and hairless. Against several of the clients he had noted one particular preference – 'chicken'.

In Amsterdam, Spinks decided to open his own brothels on boats outside the central city, well beyond the sight and hearing of neighbours. Edward saw Spinks the pimp in action one afternoon when he appeared outside the Gay Place with a young boy, probably aged seven or eight, blond with blue eyes. Spinks was holding the boy's hand.

Edward asked him what he was doing. 'He glanced down at the boy and said, "I've got to make a delivery, I'm going to be another half an hour." I don't know what happened to that boy. I never saw the boy again and I decided not to ask Warwick what he meant by making a delivery.'

Spinks was not the only British man who was procuring boys this way. One of his friends in Amsterdam, Peter Howells, was involved in a particularly effective honey trap. He owned a theatrical agency for children, with offices in London and Amsterdam. It was called Bovver Boots. Howells is a convicted paedophile who has also been named in police statements by children from Hackney in north London who say that they were abused, photographed and filmed. These children were initially befriended by an amiable old man, known to his neighbours in Hackney as 'Uncle Harry'.

His real name is Owen Jeffries, he is 71 years old and he too is a convicted paedophile. He told children he was the official photographer for Bovver Boots, he gave them sweets and drinks and a chance to become film stars. He conned them into posing in swimming trunks, rubbed oil on their bodies, saying 'it enhances the picture', and cajoled or threatened the children into stripping completely. Once he had his first nude pictures, he warned the children that he would show them to their parents and their friends on the estate if they did not do as he told them.

The youngest child photographed by Jeffries was only five. The children were prodded with a metal stick to make them strike the right pose. One of the victims, Matthew, says there was a hole in the wall between the room where the children were photographed and the next room, where Harry's friends could watch.

After five years of abuse, Matthew, who was then 14, went to the police, with the result that Jeffries was jailed. Detective Inspector Ian Delbarre, who led that inquiry, believes many of Uncle Harry's pictures found their way to Amsterdam. Dutch police who visited Howells's houseboat on a quiet canal in central Amsterdam found the walls papered with obscene photographs of young boys.

While men like Peter Howells treated children as sex objects, Warwick Spinks and some of his Amsterdam friends broke new boundaries in treating them also as marketable goods. Some of those most closely involved have spoken of a house in north London where boys, aged between 11 and 14, were bound and buggered for the camera by two British paedophiles. They say that boys were imported to Amsterdam for more film-making. They recall Spinks trying to charge £4,000 for a video of an eight-year-old boy being sexually abused and tortured by two men and they describe him showing a video in which a pre-pubescent boy was tortured, castrated and murdered.

The claims of these anonymous associates may stretch belief. They may be nothing but malice. Yet the allegations that Spinks was distributing such films is supported by others and, most significantly, by the words of Warwick Spinks himself. The undercover police officer asked Spinks if he could obtain a sadomasochistic video involving some very young 'chickens'. Unaware that he was being recorded, Spinks said he thought he could.

'How young is young?' he asked.

'Pretty young,' said the officer.

'What? Ten?'

'Yes, that sort of age.'

'I know people in Amsterdam,' said Spinks. 'I might even have one myself. I'll have a look. I think I might have one hidden away in my cellar downstairs.'

The officer went on to tease more out of Spinks, telling him that friends had been offered a snuff movie, in which someone was tortured to death, for £6,000. Spinks spoke with the voice of an expert.

'They're not six grand,' he said. 'I know – I knew – some people who were involved in making snuff movies and how they did it was they only sold them in limited editions, made 10 copies or something, 10 very rich customers in America, who paid $5,000 each, which is a lot of money to watch some kids being snuffed. I mean, I steer a wide berth from those people. I know somebody who was in a snuff movie and somebody got snuffed in front of him and he never knew it was a snuff movie. They had tied him up and done terrible things to him and killed him.'

'Did they?' asked the officer.

'And he has been really petrified since, because he was like from Birmingham, middle twenties. I know the person who made the film. I felt sorry for this boy, it was a German boy.'

'How old?' asked the officer, nudging Spinks along.

'About 13, 15. He thought he was going to make 200 guilders and ended up being dead.'

What was Spinks talking about? Was he involved only in the distribution of these films, or did he know something about their production?

This week Spinks denied any involvement. Speaking from his prison cell, he said, 'I had three brothels in Amsterdam but that does not make me a murderer. It does not make me an associate of murders. It does not mean I'm in a paedophile ring, because I've never had anything to do with anything like that.'

This is contradicted by others. One of Spinks's closest friends in Amsterdam is a convicted international drug dealer, 'Frank' (not his real name), who lived with his boyfriend just outside the city. The boyfriend was in his mid-twenties when Spinks knew them. Frank has since told British police that Spinks and his friends were involved in producing films in which children were raped and killed.

Edward too was close to Spinks at this time. He claims to have seen five videos which were produced by Spinks and Frank and Frank's boyfriend, in which young boys were abused and murdered. Frank denies this.

There is one particular video which Edward has described for *Network First* with terrible clarity. There was a man, he says, 'who was allowed to do anything he wanted' to a boy: 'There was sound on the camera. You could hear the waves slapping against the side of the boat, you could hear noises of water-fowl in the background . . . You saw the guy trying to shake the boy and the boy was a rag doll, the boy couldn't move at all, and he left him lying down on the seats, going around to the left in a half-circle. The boy was actually flopped across the seat, faced towards the camera. Then there was panic. There was a lot of running in and out, the camera got hit from the side and got blanked out.'

Network First has passed all of the information to British and Dutch police, who examined it and decided to launch an inquiry. Edward has given detailed statements to both forces and identified a house in Hoofdorp near Amsterdam where, he says, some of the videos were made and a second house where, he claims, Spinks was living with Frank and his boyfriend. He has taken police to a lake where, he says, Frank's boyfriend told him that the bodies of the dead children were dumped. He has named two Dutch criminals who are said to have sold the tapes in sections, starting with the death and charging more and more for the preceding clips. One of these criminals is believed to be a leading member of the Dutch Mafia; the other is a Dutch paedophile who has run his own brothels in Amsterdam.

Edward describes the children he says he saw in all five videos. 'There was a boy with sallow skin and brown hair, brown eyes, which is unusual for Amsterdam. I've no idea where they got him from. There were two blond-haired boys and a strawberry-blond boy, and a boy with a very distinctive haircut.'

Police in London and Amsterdam confirm that Edward was a known associate of Warwick Spinks and of Frank, and that he approached British Customs officers several years ago to make these allegations. Dutch police confirm that Spinks was living at one of the houses identified by Edward with two British men.

Scotland Yard and the Dutch police are believed also to be looking for links between Spinks and the 'Bjorn Tape'. The fate of Bjorn is not known. Detective Constable Terry Bailey, who has searched for clues in the tape, told us, 'When you see the terror that is on the child's face, and the fear that is there . . . It is so horrific.'

This summer, Warwick Spinks is due to be released from prison. The Appeal Court cut his sentence from seven years to five. As Spinks boasted to the undercover officer, 'I know I'm a fat old queen, but I get away with it. I get away with murder.' •

The names of Gary and Peter are false, to protect their privacy as the victims of sex offences.

AP

Foreign parts

'No decolonisation has been longer in the making or more exactly timed. But then no decolonisation has consisted of passing a people from freedom into bondage.'
Hugo Young on the handover of Hong Kong

27 June 1997

John Gittings

Serious excuse for a good party

The most important part of the South Lamma Grand Reunification Carnival was the food – the duck and scallop with celery, the garoupa with peach in batter, and the fresh lobster. In a place where having a good time means eating a multiplicity of dishes, here was a feast.

Most of Sok Kwu Wan village on this island, unspoilt by Hong Kong standards, turned out at 11 a.m. yesterday to watch the dragon-boat racing and lion dance in the first local event to celebrate the handover to China.

The fish pens in the small bay were decorated with the Chinese and new Hong Kong flags. The only British emblem was a blue ensign on the launch which brought the island's district officer to the celebration.

The DO searched for something suitable to say. 'The efforts of the local community in staging this event show how seriously they treat the handover.' But they were not at all serious, and there were no sonorous speeches about the Joint Declaration or One Country Two Systems. With the regional council footing half the bill, Hong Kong's return to China looked more like a good excuse for a party. By 12.30 p.m. everyone was eating, and kept at it until mid-afternoon.

Sok Kwu Wan can still seem remote, in spite of a cement factory which is chewing up the hill across the bay. The little temple to Tin Hau, the fishermen's goddess, at the entrance to the village, was built before Lamma was leased to Britain in 1898 as part of the New Territories. There are Stone Age burial sites in the hills.

Perhaps its fishermen feel somewhat closer to mainland China because they can roam freely along its coast. 'It's a red-letter day,' said the master of ceremonies, James Lau – an islander and civil servant. 'We're all pleased to be going back.'

The lion dancers disgorged streamers with the inscription 'The Pearl of the East is Made Whole Again'. And the music system played 'Our Great Country' – the tune which starts transmissions for Radio Beijing. But that was about the sum total of the political content. Everyone then sat down to lunch in the Rainbow Seafood Restaurant – 30 tables with 12 seats at each. The music changed to karaoke Cantopop.

An overflow catered for 100 or so dragon-boat paddlemen. If anything is serious in Sok Kwu Wan, it is the racing. The Rainbow Restaurant was clearly delighted at the custom: the empty restaurants on either side were less so. Tiger Beer provided the drinks, some superior waitresses and lucky-dip gifts: its manager got a round of applause.

The occasion had been billed as a carnival in the regional council's calendar of local activities. The local advertisements simply called it a feast – tickets on sale for about £14 a head, with two free gifts guaranteed.

The VIPs left, drummed out by the lion dancers. They included some low-level officials from the New China News Agency, China's unofficial embassy (till next Tuesday) in Hong Kong.

The eating continued. The singers shifted from Cantopop to karaoke Cantonese opera – definitely a new experience. A small girl clutching half a dozen 'Welcome the Reunification' balloons was held up, biting her lip because everyone laughed. 'We're happy, very happy,' chorused her parents.

That was all that anyone said on the great subject of the day. •

1 July 1997

Andrew Higgins
A last hurrah — and an empire closes down

With a clenched-jaw nod from the Prince of Wales, a last rendition of 'God Save the Queen', and a wind machine to keep the Union flag flying for a final 16 minutes of indoor pomp, Britain last night at midnight shut down the empire that once encompassed a quarter of the globe.

Nearly five centuries after Vasco da Gama launched an era of European empire-building in Asia, and 50 years after Britain put the process in reverse with independence in India, it took only a quarter of an hour of martial pomp and minutely scripted ceremony to end 156 years of British colonial rule in Hong Kong.

At dawn today, China stamped its authority on its new possession when 4,000 troops, backed by armoured cars and helicopters, crossed into the territory. But the army, struggling to shake off the stigma of the Tiananmen Square massacre, projected a softer image, with many troops wearing ties and white gloves rather than combat gear.

In Beijing last night, more than 100,000 people gathered in the square to count down the last seconds of British rule, the biggest gathering there since the 1989 massacre, and proclaim the emergence of China as a great power cleansed of colonial shame.

At the formal handover ceremony, Prince Charles bequeathed Britain's last big overseas domain to Jiang Zemin, a former trainee at the Stalin Auto Works in Moscow and now head of the world's last major, albeit zealously capitalist, Communist Party.

The occasion, planned since an accord signed by Margaret Thatcher in 1984, was conducted in English and Mandarin, languages that most people of Cantonese-speaking Hong Kong do not understand – a blunt reminder that, unlike previous acts of imperial retreat, the start of Chinese rule thrusts 6.4 million people into the embrace of a new master sometimes as alien as the departing power.

'We shall not forget you, and we shall watch with the closest interest as you embark on this new era of your remarkable history,' promised Prince Charles.

The transfer, completed in a glass-encased hall overlooking the harbour that first attracted the covetous eye of British opium traffickers, climaxed a day of rain and tear-soaked British pageantry, Sino-British summitry and carefully calibrated discourtesies.

Less than an hour into Chinese rule, as the royal yacht *Britannia* slipped its moorings, carrying Prince Charles and the twenty-eighth and last British governor, Chris Patten, out of Victoria Harbour at the head of a flotilla of British ships bound for Manila, pro-democracy politicians gathered on the balcony of the Legislative Council to protest at China's abolition of Hong Kong's elected assembly.

'Why must we pay such a high price to be Chinese?' asked Martin Lee, leader of the Democratic Party. 'We are proud to be Chinese, more proud than ever before. But why is it that our leaders in China will not give us more democracy, but take away the modest democracy we have fought so hard to win from the British Government.'

A crowd, swelled by television crews, engulfed Statue Square, an adjacent plaza dominated by a bronze likeness of a dour Victorian banker.

Throughout the day Britain stressed its own contribution to Hong Kong's prosperity, while China barely acknowledged Britain's presence. 'This is a Chinese city, a very Chinese city with British characteristics,' said Mr Patten, at a British farewell festival, held next to the Prince of Wales Barracks, now stripped of its name and full of Chinese soldiers. Radio frequencies used by British Armed Forces Radio now only crackle with static.

Chinese leaders arrived by air too late to attend a rain-drenched British farewell festival at sunset and then skipped a British banquet. But in a small but unexpected gesture, Mr Jiang shook the hand of Mr Patten, vilified by Beijing as a 'sinner for a thousand generations' because of the modest political reforms he introduced.

Tony Blair, in Hong Kong for barely 12 hours, and the Foreign Secretary, Robin Cook, both later stayed away from a Chinese ceremony to swear in a new puppet legislature. It was a civil, correct exchange of property but a far cry from the warmth and passions – quickly followed by bloodshed – that accompanied Britain's exit from India.

While Hong Kong's democrats protested, Chinese leaders swore in their handpicked substitute legislature in a Hong Kong hall redolent of the Great Hall of the People in Beijing. Again, no Cantonese was spoken, with 60 Beijing-selected legislators, the new post-colonial governor, chief executive Tung Chee-hwa, and his senior officials all taking their oaths of office in Mandarin.

The substitute legislature immediately began its first formal session, ready to pass an omnibus law activating a string of legislation, including curbs on protests and the funding of political parties, which had been approved before the handover.

'This is a momentous and historic day after 156 years of separation. Hong Kong and China are whole again,' said Mr Tung, a shipping tycoon born in Shanghai and educated at Liverpool University. 'We are here to announce to the world on our own terms and in our own language that Hong Kong has entered a new era.' What ordinary Hong Kongers regard as their own language, though, will not be heard until Mr Tung makes a separate address later today.

When Mr Blair met the Chinese leader, Jiang Zemin, earlier in the day, he called for a new start after the squabbles that have dogged Sino-British ties. 'We want a relationship based on the twenty-first century, putting the battles and struggles of the past behind us,' he told Jiang during a 45-minute meeting. Mr Blair accepted an invitation to visit China. He later left Hong Kong to return to London, avoiding the arrival of Chinese armoured cars, warships and military helicopters.

In Beijing, celebratory fireworks lit the sky and huge crowds in Tiananmen sang the Chinese national anthem.

Hong Kong's democrats, their seats now taken by unelected substitutes chosen by China, also vowed defiance. 'The lustre of the pearl is our freedom. If we lose our freedom, that pearl loses its lustre,' said Mr Lee. 'Some people say democracy is finished in Hong Kong. This is absolutely not true, because the flame of democracy burns in the heart of Hong Kong. We will continue to fight harder and harder. Or to paraphrase [Gen Douglas] MacArthur, I will be back.' •

1 July 1997

Hugo Young
Handover confounds the chorus of elders

A free country was handed over to the only Communist superpower, with due and doleful ceremony, at the stroke of midnight, and nothing palpably changed. The British side looked bleak. Somewhere out in the territories, 4,000 Chinese troops were moving in, and armoured trucks were giving a profile to China's presence that the British army was careful never to display. No decolonisation has been longer in the making or more exactly timed. But then no decolonisation has consisted of passing a people from freedom into bondage.

It was bound to be something like this, with the Prince of Wales doing the honours, and one lot of owners shaking hands with another as the lease falls in. The scenes on the ground were chaotic, as thousands of dignitaries sat in engulfing rain watching what an old nation does best: beating the retreat with wonderful military precision and playing all the old tunes. Tears were jerked from even the stoniest heart. But they weren't tears of pity or regret. All in all, the run-up to the due transfer of Hong Kong has been, against every prediction 10 years ago, a triumph: economy booming, construction rocketing, people alerted, by late British insistence, to the meaning of democratic freedom.

Yet not everybody was pleased. Behind the ceremonial rituals, a chorus of elders was chanting the omens. This wasn't the Hong Kong Democrats, though they could be heard, and made their own gestures of rejection. The lamenting came from the people with whom all this began: British officials who got it under way in the 1980s, now standing watch over the final act and hating what they see. They tell one a lot about the peculiar *schadenfreude* of the official mind.

Plenty of them came. I didn't see Sir Percy Cradock, but Geoffrey Howe, the point man on the 1984 Joint Declaration, Sir Alan Donald, a prime Foreign and Commonwealth Office sinologue, Lord Wilson, former governor and the sinuous epitome of a British version of the Chinese mind, and quite a few others were here, all attending the obsequies not so much of Hong Kong as of their own delicate handiwork: the Ming vase they made, which Governor Patten, grandstanding for democracy, shattered.

Lord Howe thinks yesterday could have been quite different. It should, he told me, have been the Asian version of the Mandela–De Klerk handover. The analogy is, frankly, fatuous. A generous optimist might see one or two De Klerks skulking on the Chinese scene, C. H. Tung, the new local boss, possibly among them. But where is Mandela?

Never mind: what some elders who crafted 1984 believe is that, handled as they had brilliantly arranged, this could have been the climax of a rapprochement between two cultures, instead of the perilous stand-off which, as they believe, is entirely Mr Patten's fault.

They think that, back then, they did something extraordinary. The Chinese could simply have walked in. Britain held no cards, yet the great FCO apparatus of sinological learning brought them to the table, patiently manoeuvred for years, agreed the procedures, fixed the timetables and built a through-train carrying legislators elected in 1995 past 1997, with only occasional rebellious passengers flung out of the door if Beijing didn't like them. All this, they think, Patten recklessly put at risk, as only a barbarian could do.

The elders do not always chant in tune. For example, they say contradictory things about the Asian attitude to democracy. Much of the attack on Patten used to claim that Hong Kongers would never care about democracy anyway. The indictment has changed. It says, instead, that Patten has put democracy itself at risk.

One former official told me that the downside of the Patten initiatives, which gave many people a fragment of a vote without Chinese permission, was that they would delay by many years the democracy the Joint Declaration provided for.

This contestable proposition is part of a wider conflict in these people, between optimism and pessimism concerning China's real intentions. Most of them, Cradock being the acme, have spent a lifetime kowtowing to a force they consider to be beyond challenge. Cradock's straight-faced verdict on the Tiananmen Square massacre, in a recent article in *Prospect*, was that 'it made the Chinese authorities even more resentful, sensitive and suspicious of British intentions in Hong Kong'. At the same time, other members of this chorus seem to have discovered new heights of lyricism, contemplating what might have been.

If only Chris had not been so honourably stubborn, Howe thinks, a glorious future stretched ahead. He had tried to secure by confrontation what had not been available by agreement. Telling the Chinese what to think about human rights constituted a kind of recidivist imperialism. Imagine how much more influence he would have carried had he been in dialogue with Beijing for the past five years. Howe's dissent from Patten had apparently persuaded him that Deng Xiaoping was on the verge of conversion to Jeffersonian democracy, courtesy of the Joint Declaration, until the governor reversed the process.

I can understand what the chorus is lamenting. What's at stake here is pride of authorship. Sitting in the audience at the handover they'd spent a decent part of their lives preparing for, they had been, to some extent, overtaken. Their version of how to deal with China had not prevailed, and Lord Howe chose to satisfy his vanity by proclaiming his attendance at China's own celebration. Lumbering alongside, Sir Edward Heath, the arch-exponent of Asia's negative attitudes to democracy, who not long ago on British television told Martin Lee, the brave leader of the Democrats here, that he had no business challenging what China wanted, cut a signal figure: the man who says, as most of them fundamentally believe, that the only proper way to close down the British empire was by following the rulebook of the twenty-first century imperialists.

So they were an unsettling presence, in their discontent. But they did not spoil the party. As yet, their prophecies have proved false. They thought things would get much nastier than they have, much sooner, as a result of Patten's unnecessary quarrel. But if anything, China eased up on its political threats and demands as the handover got closer.

Nobody can foresee the future, but then nobody ever could. *Le tout* Hong Kong were there last night, when the British said goodbye, and few of them were mourning. The identical crowd will be there today, when the new chief executive of the Special Administrative Region, Mr Tung, gives his own first party. In the end, most people needed neither Geoffrey Howe nor Chris Patten to teach them about reality. •

....

28 May 1997

Andrew Higgins
Crazy for red chips

In a speculative frenzy wild even by the standards of a city where betting on horses averages more than £1,000 a year for every resident, the cash equivalent of former Zaïre's entire economic output has been stumped up for a single roll of the dice at the Hong Kong stock exchange.

The bet is, basically, that Communist Party connections will make more money faster than proven business acumen. With only 35 days before Hong Kong reverts to Chinese rule, the proposition has been judged a sure thing – or what *aficionados* of high finance call a 'no-brainer'.

While the share prices of many of Hong Kong's traditional blue-chip conglomerates languish – despite healthy profits – because of concern about their colonial tincture, investors have gone wild over so-called red chips: politically correct mainland-backed enterprises.

'You don't need an MBA to follow red chips, for this you need a degree in psychology,' said David Webb, a director of Wheelock Capital. 'It is the emperor's clothes syndrome. As long as we all agree the clothes are golden and wonderful, then prices might hold up in the short term.'

Instead of people rushing to get their money out of local banks before the 1 July handover, as they did in Shanghai in 1949, the longest queues in Hong Kong over the past week have been of investors wanting to buy into Beijing Enterprises, an assortment of unconnected assets conglomerated by a party fiat.

The firm boasts a stretch of the Great Wall, a slice of Big Mac profits, part of a brewery, a dowdy luxury hotel and other holdings. Only three months old, it is controlled by the Beijing People's Municipal Government, a body probably best known for having spawned China's biggest corruption scandal in 1995.

Hu Shaoguang, the chairman of Beijing Enterprises, told the pro-Communist Hong Kong newspaper *Wen Wei Po* yesterday that the management had been put under 'great pressure' by the huge demand for a stake in his untested company. Not mentioned is the fact that senior managers look set to become millionaires thanks to share options and other privileges.

The paper said the share offer was oversubscribed 1,600 times, would-be investors putting HK$220 billion (more than £18 billion) – more than twice the total amount of cash in circulation in the colony – into a ballot for shares.

'This is a vote of confidence from international investors in the return of Hong Kong to the motherland,' said Mr Hu. 'It is also a vote of confidence in the reform and open door policy of China and Beijing.'

It is also a very easy way to make quick money. The deadline for share applications was last Friday. By the time unsuccessful applicants get their money back this week, Beijing Enterprises will have made some £15 million in interest on their money. In six days it will have made more than half its projected annual profit.

'We have a crazy market at the moment,' said Tom Grimmer, a director at Peregrines, an investment company which with Morgan Stanley is sponsoring the Beijing Enterprises launch. 'There is a frenzy for red chips. Frankly, it is not very easy to explain. Perhaps it's an alignment of the planets.' •

21 December 1996

Ruaridh Nicoll
The art of getting by

t is the end of term. The teachers hover in the laboratory at the Institute Vdjili, a high school specialising in science on the outskirts of Kinshasa. The room is filthy and very hot, just a shack with a long bench of smashed tiles running down the centre. One of the teachers points towards the ceiling, where the equatorial sky can be seen beyond. 'When it rains the teacher cannot stand at the blackboard,' he says.

Even Zaïre's leaden corruption cannot slow time, and with each of the past six years life has become more difficult for the people who teach here. The world may be watching Zaïre, expecting its disintegration, and President Mobutu Sésé Séko may have returned after a long absence, full of promises to fight and win the war in the east. But in the school these things are just politics, nothing compared to facing the daily evil.

Each morning André Mashikote, the school's attendant, turns his harrowed face to the ledger on his desk. A column falls alongside the names of the 1,200 students; his pen runs down, checking for those without a tick. Then he walks to the classrooms where between 80 and 100 students sit three to a desk. There are no pens, books or jotters and the teacher stops as the attendant walks in.

Mr Mashikote calls the names of the children on his list – kids whose parents have failed to pay the £3 monthly fee – and then escorts them from the school grounds. 'They come the next day because they want to learn, but since they have no financial means they are not allowed in,' he says. 'It is very sad. They stand around until the classes are over.' Mr Mashikote cuts a miserable figure in his plyboard cubbyhole.

That schools used to have facilities like a laboratory tells a tale. Adult literacy has always been reasonably good, but in 1990 the government began its transition to democracy and, more than 14 governments later, everything has gone to hell. One in three children now receives no schooling. But education would not exist in Zaïre if the teachers and parents had not taken over responsibility for the schools in the vacuum that was left when, in 1993, the government cheques stopped arriving.

There is unlikely to be an election, as promised, next year. The war in the east has already given the government its excuse to back away from its promises. What the transition has brought instead is misery. 'Leadership has been suppressed, the military is disorganised, the government is weak and the political class is totally irresponsible,' says Cleophas Kamitatu-Massamba, a former minister and ambassador, who sits in a room surrounded by portraits of himself. 'Because of the vacuum, the president has complete, total and absolute power.'

It is easy to see where the money the school needs has gone. On the slopes of Binza Hill stand the grey guts of a large half-built house. It is nicknamed the White House by Kinshasa's residents, who recognise the vast bow front in the skeletal structure. Around it, beautiful homes in lush gardens spread away into the distance. The unfinished house belongs to the prime minister, Kengo wa Dondo.

It is almost impossible to describe the way this country operates. Foreigners are robbed by officials at the airport and £130 for accreditation is placed in a folder marked '*pour le ministre*'. But this is nothing to what the population have to put up with. 'The soldiers are our enemy,' says one resident. 'They stop you, strip you naked and steal everything. Last week they even took my shirt.'

It is just the beginning. There are no human rights, the hospital barely functions, there is no transport and little communication. The American and the Portuguese ambassadors could only watch as the government sold half of a well-known avenue outside their embassies to a supermarket looking for parking space.

Yet the people endure, hospitable and friendly, and unwilling to criticise their president because it would be rude to pick on a man who is ill with prostate cancer.

There is laughter when people here talk of coups and revolution. 'The situation here could never happen in another country,' a Western diplomat says. 'There would have been a bloody revolution. But these are quiet people. It is a country that is used to living away from power.'

Mr Kamitatu-Massamba continues his analysis: 'The population is living in indescribable misery, but since Rwanda and the rebels attacked there has been a great rise in nationalistic feeling. The president appears like the man who has saved the country's integrity in the past, so now the people look to him.'

In the east, the war seems to have ground to a halt. The rebels' advance has stalled despite Zaïrean forces falling back to the regional capital of Kisangani. There is a vast 'grey area' between the armies, awash with refugees.

Meanwhile, the good people of Kinshasa get on with their lives. It seems the only thing worse than Zaïre disintegrating is that it might remain the same.

Lema Kiensidna, a father of 11, holds some plants with which he is going to make a stomach potion that he hopes to sell. He used to be a tailor but people are too poor to ask for his services these days. 'Every time I have any money it is quickly gone,' he says. 'Now I don't have enough to feed my family or educate them.'

Asked how he copes, he shrugs. What he means is that he believes in the *débrouillardise* – the art of getting by. •

4 April 1997

Chris McGreal
Waiting for Kabila

Kaiser Nzengu flits between his customers, shamelessly lifting the latest rumour from anxious soldiers or lorry drivers before passing it on to the next table in a half-whisper.

The head waiter of the Mokador café confides that it cannot be long now before Zaïre's rebels arrive. They have already secretly infiltrated Lubumbashi, he says. Across the city there is a sense that liberation (as most people call it) is close.

In a country so often thought of in terms of Joseph Conrad's *Heart of Darkness*, the prospect of war has brought more hope than fear to Zaïre's second-largest city. There is not even the scent of an enemy, unless it is President Mobutu Sésé Séko.

Mr Nzengu makes no bones about his loyalties. 'You ask anybody, ask a child this high, and he'll tell you Mobutu is the devil,' he said.

But there is a sense of uncertainty. Moneychangers prop themselves up in one corner of the decrepit café, with an ear open for anything which might affect the ever-sensitive exchange rate. Fat men waddle up with fatter briefcases to carry away packs of Zaïre's near-worthless banknotes.

The tales of rebel movements arrive with the lorry drivers bringing food and people from beyond the city, or soldiers who fled the last battle, or businessmen who are close to some army general or other. The information is swiftly channelled around Lubumbashi by the ubiquitous cellular phones. But no one is certain of anything. The northern city of Kisangani waited three uneasy weeks before the rebels struck.

The uncertainty is part of the insurgent strategy to build tension and it frustrates Mr Nzengu. 'People just wish it was over. Not because they are scared but because this confusion leaves everyone wondering what to do, whether to go out. Should we do business? I don't know whether I should buy this thing or that, or wait until the rebels have come.'

So many people turned out for a wake for the regional governor's son, who died last week, that a rumour spread that the rebels had arrived. Within minutes the market emptied as people fled to their homes.

There is no doubt that Lubumbashi has already been infiltrated by rebels who have slipped in on lorries carrying workers from surrounding villages. People talk about the number of unrecognised men in some parts of town. The security police (known as the 'Snip') are at a loss. By rights they should serve the same master they have bowed to for three decades. But no one doubts that change is at hand and few want to be the ones to agitate the coming new order. •

··

2 June 1997

Chris McGreal
Kinshasa Diary

Breakfast will never be the same at Kinshasa's Intercontinental hotel. First the rebels' arrival heralded the end of the almond croissants. Then came the business with the grenade.

Just about the only person not disturbed by the little metal ball clattering on to the tiled floor and wandering its way laboriously under the breakfast tables was the young soldier who dropped it. The sun was just up and he was more interested in opening his first beer of the day.

The regular clientele of local businessmen and foreign diplomats sat frozen and incredulous until their liberator finally slouched his way over to recover his misplaced explosive and made off to blitz the buffet.

Most of the leaders of the revolution which revived Zaïre as the rechristened Congo are now basking in Kinshasa's top hotel. With them have come young soldiers from the rural interior who have seen nothing like it. And, for all the decrepit state of Mobutu Sésé Séko's defeated troops, the hotel has never seen anything quite like their conquerors.

One regular guest to the breakfast table specialises in the Mexican-bandit look, with wads of ammunition strung across his chest while humping a machine gun almost as tall as him which he refuses to let go of even as he loads up his bowl with tinned fruit. It could wipe out most of the clientele in a matter of seconds. They tend to wait their turn at a distance.

Laden under an array of weaponry, rebels wander the lobby wide-eyed at the fine suits and electronic gadgets decorating the opulent shops. The lifts are a particular source of fascination and confusion. And the prostitutes have left some rebels close to apoplectic at the sight of miniskirts and make-up.

The 'Inter' – as the hotel is universally known in Kinshasa – had not filled more than a few dozen rooms at a time in years. The end of the war has brought a new boom, if filling the hundreds of rooms is what matters. Quite who is paying is something else.

Half the hotel is owned by the government, which used to mean Mr Mobutu. His much despised son, Kongulu – nicknamed Saddam Hussein for his ruthlessness – found it a favourite hangout for entertaining whoever took his fancy at someone else's cost.

The younger Mobutu's final visit to the 'Inter' began at 3 a. m. the morning the rebels moved into Kinshasa. He jumped from an armoured car and stormed into the hotel in search of an errant army captain and the prime minister's family to settle old scores. Kongulu found neither and a few hours later bolted across the river to Brazzaville. He left behind a $1 million hotel bill.

The Intercontinental's Palestinian-Jordanian manager is uncertain if the new order is any more credit-worthy as it does its best to compete with Kongulu's spending. The rebels even got the hotel to arrange Laurent Kabila's inauguration last week, in the absence of anyone in Kinshasa with recent first-hand experience of swearing-in presidents.

The 'Inter' may come to regret the breakfast buffet in particular. After ordering their first beers, soldiers sweep the platters clean before making full use of the numerous baggy pockets on their uniforms to stock up for the rest of the day.

Security outside the hotel is tight, if you don't have a gun. While men dripping in weapons wander in and out unhindered, everyone else is searched with the exception of some of Mr Mobutu's former associates. The security guards are having a hard time shedding old habits, so they dutifully salute and wave them through the doors untroubled.

When the bar toilets overflowed, the plumbers discovered they were blocked with ripped-up documents discarded by a few of the deposed despot's cronies who stayed on in the hope of finding a role in the new regime. One of Mr Mobutu's army generals is even living in the hotel, hoping to ingratiate himself. It is not clear if he has been successful or is on his way to a prison cell. •

Past Notes

27 February 1997

Spion Kop's acre of massacre

27 February 1900, by J. B. Atkins

If you looked up from Tugela to the hills where Sir Charles Warren fought, you would say they rose in a continuous slope to the top. But South African hills are like the sea: at a distance they seem smooth, but look close into them and you will find unexpected valleys and crests. Nothing on the face of South African nature is what it seems. You see the British trenches up there seeming to lie immediately under the Boer trenches, but if you go up you will find that they are on different hills and a deep valley lies between them.

Spion Kop, properly used, was the key of the position, and the key that would open the door of Ladysmith. Patrols had reported that there were only a few Boers on it. Soon after dusk a party set out to make a night attack on the hill. The force was three-quarters of the way up before it was discovered. Then a Boer sentry challenged it for the password.

'Waterloo,' said an officer. The sentry turned to flee, but fell bayoneted. 'Fire and charge' came the order.

When dawn came the party found it was in the clouds. It could see nothing but the plateau. The Boers were invisible; our own troops below were invisible. The curtain rose upon the performance of a tragedy. The Boers on another ridge of Spion Kop began to fire heavily and our men seemed to have no sufficient protection in the trenches. The space was small; they were crowded together.

I shall always have in my memory the scene as I saw it from below – that acre of massacre, that complete shambles, at the top of a rich, green gully, with cool granite walls. To me it seemed that our men were all in a small square patch; there were brown men and browner trenches, the whole like an over-ripe barley field. I saw three shells hit a certain trench within a minute. The trench was toothed against the sky like a saw and then – heavens! – the trench rose up and moved forward. The trench was men, the teeth against the sky were men. •

20 March 1997

Suzanne Goldenberg
Food runs out in Sargadi

Hema Chura takes a seat on a pile of bricks that is about to be turned into her new home – a gift from a contrite government after her husband starved to death when he could not find food for his family. The family already had a two-roomed house, but it had to be demolished to make way for the new one: government regulations decree that a destitute widow is entitled to 5,000 rupees (£87) in compensation and a roof over her head.

Ms Chura, bewildered at the sudden change in her fortunes, shrugs. 'I kept my old house very nice,' she says. 'I plastered it every year, but that was the government provision.'

The official largesse owes more to embarrassment and guilt than attention to the needs of Ms Chura and her six children: the family has no breadwinner and no land.

When Ms Chura's husband, Baida, died last month, he had not eaten for two days. Villagers say his was the seventh death from starvation in Sargadi, in western Orissa, since the autumn, when the village's last food stocks ran out. Even the children are listless, too dispirited to run or play. But the local government believes their slow decline does not constitute starvation.

'There is a difference,' says Prashant Kumar Mishra, the development officer in Khariar block, the administrative unit which includes Sargadi. 'In one case, a man doesn't take food, and in the other he does not take nutritious food.'

His senior officer, Satyabrata Sahu, is even more categorical. 'Starvation is impossible,' he says. 'At best, it can be said that it is poverty or destitution, but in many cases they are dying because of tuberculosis.' He dismisses an unpublished report by the National Human Rights Commission which largely supports allegations that this year's drought has brought deaths from starvation in western Orissa.

Mr Sahu, who has yet to visit Sargadi, points out that Baida had land a decade ago and suffered from tuberculosis. He reads aloud a pitiful inventory from the family home: 'One pot, one rolling-pin, one spoon . . . If they were really hungry, they could have sold these earlier.'

While local officials are understandably loath to admit deaths from starvation on their terrain, the government's efforts to appease the families of the dead highlight its failure to adopt a systematic approach to prevent such tragedies. The result is a population too cowed to help itself and a local administration little inclined to sympathy.

'Human life is worth very little here,' says Vijay Aurora, the collector of the neighbouring district of Balangir. 'They have four, five, six children and if one dies of starvation it doesn't matter to them at all. That's their mentality.'

Since independence 50 years ago, poverty in much of India has decreased, but academics say the proportion of those who are destitute is rising. In this part of western Orissa, 90 per cent of the population earn less than 1,500 rupees (£26) a year.

The village of Bahabal, in Balangir, won brief notoriety in January after newspapers reported that in November a widowed mother of five had sold her daughter as a bonded servant for 150 rupees (less than £3) and two sacks of grain. It was not a hasty decision. After her husband became too ill to work, Nura Gohir grew poorer over several months. By the time she put Sanju, aged 10, up for sale in a neighbouring village, there was nothing left to sell. 'I had to look after my sick children and husband,' she says.

After the national press ran the story, an embarrassed administration gave her a widow's compensation of 5,000 rupees, and feminists in New Delhi sent another 3,000. Other widows in the village entitled to the same compensation are still waiting.

'We are also in need. There are no crops in the field, no water. If you come to our house you will see we have nothing,' said a neighbour, Gomati Gohir.

Nura Gohir listens in sullen silence, then calls out, 'Do you think that money will last for ever? I have five children. If I can't fill our bellies, I will sell another one.' •

26 December 1996

Martin Woollacott
Bangladesh's story written in blood

The road from the Indian border to Faridpur in Bangladesh is a long necklace of battered tarmac, on which villages are closely strung like beads. Every half-mile or so, among the green of paddy field and coconut grove, there is a scatter of huts, with beaten-earth paths to each doorway, or the clutter of bazaar shops with tea, grain and soap laid out on open boards, that marks a larger settlement.

In early 1971 it was a road of fear, anger and a kind of hope. The Pakistani troops, who a month before had smashed the Bangladeshi autonomy movement, massacred intellectuals and student leaders, and imprisoned Sheikh Mujibur Rahman, were fanning out from Dhaka in an occupation of the provinces as brutal as it was ultimately to prove ineffective. Bangladeshis feared their arrival, then only days away, but they had an unswerving conviction that the world would come to their rescue. This world had to be told what was going on and, for one village along that road, the messengers to hand were two young men who rode in on a motorbike and had stopped for a drink of green coconut juice. I and a reporter for Danish Radio, Lasse Jensen, were on our way to Faridpur, where we thought we would be able to meet Awami League leaders and resistance fighters before the Pakistani army got over the Padma River and into the town. We were in a hurry, but this village would not let us go.

There, in the middle of the road, a table and chair were brought and planted down. Pen, paper and ink followed. Under the noonday sun, a local politician and a schoolteacher wrestled with the composition, in English, of an appeal to the world, surrounded by a swelling crowd of every age, the more senior calling out suggestions as to wording while the more junior fixed on the visitors an unwavering Bengali stare.

When the document was finished and after a suitably large envelope for it had, with some difficulty, been located, it was ceremoniously handed to me. As I put it in my bag, there was an audible gasp of satisfaction from the villagers. There was nothing in the letter that the world did not, in a general way, already know, yet as it was passed to us the weight of this village's simple expectation that justice would be done was passed on as well.

But Bangladesh turned out to be far from a simple case of a wrong set right. That objective was achieved 25 years ago this week, when the Pakistani commanding general signed an instrument of surrender on the spot where Sheikh Mujibur Rahman had proclaimed Bangladesh's right to freedom. That was joyfully recalled in Bangladesh this week, in rallies, meetings and processions, one of them at that same spot, organised by the government of Sheikh Hasina, Sheikh Mujib's daughter. However, Bangladesh also offers a lesson on the intractable nature of violence – on its terrible attractions and frequent uselessness, and on the difficulty of eradicating it once certain sequences have been set in motion.

The Bangladesh victory was followed by a dangerous, bloody period in the subcontinent, during which many of those who had been actors in the Bangladesh drama lost their lives. They included Sheikh Mujib himself, nearly all his immediate family, the principal Awami League leaders and many prominent liberation fighters, including General Zia-ur Rahman. In Pakistan and India, Zulfikar Ali Bhutto and Mrs Indira Gandhi were amongst the victims. To what extent the humiliation of the Pakistani army in Bangladesh contributed to Bhutto's death, or the encouragement to Sikh separatism represented by Bangladesh's independence contributed to Mrs Gandhi's, is hard to determine. But they were undoubtedly among the causes, as was the precedent of head-of-state asassination.

Naturally, it was not only the great who lost their lives. It is hard to reconcile those deaths which seemed worthwhile, when the war was being fought, with those which seemed pointless in its aftermath. It's also hard to avoid the conclusion that there was some connection between the two. In late 1971, in Dhaka, I went down at night to a bazaar area after hearing that the Mukti Bahini, the Bangladeshi resistance fighters, had been firing on Pakistani auxiliaries. The car, bumping down narrow unlit lanes, brought us eventually to a muddied piece of open ground between shuttered stalls. It was absolutely empty except for the dead body of a young man who had been recently shot in the chest. He was good-looking and well made, dressed in a khaki military shirt and trousers, a middle-class boy of perhaps 22. Bodies seen at a distance or contorted and thrown about are one thing, but this was a strange moment of intimacy of a very different kind. We stood over him like mourners. For a second or two I saw him as his mother, father or sister would have seen him, as a loved one lost and gone, his male beauty wasted in the dirt. I had not fully understood, till then, the price that Bangladesh was paying.

But it did not stop being paid. Earlier that year, I had spent two days in a Mukti Bahini camp on the border commanded by Captain Najmul Huda. He discussed the war with us over an open-air dinner before sending us into Bangladesh on what was called a firing party. In his tent he gave us Nivea for cracked lips, and I noticed at the side of his cot some kind of family photograph and an exercise book with notes and drawings on the use of the mortar. These almost domestic details, particularly the little blue jar of precious Nivea, stuck in the mind. Things to be joked about later, when encountering Captain Huda again. But that can never be, since he was killed, barbarously, in one of the coups and counter-coups which followed Sheikh Mujib's death.

The Pakistanis, like other oppressors before them, were caught in a trap in Bangladesh. There was nothing they could do that could bring them success. Yet they were doomed to try. In the broadest sense, both Pakistanis and Bengalis were victims of an unnatural union which could not be sustained on terms either side could accept. War performed the function it often discharges, of demonstrating what ought already to have been obvious by writing it in blood. The sacrifices of the war, which these memories are meant to recall, went on long afterwards. The difficult politics of Bangladesh, in which power and legitimacy have been contested between military rulers and civilian politicians, particularly those of the Awami League, now again the government after a gap of 20 years, were also born in the war. Nevertheless, the victory of 1971 was a necessary one which, at a time when other struggles, like Bosnia and Kurdistan, are far from proper resolution, is worthy of celebration. •

....

26 May 1997

Larry Elliott
We're all Californian now

Well, East Coast girls are hip,
I really dig those styles they wear . . .

Twenty years ago, a British visitor to the US would have noticed the difference straight away. The language, the movies and the music were the same, but America had a different feel. Strip developments, shopping malls, drive-through McDonald's, orbital freeways, towers of steel and glass all jarred with the dowdy Britain of the late 1970s. But no longer. Britain in 1997 has been Americanised. Almost every provincial town has a greenfield development complete with multiplex cinema, tenpin bowling, a fast-food joint and acres of parking space.

This is just the outward show of a much deeper colonisation of the Western industrial world by American ideas, business mores and culture. It is hard to accept for some, particularly those on the left, who grew up in the 1960s when America was the Great Satan.

Thirty years ago, Europe was credible as a third way between American imperialism and Soviet repression, but just as Communism was vanquished in the 1980s, so the 1990s have seen the static European model pushed on to the defensive by the United States' expansionism.

Despite this, or perhaps because of it, the anti-American left has high hopes that the new Government will 'move closer to the heart of Europe' and reject Atlanticism. But everything the Blair administration has done in its first, whirlwind three weeks in office suggests that the links with America will be as strong, if not stronger, than in the Thatcher–Reagan era. It is no surprise that Bill Clinton is to address the Cabinet this week; after all, he has been like Banquo's ghost in Downing Street since 1 May.

At this weekend's summit at Noordwijk in Holland, the Prime Minister made it clear that he would support an employment chapter in the son of Maastricht treaty only provided it encourages flexible labour markets. There had to be 'less obsession with our-selves and our institutions, more focus on the things that matter to people'.

This was entirely sensible. Labour is pragmatic and will cherry-pick ideas from any-where provided they work. As far as Labour is concerned, America works when it comes to job creation and Europe doesn't.

The Prime Minister and the Chancellor are convinced that globalisation is here to stay and that the challenge for policymakers is to ensure that their societies can com-pete. That means a macro-economic policy which encourages growth, balanced bud-gets, a better-educated workforce, a retooled welfare state and flexible labour markets. From the Whitehall perspective, Bill Clinton seems to be doing a lot better than Jacques Chirac or Helmut Kohl.

Delving deeper into Labour's psyche, it is evident that its intellectual drive comes from the East Coast. Key advisers, like David Miliband and Ed Balls, studied at Mass-achusetts Institute of Technology and Harvard, and are still plugged into US acade-mia's fecund world. Almost every idea floated since the election – operational inde-pendence for the Bank of England, a beefed-up Securities and Investment Board, Welfare to Work, hit squads in schools, an elected mayor for London – has its origins on the other side of the Atlantic. It would be no surprise if Gordon Brown chose one of the top US Keynesians – Paul Krugman, Lester Thurow, Robert Frank, Robert Reich – for the Bank of England's monetary policy committee.

And the southern girls,
with the way they talk,
They knock me out when I'm down there ...

Offhand, it's hard to think of a single Labour idea originating on the other side of the Channel. After embracing the thinking of the Enlightenment in the eighteenth century and the migrant millions from Italy, Ireland and Scandinavia in the nineteenth century, America has barely imported anything from Europe. In terms of culture, it has been pretty much one-way traffic, with even Britain's pop invasion of the 1960s a re-export of the original American musical forms of R&B and rock 'n' roll.

Britain has always found it hard to understand trends – either social democratic or Christian democratic – in mainstream European politics. By contrast, Labour mod-ernisers quickly latched on to what Bill Clinton was doing, and saw that the somewhat anomalous mixture of liberalism and authoritarianism could be transplanted. The Prime Minister will be Tony, just as Bill Gates of Microsoft is Bill, but the jeans and open-necked shirt approach has to coexist with ruthlessness and 'tough love'.

The Mid West farmers' daughters
Will really make you feel all right ...

The signs are that Labour is drawing heavily on the puritanical side of the

American dream. The central idea is to create an opportunity society, with individuals encouraged to be self-reliant and to live according to a set of established rules. There will be no room in Blair's Britain for the three-Martini lunch, any more than there is in Clinton's America. Instead, as is already happening, smokers will have to huddle on the pavement if they want to indulge their craving, applicants will be turned down for jobs if their alcohol consumption is deemed to be excessive and there will be health targets to make us leaner and fitter as a nation.

In the 1980s, American management culture gradually seeped into Britain, first influencing business and then politics. No government department is without its mission statement, just as no industry has escaped downsizing and outsourcing. In the election campaign, the buzzwords were 'rapid rebuttal' and the 'message'.

And the northern girls, with the way they kiss,
They keep their boyfriends warm at night . . .

Even the counter-culture against Americanisation is American-bred. The template for the direct-action environmental protests at Newbury and Manchester was the fight against loggers in the Pacific states at the start of the 1990s. Those who are downsized, traumatised and victimised by the onward process of globalisation have recourse to that other great American export – counselling. While France is one of the least politically correct countries in the world, Britain is fast catching on to the new etiquette involved in rooting out sexism, racism, stoutism and heightism, wherever it exists.

I wish they all could be California girls . . .

The logical conclusion of all this is that Britain should make a virtue of reality and become even more American. That too is the conclusion drawn by Charlie Leadbeater in an essay published today by the Demos think-tank. Leadbeater's argument is that Britain should become the California of Europe. He points out that the golden state, similar in size to the UK, has been more successful than any other Western economy in restructuring away from the old, declining industries and into computers, the Internet, biotechnology, multimedia entertainment and design. Quite simply, California is forging ahead in the knowledge-based industries of the future: in 1975, it accounted for 15 per cent of America's high-tech jobs; last year that figure had increased to 22 per cent.

Could Britain follow the Californian route? Leadbeater argues it could. Both economies are at the western edge of large regional markets. Both have strengths in the 'soft, knowledge-based industries which are likely to be the engines of growth in the next century'. Britain shares with California a strain of individualism, flexibility and decentralised culture and, like the West Coast, has a tradition of free trade and an openness to immigrants and new ideas.

The down side of California, as with America generally, is that the infrastructure is poor, the education system fails too many people and there is grinding and growing poverty among the underclass. These are real disadvantages. But Europe has its own underclass and it is getting bigger. It is no longer the haven of social solidarity it once was and has come up with only one answer for solving the problem – ever-stronger doses of deflation to prepare for the single currency. And anybody who thinks that is going to do the trick is 'off message'. Way off message. •

3 June 1997

Hugo Young
No going back on Project Europe

O n the British right, reaction to the French left's victory [in parliamentary elections on 1 June] is one of pleasure. On the left, behind the polite phone calls to Lionel Jospin, it is one of pain. These paradoxical responses have different reasons. Of the two, the right's, in which some elements of the left also join, is the more absurdly erroneous.

New Labour's private reaction derives from the rebuke the French people seem to have offered to the notion that socialism is dead. Jospin won with the kind of programme Tony Blair said spelled electoral and economic disaster – higher public spending, huge jobs programmes and a massive increase in social protection via a shorter working week. This does not bode well for Mr Blair's ambition to forge a New Europe based on flexible labour markets. It may be a mythic programme that won't happen, rather like Chirac's in 1995. But such a degeneration of French politics holds little promise for a new left axis pursuing the liberal reform of 'Europe'.

The Tories' pleasure, by contrast, derives from their own travails over Europe. The hard right see a decisive reverse for economic and monetary union, and the soft right think they see an easing of the pressure on Kenneth Clarke now that EMU looks likely to be postponed. All in all, in the daily gamble on EMU, with the odds changing as fast as the analyses appear, Jospin's victory is presented on many sides as though it may begin to absolve British politicians from the choice that has dominated politics for the last few years: yes to EMU some time, or no at any time?

Any such conclusion is wishful thinking. The British talk incessantly about the dangers of EMU but resist a fact they find incomprehensible: that other people regard the dangers of EMU not happening as far more calamitous. Politically, the project is a done deal. So many politicians have staked so much on EMU, imposing on their people such pain to achieve the conditions required for it, that aborting it has become unthinkable. And economically, a working EMU has come to seem essential to the very existence of the single market. Because, in the parochial world of Westminster, both the politics and the economics remain bitterly moot, we forget that elsewhere the argument is over.

It may have been the wrong project to choose for the next leap forward for European integration. I know integrationists who regard the Maastricht treaty, which exalted the principle as well as fixing the terms of EMU, with disillusion. But they see no going back. Abandoning EMU now would be a setback of massive proportions, imperilling not only the single market but the EU itself. The fact that going ahead is also a risk doesn't alter that larger truth, which is acknowledged by all mainstream European politicians, including Jospin, Clarke and Blair. If the momentum stopped, enlargement could rapidly become vulnerable to French obstruction, and the whole of west Europe to recrudescent nationalisms.

In the real world, therefore, the choice excludes abandonment. It's a matter only of timing and terms. Will the appointed day, 1 January 1999, be kept to, or will delay seem the prudent course? Even here, the options can be exaggerated. The political leaders who have staked everything on EMU cannot allow postponement to last too long, without risking some of the same consequences as total breakdown: waves of popular anger at further sacrifices, for a project that may be null and void, on which the markets are likely to pass a mordant judgement if the politicians seem to be losing faith in it.

Modest delay has its attractions. Kenneth Clarke used to call it 'controlled delay', which he favoured as long as its end point was matched by a solemn and unalterable pledge to begin EMU then. Such a framework might accommodate more easily the convergence demands on Germany and France, not to mention the Mediterranean currencies, and thus do something to ensure the hard euro the Germans want. But there are those who think that even a 12-month delay would push at the edge of the ultimate credibility of a currency which, for political reasons, most EU leaders remain committed to bringing to birth. Judgement day remains pretty close at hand.

The prospect before the British Government, therefore, is not radically altered by the French election. The risks and benefits of EMU remain as they were, and the need to weigh them imposes a no less perilous choice of scenarios on Mr Blair.

On the one hand, he can remain a committed outsider, in the hallowed bipartisan position of waiting and seeing, until past the moment when the first wave of entrants identifies itself. The French election offers support for that, in so far as it leads to an emphasis on the flexibility rather than the precision of the Maastricht criteria. The much-abominated fudge is now, in some degree, certain to happen, and there are texts from Mr Blair, as from Mr Clarke, saying that the British could not be part of such a dangerous compromise. The domestic politics of EMU, furthermore, may seem to require that. The Government is committed to a referendum. Though the referendum has a better chance of being won at the start than the end of the first Blair term, it will be surprising, to say the least, if the leader draws that conclusion and stakes his life on it.

On the other hand, the cost of outsiderdom will stare him in the face. No longer can Britain expect to be leader of a substantial group of outs. That was John Major's dream, but the inclusiveness permitted by more flexible terms puts an end to it. A rather solitary isolation beckons, at the end of which, if ever, Britain will once again be the supplicant for entry into the project that 'Europe' now consists of. In that circumstance, the pound's entry parity is only the largest of many issues on which the British negotiating position will not make it easy to maximise the national interest. Meanwhile, the warnings by Toyota, Siemens and other major industrial employers, dismissed so cavalierly by a Euro-sceptic government before the election, will begin to take undeniable shape through the withdrawal of such businesses into more EU-friendly territory.

Such is the prospect. Blair has been careful to keep open the possibility of public endorsement for EMU being sought through the next election rather than by referendum. That would be soon enough for entry in 2002, when the coinage goes euro. But no safe haven is available. Nothing will divert EMU, yes or no, from being the biggest decision this Government has to take. •

Sex and shopping

'. . . *Marrying a childhood sweetheart is not a good plan.*'
Chris Mihill

'*What odd bedfellows we make, ditched from Radio 1 . . .*
This is us, we cry, we who once obsessively played and replayed
Frank Zappa's Weasels Ripped My Flesh *in our college study-bedrooms.*'
Linda Grant

'*I didn't want the superstore five years ago, signing all the usual petitions . . .*
But now (funny thing) it's a necessary adjunct to existence:
the corner shop, a two-minute trot away.'
Peter Preston

• •

5 April 1997

Chris Mihill

The perfect mate

I t was a bad day for agony aunts, hopeless romantics and childhood sweethearts. Turning centuries of mush on its head, a psychologist yesterday claimed the key to true love lies in a simple mathematical formula. In a revelation which brings science to the choice of a lifetime partner, Peter Todd said experience of 12 partners provides enough information to select the ideal mate.

His mathematical model indicates that the search for the perfect partner need not be as long or heart-rending as the likes of Barbara Cartland imply: after 12 boyfriends or girlfriends, choose the next person better than the 12 and stick with that one.

'The dozen will be your emotional benchmark,' said Dr Todd, of the Max Planck Institute for Psychological Research in Munich, in an address to the annual conference of the British Psychological Society in Edinburgh.

His 'try a dozen' rule means that marrying a childhood sweetheart is not a good plan because a lack of experience of anyone else can be a problem. He believes that choosing a lifetime's partner is a more rational process than most people believe.

People employed what he called a 'subconscious mate-rating system' whereby they compared the new person with previous partners and also assessed their compatibility in terms of leisure interests and social and educational backgrounds. His research found that, usually, it was only if the person passed those standards that they fall in love.

'People will say they just fell in love, but we think there is an underlying rationality beneath the mate-choice process,' added Dr Todd. •

• •

8 April 1997

The Smoke *

Time to split up when . . .

Family matters ❤ Your girlfriend tells you that she is carrying your best friend's baby. ❤ Your girlfriend is carrying a baby, but doesn't know whose it is because she was 'shit faced' when it happened.

Sex ❤ During orgasm you shout, 'Oh Sarah, yes. Oh Sarah!', when your girlfriend is not called Sarah . . . ❤ During orgasm you shout, 'The fiscal policy, oh, of Brussels will, yes, never be in line with Britain's, oh yes!, inclusion in the ERM!' ❤ During orgasm you shout, 'My baby takes the morning train, yes, he works from nine till five and then!'

The 'L' word ❤ You tell your partner that you love them and they laugh in your face. ❤ You tell your partner that you love them and they pretend to be deaf, shouting, 'What, What?!' at the top of their voice. ❤ You pretend to be dead and your partner prefers you that way.

Taste ❤ Your partner collects stamps. ❤ Your partner collects stumps. ❤ Your partner collects Phil Collins records.

Questions of scale ❤ You tell your boyfriend that he has a small penis. ❤ You tell all your mates that your boyfriend has a small penis. ❤ Your boyfriend finds out that he has a small penis by reading it on a toilet wall. ❤ Your girlfriend appears on *The Ricky Lake Show* to tell the world about her 'small penis hell'.

Religion ❤ Your girlfriend becomes a disciple of the Hare Krishna. ❤ Your boyfriend becomes a disciple of the Partridge Family. ❤ Your girlfriend becomes a disciple of Des Lynam. ❤ Your boyfriend becomes a disciple of an inflatable woman. ❤ Your boyfriend tells you that the inflatable woman is a more giving lover. •

* Student newspaper, University of Westminster

....

8 April 1997

Linda Grant
Will you still need me?

Allen Ginsberg is dead at 70. The unstately young homo and poet laureate of the successive beat and flower-power generations has finally succumbed to old age in a walk-up apartment in the dangerously louche East Village, radical to the end.

This year has other stomach-churning moments yet to come. The most sobering anniversary of 1997 will mark the meeting, 40 years ago, of John Lennon and Paul McCartney at the Quarrybank Grammar School annual fête, after which the boys formed the Quarrymen, whose name was later changed to the Beatles. Forty years on! Forty years before that date it was 1917, the Russian Revolution, the carnage of the pre-tank trenches, an agricultural England where farm machinery was pulled by horses and women's skirts were still at their ankles.

The generation that was young in the 1960s, which believed that it was the first on earth that was born to be young for ever and in the eyeteeth of modernity, is now not only middle-aged but moving beyond that ghastly state towards obsolescence. John Carter and Judith Chalmers, both 61, have just been sacked from the ITV travel programme, *Wish You Were Here*. 'They do not want a presenter who is a grandfather,' Carter says, 'and there is absolutely nothing I can do about being old.'

In their private lives too sixties swingers are facing redundancy. Jilly Cooper, now 60 herself, fearfully thinks aloud: 'I sometimes wonder what would happen to me if Leo died. Would anyone else ever love me again? That's what I think I'm frightened of.'

Will anyone else love her? Who has ever before lusted after post-menopausal women? And there are other minor shocks. Twirling the dial on my radio in the middle of an insomniac night I heard a run of Tamla Motown songs, followed by a Joan Armatrading, and thought, 'This is it. This is my station.' What dire humiliation followed when I realised it was Radio 2, home of *Sing Something Simple*. Keep this quiet, I told myself. Then Bob Harris, who 20 years ago fronted *The Old Grey Whistle Test*, moved to Radio 2 because the network's controller, Jim Moir, wanted to attract the 40-plus generation. 'The key factor was that they let me play my own music,' Harris told me. 'Though all in a fairly mellowish style.'

It was Elton John's fiftieth birthday last week, Eric Clapton's the week before, an anniversary of 'Black Magic Woman' this week. Saturday nights on Radio 2 are now given over to Bryan Ferry, Fairground Attraction, Mark Knopfler, The Beautiful South, Lyle Lovett and Crosby, Stills and Nash. What odd bedfellows we make, ditched from Radio 1 to rave alongside our own mums and dads, who want nostalgic reruns of Bing Crosby singing 'White Christmas'.

This is us, we cry, we who once obsessively played and replayed Frank Zappa's *Weasels Ripped My Flesh* in our college study-bedrooms. Twenty years on and the baby-boomers are in the same cultural geriatric ward as the parents we rebelled against, and our drugs are what the doctor gives you for a hernia. Last year, the EC issued a report forecasting that in 30 years' time there will be nearly 50 per cent more people over the age of 60 (43 per cent in Britain), with a tiny base of the working young to support them.

Once again, we are the future. We are the future shock. So are we also able to radically transform old age, bolshie revolutionaries to the last? Or are we going to be just like those before us, standing in the grocer's exclaiming over the price of a bag of sugar, moaning about our operations and how there's no respect these days?

The real gulf that divides us from today's old is that they were the generation formed by the school of hard knocks rather than plate-glass universities – a childhood in the 1920s, fatherless or with fathers damaged by the war, their youth during the Depression, young adulthood in wartime, pensionable just as the Tories decided to asset-strip the welfare state. In the very little research that has been done on the curious crime of the rape of elderly women, there is evidence that this group is far less traumatised by sexual violence than young girls. 'I've been through worse than this,' the victims say. Real hunger, being bombed out of your house, the black-bordered letter from the army authorities. Today's old were stoically reared on trauma.

The difference between us and our parents and grandparents is more than the music we listen to. It is that we have always had great expectations. We have taken for granted expanded educational opportunities, home ownership, foreign holidays, fancy food. We have learned to take care of our health, and really, deep down, some of us think we might just be able to live for ever. Poverty in old age is not on our confident agenda, just as redundancy and enforced early retirement weren't either. We do not intend to age with grace. Who will dare to patronisingly call Janet Street-Porter a little old lady or Germaine Greer a battling granny?

Medical advances promise to conquer some scourges of ageing. HRT has blown out of the water the post-menopausal sexual shutdown, though it may leave older single women stranded with desires that cannot be fulfilled. Alzheimer's Disease researchers are adamant that within 10 years there will be treatment for dementia. No senility for us. Free NHS dentistry should see most of us at 70 with all our own teeth.

The Conservative insistence on self-reliance that has forced many to take out private pension plans should ensure the kind of financial security that will see us on the Riviera at 70. Or, if the stock market goes horribly wrong, then the ongoing story 40 years on will be the scourge of elderly beggars on the streets. Will you still need me, will you still feed me, when I'm 64? It should be possible for the young of the sixties to create radical alternatives to the isolation, loneliness, poverty and discrimination of old age, were it not for the fact that there is no group that we more despise than the elderly, which we still think of as our own antithesis. Wrinklies, crumblies, the group that no advertiser wants to pursue – we have created the culture which has successfully marginalised the old, ruthlessly reducing the age at which one's skills cease to be of any value. Fighting against racism, sexism, homophobia, we have made a world in which the old are as excluded as in the segregated South from restaurants, clubs, TV and newspapers.

Few people who are oppressed have any choice in the matter. Black people cannot undress from their skin, even if they wanted to. Yet we behave as if old age is somehow excluded from the category of unchosen oppression. We will all one day be old, and the only alternative is not to be at all. The baby-boomers are the ones who think we rewrote the rulebook, priding ourselves on having transformed everything we have touched. Of course, the people who campaigned for legal abortion, divorce and homosexuality were the men and women born before 1930 – those whom we, their beneficiaries, have airbrushed out of the victory photographs.

Forty years on, when the Beatles are a sepia memory of a long-distant past, we old will be going ungently into the night, furious that we have been cheated of our birthright, eternal youth, and that no one fought against the stigma of old age on our behalf as the generation before us once gave us abortion and free love and the Pill. Howl, as Ginsberg advised. But it will be too late. •

Pass Notes

BBC

27 February 1997

Simone de Beauvoir

Profession: Feminist icon (deceased, 1986).

Author of: Seminal 1949 feminist tract *The Second Sex*.

What was that about then? De Beauvoir argued that marriage and motherhood constitute submission to male domination. And she differentiated between sex, which is biologically defined, and gender, which is a social construct. As in: 'One is not born a woman, one becomes one.'

Wow. She had brains. And was a bit of a party girl too. She used to hang out with Jean-Paul ('They go for my intellect not my looks') Sartre in the Left Bank cafés of Paris, drinking very black coffee, smoking very black fags, talking *l'existentialisme* deep into the night.

So she wasn't one of those feminists who hate men? You don't understand this feminism lark, do you? Simone loved Jean-Paul – 'I would rather die than leave Sartre' – and being something of a saucy radical (sexual freedom equals political freedom, we're all alone but we might as well get laid) she had a few other fellows on the side.

More namby philosophers? Yes, plus the odd lesbian affair, a romp with a Marxist toy-boy, etc. But she went for the beef with her 17-year fling with American writer Nelson Algren, a slum-raised hard man of words who wrote books about gambling, the Depression and the criminal underworld.

Since she was so right-on, I suppose their relationship was all about joint bank accounts, equal hoovering duties, taking it in turns to go on top? Afraid not. Her love letters to Algren have just been published, and France's First Feminist submissively calls her boyfriend 'the crocodile', 'The Brute' and 'my dearest husband'. She describes herself as 'your obedient Arab wife'.

You'll be saying next she liked to clean up after him. Well, she says she'd like to do his washing up. She offers to make him cakes. She calls herself his 'little loving frog' and agrees to obey the 'seven frog commandments' he set her. She even said, 'I was surprised by how much I enjoyed it.'

You're crushing all the feminist ethics I hold dear. You are debunking the reputation of a heroine of women's liberation. How dare you! At least she was aware of how she was behaving. She once said, 'How come you get to be the big crocodile when I am just the little frog?' And poignantly: 'If it's true that men despise women who worship them, then I am on the wrong track.'

Perhaps we should look to her novel Tous les hommes sont mortel (All Men are Mortal). **In it she wrote, 'If you'll live long enough, you'll see that every victory turns into defeat.'** Enter Simone the Realist, Simone the Psychic, Mystic Simone.

Most likely to say at dinner with Sartre: *'L'Enfer c'est les autres.'*

Most likely to say at dinner with Algren: 'Would beefy butchboy care for a little steak-frites made by little babykins bunny?' •

20 March 1997

Shane Watson
No sex, please, we're single

I t is hard to remember that we spent the late 1970s, the entire 1980s and a bit of the 1990s doing it as if our lives depended on it. It's hard to imagine that while our lives didn't depend on it, they more or less revolved around it, that a large part of our working hours were spent mooching around being in love or mooning about X-rated day-dreaming. Lunchbreaks were for buying stockings and leg-waxing and going to the family planning clinic. But now that time when regular sex seemed like a democratic right is like another world.

It isn't only me, because today the General Household Survey publishes its annual report with the finding that 39 per cent of single women between the age of consent and 49 aren't getting any either. Forget that famously ridiculous American statistic about women of 40 being more likely to get killed by a terrorist than to get married – now almost half the single female population aren't even getting close enough to find out if they're with a commitment phobe.

The fact that you're as likely to be 16 and on the shelf is rather comforting to us thirty-somethings who had assumed it must be to do with our age. Actually, we've always known there had to be more to it. True, the singles market is drastically depleted, but as my friends and I have become less pudgy and cigarette-skinned, better-dressed (hmm) and more at ease with ourselves, so sex has become increasingly separate from real life, like Third World trips.

Of course, once you've realised you're on sexual sabbatical, it is all the more difficult to get back to work: you've waited this long, so suddenly it has to be worth it. You've per-suaded yourself that after a drought you will settle only for the purest mountain spring (naturally fizzy). On top of this, because you are a born-again virgin, you must delib-erately adopt an attitude that couldn't possibly be mistaken for desperation, so you end up behaving like a supermodel at a soirée. You won't meet the eye of anyone single in case they should get the impression you are on the pull. Multiply this *faux* disinterest by two for the single men and you've got a no-contact situation.

Besides the 'Who said I wanted to anyway?' posturing, it's hard to work out what fac-tors are responsible. It's certainly not the obvious ones like pressure of work (look at the 1980s, when everyone had an overnight bag with them in the wine bar). Or fear of con-tracting something filthy (we know the routine). And while all this future-is-feminine stuff has probably knocked a bit of stuffing out of the neighbourhood studs' egos, it surely hasn't affected their sex drives? No, there are only two real reasons for the new sex embargo and the first is control.

Control has to be the obsession of the 1990s, from which so many things follow – commitment phobia, the cult of self-awareness, our fixation with looks and style and using our telephone like security screening. Get dressed up, look good, go to the party and flirt by all means, but can you really afford to take it all off and let go? Simply by consenting, you've given up control of the situation; if you go to their place, you're another notch down; and if you appear to have enjoyed yourself too much, the delicate power balance has swung right in their favour – who in their right mind is going to risk being branded needy and clingy by actually asking if you might do it again? According to Anna, recently divorced, the hardest part of sex in 1997 is the conversations that ensue immediately after, regardless. 'You get a lecture that is partly the can't-offer-you-commitment speech, but with a different slant – sort of noncommitment, with conditions: "I have to be on my own at weekends; I have to sleep at my flat; I'm not the kind of person who can plan what I'm doing tomorrow."' Tom Hanks, out of practice in the sex stakes in *Sleepless in Seattle*, was worried that his date might expect tiramisu, but now you've both got to anticipate a vigorous power struggle in the first 24 hours.

You don't have to be a commitment phobe to draw the conclusion that sex at this price is hardly worth it, which explains the biggest reason for the sex slump: apathy. 'You just think, I can't be bothered, I'd rather go home and read a book,' says Jo. 'Life is complicated enough. The last thing you want these days is trouble.' (For which read anything that reduces your control over your life.) You have got someone else's expectations and demands to deal with – they'll be there in the morning. 'Sex is such a big deal now,' Jo says. 'There's no such thing as guilt-free, stress-free sex.'

The solution in the 1990s is to behave as if you're sleeping with someone without actually doing it. Accessorise yourself with an apparently louche person of the opposite sex (ideally ex-boyfriend or gay) and do a bit of public stroking and hugging, à la Amanda de Cadenet. You feel vaguely wanted and no one has got near enough to tell if that's really you or your Wonderbra. It's not the same, but it's certainly very now. •

* * *

25 February 1997

Matthew Norman
Diary

How do you put a price on love's young dream? Very easily, it seems, if you are Christopher Bacon, headmaster of Cheltenham's Dean Close School. Mr Bacon has imposed bail in the sum of £500 (the alternative being expulsion) for two sixth-formers caught snogging in a corridor. Mr Bacon seems quite a character: two years ago he caused a little excitement by withholding an 18-year-old girl's A-level results until her father had paid the fees, which now come to a tidy £12,000 a year. In this case, although the pair caught kissing will get the money back if they behave themselves until leaving, the headmaster's secretary takes mild umbrage at the term bail. 'He wouldn't actually call it bail himself,' she insists. 'The headmaster calls it caution money.' He sounds a bit of a caution himself, doesn't he? Alas, since he has been unable to call back, we have been unable to ask him the obvious question – if it's a monkey for a kiss, what in God's name does it cost at Dean Close for a shag? •

25 February 1997

Alex Bellos
The Republic of Tesco

What do you think Tesco is? A supermarket, a temple of consumerism, a capitalist superpower? Ask Blessing Chingwaru, who supervises the picking of Tesco's mange-tout peas at a farm in Zimbabwe and he replies, 'I take it to be quite a superior country, quite magnificent, even more than what I can see Zimbabwe is.' Blessing makes his comments in a BBC2 *Modern Times* documentary which, in tracing the humble mange-tout from plant to plate, subjects the supermarket chain to intimate scrutiny.

You see why it's not outrageous for Zimbabweans to believe in the Republic of Tesco. The trip of one of the company's produce buyers to the farm where Blessing works has more in common with a royal visit. A Tesco flag is hoisted above the farm, there is a welcome party of hundreds, children offer gifts and a school choir sings 'Down the valley, Up the mountain, Tesco is our dear friend.' You see how dependent the workers are on the supermarket's business. 'If the king is not satisfied, you simply do away with the community,' says Blessing, recognising that the social fabric of the surrounding area is at the produce buyer's mercy.

Tesco shareholders will presumably be overjoyed at the portrayal of the company. Its staff come across as hard-headed, consistently pushing for higher quality, higher sales and higher margins. 'We're not a charity,' replies Mark Dady, the produce buyer, when pushed to defend the quest for more profits.

But those with a more humanitarian outlook will feel uneasy seeing a system where more care and attention is given to a vegetable than to the workers producing it. Over the last few years 'ethical sourcing' – jargon for making sure foreign suppliers are well treated – has become a hot issue for campaigning groups hoping to improve the lot of workers in the Third World. Only last week, a unique combination of manufacturers and aid agencies got together to try to eradicate child labour in Pakistan. It was a reaction to the high-profile allegations during the Euro '96 football championships in England that 7,000 Pakistani children were stitching the leather balls being sold as official merchandise.

Supermarkets were targeted because of their 'money, muscle and mechanisms'. The

BBC

Keeping the flag flying ... workers such as Blessing Chingwaru, a supervisor of mange-tout picking in Zimbabwe, know they must keep the King of Tesco satisfied

economic power of supermarkets is immense: Tesco's annual turnover is almost four times Zimbabwe's GDP. The idea was that if customers sent back till receipts saying, 'That's the value of my custom – what are you doing about it?', supermarkets might feel it commercially prudent to implement new codes of conduct.

The Global Supermarket built on work started in 1994 by the Fair Trade Foundation, which was one of the first independent initiatives that tried to use consumer power to promote ethical trading. It set up a fair trade label for products that fit its criteria for addressing social, environmental and labour concerns. But of the products that bear the FTF symbol, you will find few in supermarkets – the exceptions including Maya Gold chocolate and Percol and Cafédirect coffee.

From 1999, B&Q will buy timber only from sustainable sources approved by an independent certifier. Also, Gap allows independent human rights workers immediate access to its clothes factories in El Salvador.

Phil Wells, FTF director, said he has had discussions with most of the leading chains, but does not appear worried that they are lukewarm on independent monitoring. 'I am not too bothered about it,' he says. 'Independent monitoring is the way the world is going. It's just a question of who joins us first. I think another couple of supermarkets will join in in the next couple of months.'

In the film, it is revealed that the result of the Tesco visit is to change the way the reapers are paid. Instead of getting something for every mange-tout picked, they will be paid only for ones good enough for export. It appears this will mean a drop in wages of 25–30 per cent. Tesco responded to the documentary by saying that the reapers would be no worse off because they would choose better mange-tout. •

21 February 1997

Peter Preston

No dancing in the aisles in Sainsbury's

There's a Sainsbury's at the bottom of my garden. And not just any old Sainsbury's: a whopper; a pile of bricks and a swathe of car-park concrete where the playing fields used to be – plus a dawn chorus of delivery vans to help you start your day thinking funny things about food.

I didn't want the super-pile five years ago, signing all the usual petitions before the council, as usual, rolled over. But now (funny thing) it's a necessary adjunct to existence: the corner shop, a two-minute trot away. What about tonight? Carrot and coriander soup and a lobster in a plastic coffin? Fresh tagliatelli with amatriciana sauce? Or mere Gorgonzola with ciabatta? You slide down the hill after work and join the JS evening clan, wandering the aisles in search of inspiration. We're a sort of ad-hoc community (maybe the one Tony Blair keeps talking about). We gather from all over south London, old friends you haven't seen for years jostling for satay strips at the deli counter. The concrete canyon has changed our lives.

Some of the change is insidious, going on malign. The streets for miles around have lost their butchers and their fishmongers, drained of trade like bodies drained of blood. The greengrocers and bakers are looking a bit waxen. Survival in the giant shadow of Sainsbury's means selling Paul Smith or turning your patch into a pet shop, so the old rhythms of human contact turn discordant. Everything – every funny thing – revolves round the Sainsbury's hub. Peripheries wither and perish.

But would you drop a bomb and flatten the site, return to a gentler potter of messy high streets and smaller queues? Not easily. The difference is all-consuming. Could I go back to making my own salad, not tipping it ready-washed from a bag? Could we go back to growing our own yoghurt culture or keeping chickens in a shed by the back fence? Could I even go back to proper cooking?

That is a funny question, which all around seems to render foolish. Our televisions are currently pavilioned in chef shows. More viewers watch expert chaps whipping something amazing from a random plastic bag of ingredients every afternoon than tune in to *Nostromo*. Pilgrims flock to worship at the Shrine of St Delia. And yet, down the corner shop, the evening clan are stuffing their baskets with cooked and chilled. They'll be eating their fishermen's pie tonight as they watch Rick Stein do amazing things with sea bream.

We clan members, you will see, have become kitchen couch potatoes, and the spuds pop polished into the pan: we're nervous with it now. For something rotten is happening in Sainsbury land; something funny afflicts our sacred acre of mange-tout and Ogen melons. The headlines are lousy. Fourteen per cent interim profit drop. The share price of our treasure, once touching 600 pence, is barely half that now. What on earth's gone wrong? The car park is as packed as ever. Every square foot of the temple turns in £20 a week – the best in the field. Who cares about the Tesco menace? Tesco lives in Brixton, on the other side of the moon. What's our management, the great and good Sainsbury family, doing that's so disastrous?

It is here that the ultimate funniness begins, where dislocated worlds collide. On the ground, your crowded Sainsbury's seems to be doing nothing different. The woe, the mounting sense of crisis, arrives from a quite different direction. Here we're into City-speak and the verdict of the analysts. Sainsbury's was a great share to hold in the late 1980s. Profits rose 20 per cent year on year, year after year. They were rolling out the concrete across the country, slaughtering butchers, sweeping fishmongers into the sea. And then the tide turned. Tesco hired a new guru. Discounters like Aldi set up on our shores. It all got a lot tougher and harder.

That, as I stuff my basket, is good news for me. But it is terrible news for the City. They don't want bitter competition. It renders the whole sector undesirable. They hate any hint of price warfare: it crucifies profit maximisation. The City and the humble customer seek precisely contradictory things. The lower the margin, the deeper the shareholders' gloom.

Funny logic, arriving ready-minced from the Square Mile machine. The headlines of doom have a quite different meaning in the car park. The headlines of Tesco triumph might be designed to send us to Sainsbury's. But the funniness does not stop there. You'll have noticed that all three parties, warming up for election, agree on one unshakeable thing. They will never put VAT on food. Europe may have it. Europe is welcome to it. But here it's an alien monstrosity.

Well, possibly. A tax on consumption hits the poorest hardest. But Europe isn't going to change its tax structure and our politicians, tinkering with VAT on the Lamont model, know that. The line may be drawn, but it's thin and squiggly.

And where, you wonder, fingering the walnut bread, can any rational line be drawn? British supermarkets, for all the City sadness, still have the highest profit ratios in the world. If Sainsbury's or Tesco had total market dominance, they'd be making over £4 billion a year in pre-tax terms. Would Gordon Brown call that a windfall?

Sainsbury's are trying to expand into America. The jury, according to the analysts, is out on that. 'US supermarkets are less profitable and more parochial than those in the UK.' Tesco is heading into Europe, where the fishmarkets still live. At home, in anxiety, the move is into telephone banking and 24-hour opening, to kill off the Asian shopkeepers. Anything but an endless price war, just carrying on.

Thus a counter full of funny things comes together. Politically, for tax, we can't differentiate between a pound of English carrots and a pound of sugar beans flown in from Guatemala. They're all food, to be defended against VAT to the end. But our retail system is rooted in margins that shame the rest of the world. Failure is finding them under pressure. Success is trying something irrelevant. We'll be the last nation on earth to keep our plasticated lobsters tax-free in the name of the suffering masses.

Funny stuff, food. I think I'll pop down for a chicken Kiev. •

23 December 1996

Andrew Moncur

Shopaphobia: a victim confesses

W hile much attention is paid to those unfortunate addicts who are unable to stop shopping, precious little is heard about we shopaphobes, who can't start in the first place.

Who knows, perhaps some of us were frightened by a department store at an early age. Maybe we had a bad experience with a chain of high-street chemists. We might have overheard alarming stories from an auntie who was short-changed in Freeman, Hardy and Willis or a granny who clashed with the man in the white trilby hat behind the cheese counter at Tesco.

I had a friend who walked into Woolworths in New Street, Birmingham, and asked for the toy counter. A shop assistant came to her aid with typical Brummie charm. My friend followed the assistant's instructions in the patois of the region and found herself in front of a display of ties.

Now, in the face of this sort of shopping-cum-language difficulty I would have given up. Or, at the very least, every child on my Christmas shopping list would have ended up with a strip of Terylene in a livid shade of green to wrap round their tiny necks.

You see, some of us will do virtually anything – at almost any price – to get out of the store as quickly as we can. While Princess Thingie is addicted to spending squillions at the shops, we're hopelessly addicted to standing on the pavement putting off the moment of entering those horrible doors that swish hot air down the back of your neck.

I was sitting in a pub, thinking about this little-understood problem and working myself up into a shopping frame of . . .

No, that's not strictly true. I had been thinking about shopaphobia, but then a little diversion occurred. In no time at all, a different, although not wholly unrelated, question had formed in the air over my head. Namely, is the letter E the pariah of the alphabet? Do we attach it, to an unusual degree, to those things we don't much care for?

It certainly touches on shopping. Can there be any greater nightmare for the butcher's shop, or its customers, than the dread E. Coli 0157? Is there anything less appetising at the grocer's than a dose of lurid E numbers?

European shoppers face a future of licking their fingers and peeling off pallid euro notes to pay for their Danish bacon, French wines, Greek cars and German olives (I may be a little muddled here). Is it mere accident that the euro, possibly the least-loved banknote in world history, is a John-Major-shade-of-grey thing, known as the E5?

E means emergency rate in the income tax bands. Shopping addicts would have more money to throw away if only their moolah were not being siphoned off at this drastic rate. E stands for Ecstasy and EMU and encephalopathy and eczema and electro-convulsive therapy and evil empire.

It also heralds the arrival of 'extraordinary' and 'event'. Which is more or less what happened next. As I say, I was sitting in this pub, pushing a potato around a plate and trying to build up sufficient courage to go shopping. At stake: a most significant present. I will not spoil any surprises by saying that a request had been made for a magnifying glass (for examining elderly pictures). Then the conversation at the next table broke in on my gloom. It was a salesman, talking about his line of business. Swipe me. This gent was selling . . . binoculars and magnifying glasses. Sure, he would be pleased to do a deal. It was simply a question of strolling around and looking in the car.

Which is how one vital item of Christmas shopping came to be accomplished without setting foot inside a shop. Eee, you could have knocked me down with an ethereally elevated *embonpoint.* •

Final calls

Rosebank, the setting for Cider with Rosie

April Rise

If I ever saw blessing in the air
I see it now in this still early day
Where lemon-green the vaporous morning drips
Wet sunlight on the powder of my eye.

Blown bubble-film of blue, the sky wraps round
Weeds of warm light whose every root and rod
Splutters with soapy green, and all the world
Sweats with the bead of summer in its bud

If ever I heard blessing it is there
Where birds in trees that shoals and shadows are
Splash with their hidden wings and drops of sound
Break on my ears their crests of throbbing air.

Pure in the haze the emerald sun dilates,
The lips of sparrows milk the mossy stones,
While white as water by the lake a girl
Swims her green hand among the gathered swans.

Now, as the almond burns its smoking wick,
Dropping small flames to to light the candled grass;
Now, as my low blood scales its second chance,
If ever world were blessèd, now it is.

From *Selected Poems,* published by Penguin Books
Laurie Lee, 1914–97

27 May 1997

George Monbiot
Cider with Rosie is a deadly brew

When Laurie Lee died [on 14 May], the heart of England missed a beat. *Cider with Rosie* is one of those very rare books which almost every literate person in Britain has read. Unlike *Richard II*, Chaucer's *Prologue* or even *Lord of the Flies*, which were also mercilessly inflicted on us at school, this small plain tale of an ordinary village boy's life enchanted almost everyone.

It is beautifully written, with an attention to the microscopic that suggests both a supernatural memory and a voluptuous imagination. But it also captures something that all of us, in this world of perpetual upheaval, crave. It is the tale of a place that, though threatened, has undergone no significant changes in millennia. 'The village,' Lee tells us, 'in fact was like a deep-running cave still linked to its past . . . we just had time to inherit, to inherit and dimly know – the blood and beliefs of generations who had been in this valley since the Stone Age.'

Cider with Rosie is the hearse at the head of a nation in mourning, bereft of the stability and continuity of which we have been so brutally and so recently deprived. It is one of the cruellest frauds ever perpetrated upon the English people.

The history of the British countryside is a story of tumultuous change. The people of Laurie Lee's village might still have been able to discern a whisper of the beliefs of the Stone Age, but they are unlikely to have possessed much of the first inhabitants' blood. The limestone valleys of southern England, being well drained and easy to cultivate with handtools, would have changed hands earlier and more often than almost anywhere else. From the early Stone Age to the Norman Conquest, periods of relative calm were terminated by violent invasion, clearance and repopulation.

The rural revolutions initiated by the Conquest still reverberate through the British countryside. The enslavement of freemen, the replacement of serfdom by tenant labour and the forcible alienation of land all precipitated massive change. Repeated rioting over tithes, game laws and enclosures and the ruthless repression that always followed; the Corn Laws and their repeal; labourers' enfranchisement and the First World War ensured that life in the countryside remained almost as uncertain as life in the towns. The period of which Laurie Lee writes was perhaps the most turbulent. The big estates were breaking up, land prices were collapsing and thousands were leaving the countryside to find work in the towns.

Of course, Laurie Lee never set out to deceive his readers. Children see – and want to see – stability, not change. Nor is he solely responsible for our misapprehensions. Bates, Housman, Vaughan Williams, Gurney, Butterworth and even Evelyn Waugh all sounded laments for the passing of an unchanged world. Strangely, thanks at least in part to their efforts, it is the traumatic interwar years whose images we cling to as the

Christopher Jones

Laurie Lee

pillars of true nationhood.

The British characteristics, 'unamendable in all essentials' – so famously evoked by John Major – are drawn from a Georgian countryside. Our veneration of the fabled immutability of the countryside has brought it nothing but harm. Laurie Lee fought for years to stop his Slad Valley from being turned into a vast housing estate, due to have been inhabited by people jostling to experience his timeless past. At weekends the roads bellow with traffic rushing to places where time stands still.

Now that the Tory Party is confined not only to England but to the English countryside, British Conservatism has been reduced to its essence: a campaign for the retention of a bogus rural tradition. The Tories have retained control of the countryside for two reasons: people retire there in the vain hope of escaping from change, and people have to be rich to live there, as the demand for second homes and rose cottages is squeezing out the poor. Attempts to challenge the snobbery and deference, the failures of accountability and accompanying destructiveness which govern rural England, are dismissed as running counter to the way the countryside and country people have always been.

Writing in *Country Life* three weeks ago, the retired Tory MP John Patten claimed that 'urban notions of the politically correct ... are swamping rural communities and rural tradition'. The cultivation of organic vegetables and laws preventing the persecution of badgers were cited as examples.

Laurie Lee recorded a world containing many of the things we seek in our countryside – rural employment, tranquillity, safety and biodiversity – and there's no question that these wonders did exist in his day. But we won't recover them by seeking either to burrow back into the past or to keep things as they are. Rural peace – and the means of enjoying it without destroying it – will only come about through noisy revolution. •

20 February 1997

John Gittings
Great leader's shaky legacy

Mao Zedong called him a little man who would go a long way. And Deng Xiaoping bounced back not once but twice in the Cultural Revolution upheaval. Then, after Mao's death in 1976, Deng enlisted the young democracy movement to sweep away Mao's successors. Ten years later, Deng allowed the tanks to sweep away the student democrats.

Now Deng finally departs to meet Marx – or Mao – leaving a China which has bounced back with him again. Hong Kong's return, which he brokered with Margaret Thatcher, satisfies a deep nationalist longing. And the new wave of economic reform that he kick-started in 1992 has broken China's inward-looking and self-sufficient mould for ever.

The third generation of Chinese leaders has been anticipating this moment for months or years. They have stitched up a new division of top posts for the Communist Party congress in the autumn. But in China's political culture the death of a great leader still creates expectations of an earthquake. The three big factions – liberal, moderate and conservative – will look nervously at one another, and at the broad masses too. Economic rewards are skewed between Chinese coast and interior, between new urban rich

The dynasty lives on . . . Deng with granddaughter in 1985

and migrant rural poor. If not an earthquake, there could still be tremors.

Born in the Sichuan countryside, Deng was a radical student in France in the early 1920s. Unlike Mao, his exposure to the outside world gave him a sense of China's global role. His first move after regaining power in 1979 was to visit the United States and firm up a new relationship with Washington.

Party reformers believed at first that Deng would establish a democratic republic. But although committed to economic modernisation, Deng retained a Leninist belief in the party's supremacy, backed by the army. 'Don't be afraid of the students,' he told senior leaders in 1989, 'because we still have several million troops.' After the Tiananmen Square massacre he congratulated them on their suppression of the 'counter-revolutionary rebellion'.

As Eastern Europe bounded into a post-Communist future, it looked as if Deng had led his country backwards. But its troubles – and later those of the former Soviet Union – only encouraged Deng and colleagues to believe they were right to stand firm. But Deng also believed that political repression would work only if there was economic liberation, and that he had little time left to achieve it. In the early spring of 1992 he dragged himself back on to the campaign trail for one last offensive.

He emerged from seclusion and set off on a tour of Guangdong, the southern province where his reforms took off in the early 1980s and where he had sheltered during the Cultural Revolution. His journey became known as his 'southern expedition', but it was in a very different style from the imperial expeditions of the past. Deng made a point of visiting the Special Economic Zones just across the border from Hong Kong, already transformed by foreign money and culture.

Deng urged people to stop worrying about whether policies were 'capitalist' or 'socialist' and follow the zones' example. He also said that while it was important to guard against 'rightism', it was more important to fight 'leftism' – the ideology that had plunged China into disasters such as the Cultural Revolution. Deng's initiative revitalised the economy and led to a growth rate of nearly 14 per cent in 1992.

Two years later Deng appeared in Shanghai – in public for the last time – looking much shakier. The economic boom had led to higher inflation and an alarming crime wave, as well as the growing urban wealth that so impressed the outside world.

Although formally retired, Deng continued to exercise an unseen influence on Chinese politics merely by staying alive. Despite his strictures against 'leftism', this past year has seen a shift back towards political conformity as the élite leaders, including President Jiang Zemin, played safe.

The question for China is whether his economic legacy is sufficient. Millions of Chinese eat well and make money, but in a population of 1.2 billion a significant minority does badly. World Bank figures show that more than one-sixth live on less than $1 a day.

Stability has been achieved at a price – but no one knows exactly what that price will be. If Communist rule is to transform itself into a more flexible system for the next century, where will it start? No one knows how to engineer what the Chinese call a 'smooth transition'. Deng transformed China's economy and society, but he did not leave a formula for fundamental political change. •

8 January 1997

Richard Williams
One last solo for Soho's favourite son

Oddly, for a jazz funeral, there was practically no music to be heard as London said goodbye to Ronnie Scott yesterday. But most of those present at his funeral had the appropriate soundtrack in their heads, from countless nights in the Soho club to which he gave his name. The music of Dizzy Gillespie, Stan Getz, Sonny Rollins and countless others formed the unheard but insistent accompaniment to an emotional gathering of family, friends and colleagues.

A large floral saxophone mounted on the roof of the hearse marked Scott's last journey, which began at the Frith Street club and ended at Golders Green Crematorium. Made of white chrysanthemums, with tiny gold roses for the keys, it was the tribute of Pete King, Scott's business partner since the club's founding in 1959. Like many of those who thronged the small hall, with 100 more forced to stand outside, straining to hear the ceremony in the dimming light and the deepening afternoon chill, King had known him far longer than that.

Old friends from an East End childhood and a Soho adolescence arrived to salute the figurehead of British modern jazz, who died on 23 December, a month before his seventieth birthday. Sonny Herman, a trombonist who grew up with him in Whitechapel, chanted a Jewish prayer. Alf Summers, a guitarist, recalled their days of roaming Archer Street for gigs. Joe Green intoned Kaddish, the prayer for the dead.

Outside there were red roses from Van Morrison – 'To my dear friend Ronnie in fondest memory' – and lilies from Charlie Watts and family. Both of them had grown up in awe of the man and the club he ran, and when they had stopped being pop stars they were proud to bring their bands into the murky Soho room with the black walls and orange lampshades, and to hear themselves introduced by the proprietor in a tone neither more nor less respectful than he would use to present an ancestral hero or a promising novice.

Musicians of many eras turned up to pay homage. The trumpeter Humphrey Lyttelton embodied the traditional forms against which Scott's generation of beboppers had rebelled. These were represented by John Dankworth, who joined Scott in taking a job on the *Queen Mary* in the 1940s so that the two of them could get to 52nd Street and witness Charlie Parker's revolution at first hand.

Tony Crombie, Scott's drummer in the early 1950s, was present, as was Peter King, the alto saxophonist who played at the opening night of the original club in 1959 and by coincidence began a season at the new one on Monday night.

The obituaries tended to overlook the helping hand Scott habitually extended to young musicians scuffling to make a living in the often inhospitable British jazz scene, giving them valuable exposure in front of an audience which had come to hear the big names. They were represented yesterday by Kenny Wheeler, Tony Coe, Evan Parker, Michael Garrick, Lol Coxhill, Art Themen, Guy Barker and many others.

The saxophonist Alan Skidmore, the son of one of Scott's contemporaries, played at the original club while still in his teens and described him as 'a second father'. He had never lost his enthusiasm for music, Skidmore said. 'We spent days, months, years talking about it,' he said, 'right up to the end.'

The singer Cleo Laine told how Scott's playing had been unfairly overshadowed by his celebrity as a club owner. 'He was a great player, which wasn't said much. But the musicians knew.'

A frail Spike Milligan, once a regular at the club, described a conversation a week before Scott's death. 'He was the same as me, a manic depressive,' the comedian said. 'He said to me, "I don't feel well." So I asked him, "What pills are you on?" He said, "Tuinol and whisky." I said, "That's no good, you'd better come down and stay with me." And that was it.'

Scott's sardonic humour was never far away. The writer and saxophonist Benny Green, who played in one of his early-1950s bands, described his jokes as a way of camouflaging deeper feelings, and told a story about the funeral of someone for whom Scott had a great affection. 'I had a slipped disc, so my wife put down the car seat and lay me down in the back. She drove me almost to the graveside and pulled up. Ronnie came over, looked down at me, and said, "Hardly worth going home, is it?"'

Some of Scott's jokes lasted decades, worn to near-extinction. Dankworth recalled one, the classic triple putdown of a customer asleep at a ringside table: 'First he'd say, "Excuse me, sir, are we bothering you?" Then, "Are you the man from Rentacorpse?" And finally, "I hope he's dead – we could do with the publicity." ' Receiving its first performance in daylight, the gag got a familiar, loving laugh. •

....

11 December 1996

John Prescott
The man who opened my mind

Raphael Samuel (Obituary, 10 December) opened my mind when I was a student in the 1960s. Until I went to Ruskin and met him, my education had come from correspondence courses, which I used to complete in a 14-bunk cabin after 20 hours' duty as a seaman on a liner. To move from that to two of you in a college room with a tutor was an experience, but Raph was never my image of a tutor.

He would turn up with his hair all over the place, in a style of dressing that was all his own and that was brilliantly captured in the photograph of him which the *Guardian* published yesterday. He arrived with bags full of poems and bits of paper and references and he would pull one out when he wanted to make a point.

He made me do something I thought I'd never do. Not just write an essay – that was difficult enough for me – but use the experience of

Raphael Samuel: a life of the mind

Stefan Wall Green

poetry to illustrate a point. Until then I had thought poetry was about them and not us.

I remember once that I did a mock exam while I was at Ruskin. I had a terrible time. I was so frustrated that I couldn't say what I wanted that I stormed out. Raph chased after me down Walton Street, but he couldn't catch me. When I got back there was a note on my desk in that big handwriting of his telling me not to worry and to come and have a talk and a cup of coffee. He was always supportive like that.

He never forgot you. When I was standing for the deputy leadership of the party in 1992 after Roy Hattersley resigned, I came under a lot of attack from people who said I could never hold the job because I might stumble over my words and say the wrong things. Completely out of the blue, Raph wrote this wonderful piece for the *Guardian* about me, recalling some very strong memories of those Ruskin years and urging support for me. It moved me to tears.

He knew what was in the heart and he knew what was in the head. He wasn't taken in by an establishment that judges just by the mouth and the glamour. I felt really proud that he felt that way about me and that he was still there after 30 years. I was devastated to hear of his death. •

21 December 1996

Martin Kettle
Death of an era

Raphael Samuel's funeral in Highgate Cemetery this week seemed more than just the funeral of a very remarkable man who has died far too early, at the age of 61. It seemed almost like the funeral of a way of thinking and a wake for an era of the human spirit. To those of us who do not believe in resurrection, it had a kind of wider finality.

If you didn't know Raphael Samuel, or if his name means nothing to you, which will be the case for many readers, then I fear it will be hard to explain why this December death seemed so much more than usually conclusive. Samuel was a learned and omnivorously enthusiastic historian. He was a tutor of many generations of working-class students at Ruskin College, an inspirational participant in many networks, and a man whose intellectual and political passions were rooted in socialism, in scholarship and in an unbounded love for the infinite and messy detail of human life.

Yet even if you didn't know him, he probably left his mark on the way that you think about the world. Samuel had an unconditional interest in the past. He believed that history was not merely a tale of kings, queens and governments, nor even of the long march of the dispossessed towards a society of all for all, though he was hugely interested in both. He loved people's memories and inheritances, yours, mine, his own, everyone's.

Final calls

Through his work in the Ruskin History Workshop, he was, in spite of his apparent aversion to his own celebrity, the presiding genius of the modern reclamation of the day before yesterday. That book of your district in old photographs is his legacy, just as much as the more learned books of his own that he never quite seemed to finish.

He wanted to be buried in Highgate Cemetery and when his final illness was diagnosed he had made sure that he would be. The choice, as Stuart Hall said in his graveside speech, was massively resonant. This corner of Highgate may not be London's equivalent of the *mur des fédérés* in Paris's Père Lachaise, yet it is the right place to lay to rest both a passionate socialist and a nonpareil chronicler of Victorian London.

Winter, too, is the right time to bury the dead. A lonely time of inner warmth and outer cold. We arrived in our ones and twos, murmuring our greetings, looking to see who else was there, and lining the muddy and gravelled avenue that winds its way across the damp and wooded hillside graveyard. Familiar figures from what was once the New Left bent nervously to lift his coffin from the hearse and then carry it, with its huge bunch of blood-red roses, on his last march.

There was a lone piper. I don't know why, but no matter. We shuffled silently along the path that takes you past Karl Marx's mysteriously troublesome monument, past the lesser and later tombs of socialists who jostle to lie in Marx's shadow, and upwards past the memorials to those who are merely part of the haphazard society that inhabits all urban cemeteries. Then, in a high corner looking down over London, we took up our places as best we could, while Hall and the others delivered their fine tributes and read heart-stopping words by Auden, MacNeice, Emily Brontë and John Donne. We didn't sing. Now there's a tell-tale sign of the confusions of the English left in 1996. We have no equivalent in this country of the ancient Russian burial hymn 'Eternal Memory'. 'The Internationale' would not have been truthful any longer, though I bet that all of us who were there knew the words. Nor, for different reasons, would a Christian hymn have done for this secular Jew, though a hymn would have come very naturally among well-educated atheists of a certain age. At least we should have sung 'Jerusalem' or, even better, 'England, Arise'.

And yet that's just it. We cannot honestly sing such songs now. We remember the words and they move us greatly, but I don't think many people believe in them any more. A new Jerusalem? Pardon me while I turn my New Labour manifesto to the wall. England, arise? The long, long night is not over and perhaps it never will be. Perhaps, perish the thought, it isn't really night after all. Perhaps too, as A. J. P. Taylor once wrote, England has risen all the same and so, in a way, it doesn't matter so much now as it once did.

Mourners tend to have grey hair. Certainly a lot of those who were there on Wednesday seemed to have. When you go to any funeral you ask yourself worrying questions, like whether anything survives and whether it all mattered as much as it seemed in your hot youth. I cannot believe that anyone who was in Highgate Cemetery last Wednesday did not ask themselves such questions under the benevolent shadow of Karl Marx. I cannot believe that many of them came up with stories with happy endings. I suspect that Raphael would not have done so either.

It isn't just romantic Ireland that's dead and gone. It's romantic, optimistic, every-man's England too. Some day, like the sleeping knights under the hill who provide the most potent image in English legend, perhaps they will rise again. But not, I thought in the cemetery, in our lifetime. •

12 December 1996

Henry Porter
An original eye for wit

Willie Rushton, who has died aged 59 after complications arising from heart surgery, looked the very picture of an easygoing *bon viveur*. He had a well-marinated voice and a taste for loud checks to go with his figure. But he was never so uncomplicated. Amongst his many gifts was an extremely sharp wit which became all the more devastating when something annoyed him. He had the convictions of a satirist although he never made a point of parading them, and an acute eye for the ridiculous which was as easily applied to his acting and cartoon work as to the rapid fire of *I'm Sorry I Haven't a Clue*, the BBC radio programme he contributed to for 20 years.

William George Rushton was born the son of a publisher. He was sent to Shrewsbury public school, where he met and befriended Richard Ingrams, who was born the day after him. Also at Shrewsbury were the young Christopher Booker and Paul Foot.

But it was Ingrams and Rushton who hit it off immediately and together they founded *The Wallopian*, a satirical version of the school magazine which was adorned by Rushton's early drawings and was to be a precursor of *Private Eye*. Rushton's other talents began to show at Shrewsbury, the first of which was acting. He was, as Ingrams recalls, extremely mature for his years and had no difficulty in playing the part of a middle-aged man in the play *The Admirable Crichton*.

His was the last generation to do National Service, which he regarded as a privilege because the army came to represent to him all that was absurd and posturing about post-war Britain. He was never one for respecting authority, but in the ordinary soldier Rushton

Willie Rushton

found a wit and resentment which he truly admired.

His acting break came in Spike Milligan's *The Bedsitting Room*. Kenneth Tynan described his performance as brilliant, a remark which Rushton hoped would be inscribed on his gravestone. And so it should. Other parts followed in film and TV, most notably in *That Was the Week That Was*, where the young Rushton performed a weekly impersonation of Harold Macmillan, which even his friends will admit was only a rough approximation of the old humbug's manner.

Rushton excelled at impersonating a type and could instantly summon the voice of a blithering judicial figure soaked in whisky. It was the archetype of callous establishment authority that inspired the satire of so many of the comics and journalists who loitered in the Soho offices of *Private Eye*. Rushton was a lifelong Labour supporter who always felt he should do something more for the party, but recognised that humour was the best support he could offer.

Unlike Ingrams and Foot, he never went to Oxford, at least not formally, but he was up there often enough to see Ingrams and to help with the magazine *Parson's Pleasure*, which was to be the immediate forebear of *Private Eye*. They both drank copiously in those days and both subsequently gave up the booze, Rushton because he developed diabetes in the early 1980s. He lost weight and found to his delight that a teetotal life gave him a lot more time for drawing and commercial voice-overs. These made him a wealthy man. Some friends believe he gave too much of himself to quiz shows and commercials. But he could fill a programme with his warmth and humour.

His greatest pleasure was drawing and in the early issues of *Private Eye*, founded by Ingrams, Booker and Rushton in 1961, it was Rushton's cartoons which supplied the magazine's distinctive look. He had a line all of his own and a fascination with incidental detail which made his covers for the *Literary Review* collector's items. He illustrated many books, among them *The Day of the Grocer*, *Willie Rushton's Greatest Moments in History* and *Pigsticking, a Joy for Life*. Most of these he wrote himself, as fluently as he drew or spoke, but the most successful match of word and illustration came in the collaboration with Auberon Waugh, first at *Private Eye* and later at the *Literary Review* and the *Daily Telegraph*. They enjoyed each other's jokes so much that somehow Rushton's style came to represent Waugh's voice.

Like his friend Peter Cook, who died last year, he had only to walk into the room for people to enjoy themselves. He was very funny but he was also generous with his own laughter and never felt the need to dominate a gathering. He always carried a shoulder bag stuffed with elegantly crafted drawings. To his colleagues at *Private Eye*, he appeared big, smiling and acute. But he hated some aspects of their journalism, particularly the gossip columnists who went to work for the *Eye* in the 1970s. He was intensely private himself and once said, 'I don't think because I appear on TV it gives people the right to shout out to me in the street or pull me about in public.' He felt for other peoples' privacies that had been invaded unless the target was a Conservative minister.

It is a testament to Rushton's extraordinary range of talents that so many in radio and newspapers, the theatre, publishing and particularly in *Private Eye* were shocked yesterday by the news of his early death. It was so unexpected. He was a big part of all their lives and they will miss his generosity and his wit. As Paul Foot said, 'I saw him just a few weeks ago at somebody's leaving do and I was struck by how genuinely clever and funny he was. He really was clever. And I think we may have underestimated him.'

William Rushton leaves a wife, Arlene, whom he married in 1968. They had three sons. •

John Wells writes: Willie Rushton joined us at Oxford at the weekends when he was a lawyer's clerk. He already looked like one of his own drawings, flourishing a broken umbrella, and since then he has been so central a figure in everyone's life who worked with him that the loss is barely comprehensible. He had such an amount of sheer comic energy it was impossible to be with him without being charged up with optimism. He drew beautifully, he wrote wonderful lyrics, he sang charmingly and danced, often in the street, and the really remarkable thing about him was that he did it all the time, for complete strangers as much as for old friends. The happiest time I spent with him was wandering back through Europe after a drunken wedding in Bavaria in the mid-1960s when we found ourselves climbing through a hedge in Liechtenstein. We walked for some way through a park, then saw a drive that rejoined the main road. It was flanked by two sentry boxes and, as we walked out, two sentries in archducal uniforms saluted us. Life was infinitely more fun when he was there. •

....

22 November 1996

Anthony Tucker
Guarding the flame of intellectual freedom

From the early 1930s, when Nazi persecution began its crusade against the free intellectual life of Europe, through the turmoil and suppression of Communist regimes in Eastern Europe and to her final years, Esther Simpson, who has died aged 93, was the first contact in the free world for many hundreds of refugee scholars. Through her work with the Society for the Protection of Science and Learning (SPSL), which was set up in Geneva by Lord Beveridge and Leo Szilard in 1933, later operated from Cambridge and ultimately jointly with the Society for Visiting Scientists in London, Esther played a key role in activities which hugely enriched the intellectual fabric of Britain.

She was totally dedicated, self-effacing, a natural linguist able to cope with mountains of paper and red tape and endowed with great empathy for people in distress. While working hours that would have killed most of us, she still found time, and an ensemble, in which she could exercise her skills as a violinist. She once led a quartet in which the great Max Rostal played cello; and she said of Vienna in the early 1930s – where she was working when recruited for the SPSL – that it was a musical paradise, with operas and concerts free and the playing of music so much a part of life that everybody did it, like brushing their teeth.

Her great achievement was holding together the lifeline for scholars before, during and in the years following the Second World War, when some of the greatest names of our time in science and the arts came to Britain, and many made it their home. One measure of the quality of this flow is that it provided more than a dozen members of the wartime British scientific team working on the atomic bomb at Los Alamos.

Over 150 of the 500 or so refugees who stayed in this country became Fellows of the Royal Society or of the Royal Society of Arts. The only published (and incomplete) list embraces at least 16 Nobel Laureates and a galaxy of famous names, with Ernst Chain, Karl Popper, Claus Moser, Hans Kornberg, Ernst Gombrich, Eric Ash and Max Perutz among them. Esther wrote with great affection about her huge family of scholars, an affection reciprocated throughout their lives by those whom she helped.

Gombrich and Perutz paid homage at a reception held at the Ciba Foundation in London in 1992 when Esther published her memoirs. It is true, as Max Perutz then said, that the flow of benefits was not a one-way affair. Many of those who came to Britain, and experienced the stimulation of academic freedom and vigour, achieved much greater eminence here than they could have done at home, even in normal times. But in the dark years before and throughout the war when Esther Simpson tended the flickering beacon of intellectual freedom, the overwhelming memory of those rescued from oppression was her welcoming friendliness, her breadth of culture, the speed at which she could process information, find academic niches and provide hope for those in despair.

Esther was born in Leeds and went to Leeds College of Music, but graduated from Leeds University with first class honours in French and German in 1924. She went first to Germany and then to Paris, where, working for a building company with an international workforce, she produced a multi-language dictionary to enable everyone to understand essential technical terms. After six years with the International Fellowship of Reconciliation, mainly in Vienna, and a brief period with the World Alliance of YMCAs in Geneva, she joined and merged her life immutably with the Academic Assistance Council (later the SPSL).

At a superficial level her work was documentation, keeping track of individuals and groups under oppression, and opening up routes for them through international academic channels. 'I am insignificant,' she used to say. Only the scholars and their freedom were of importance. At times of crisis, such as 1940 when, in fear of invasion, the Home Office interned several hundred foreign academics, others might have been overwhelmed. But, from the new SPSL office in Cambridge, Esther fought on their behalf and, in the end and to the great benefit of Britain, won.

She gave her entire life to such corrosive work and, for relaxation, to demanding music. She never thought of marriage, had few possessions and never had a holiday in the conventional sense. As Sir Eric Ashby recorded, she achieved that very rare level of distinction for which there exists no obvious formula, for it is based on intrinsic character and worth. Nowadays, some might regard the entire SPSL operation as élitist, a view which Esther dismissed. 'We could not save them all. Lawyers, writers and other groups had their own channels. We did what we could,' she once said. And what she did, often under great pressure, was to save substantial segments of the intellectual life of Europe. •

21 July 1997

Richard Ingrams
Punter who lost at politics

Sir James Goldsmith, who has died from a heart attack aged 64, was not the first powerful man to discover that there is nothing like suing for libel for drawing attention to yourself. Until he issued 60 writs against *Private Eye* in 1975 he was scarcely known at all in this country. The Anglo-French owner of a huge grocery chain, his only previous experience of front-page publicity came in 1953 when he eloped with his first wife, Isabel Patino, the young daughter of a Bolivian tin magnate. She died shortly after giving birth to their daughter the following year.

Goldsmith's sudden passion for litigation forced journalists, including myself, to investigate his background. He was born the second son of Major Frank Goldsmith (a famous hotelier in France and England) and his French wife, Marcelle, described by her son as a 'peasant from the Auvergne'. The Goldsmiths had no fixed income and Jimmy was brought up in the foyers of his father's hotels in an atmosphere of loose women and bouncing cheques. At a very early age he showed a passion for gambling, first with the fruit machines in his father's hotels, then later at Millfield Prep School where with postal orders he placed bets on horses. He was sent to Eton, but left after winning £8,000 on an accumulator at Lewes races. Visiting Oxford, where his elder brother Teddy was a student, Goldsmith first met his lifelong friend John Aspinall who, with his mother, organised gambling parties in the days when it was still illegal.

It is possible to interpret everything Goldsmith did in later life as the act of a gambler. More than anything he resembled a restless punter moving from table to table in a casino, losing money here, making it there, from time to time cashing in his chips out of boredom and moving on to another gaming room. Yet in his youth he was a gambler pure and simple, a rich spoilt playboy interested only in women and roulette. But the elopement experience and his subsequent battle with Isabel's father, who represented in many ways the kind of man he was to become, steeled his nerve and he set out to make himself a very rich man. Early business ventures, however, failed and it was not until 1962 when he teamed up with a distant relative, Baron Alexis de Gunzburg, that he began to make serious money. He moved into groceries and by 1962 his company Cavenham controlled a huge empire varying from biscuits and snuff to Marmite and marzipan mice. By the time he was 40, Goldsmith was a multi-millionaire.

But like many rich men before and since, Goldsmith hankered after a more influential role. He made friends with the Tory Prime Minister Edward Heath (later to be cast as chief villain by the Referendum Party) and helped to raise money for the Conservatives. When Heath lost office, Goldsmith was introduced to his Labour successor Harold Wilson by their mutual friend David Frost, making friends especially with Wilson's powerful secretary Marcia Williams (Lady Falkender). When he threw the book at *Private Eye* in 1975 – when I was editor – Goldsmith did so partly to endear himself to the Wilsons, but from his own point of view it did nothing but harm. His conduct of the case was ruthless. He employed private detectives to search through dustbins and threatened two senior professional men into swearing false affidavits. At the height of the long-running legal battle, he was named as one of the beneficiaries of Lady Falkender's famous Lavender List of honours. By the time Wilson resigned, Goldsmith, by his own actions, had put paid to any immediate hopes of a political career.

Instead, he tried another game – becoming a press lord. It was a scarcely logical move by one who had already shown himself to have an almost paranoid attitude to journalists, many of them, in his view, members of a sinister Marxist conspiracy working to destroy the system. (Later, in collaboration with the famous libel lawyer Peter Carter-Ruck he established a fund to enable victims of unwelcome press attention to bring libel actions, the beneficiaries including Neil Hamilton and Dr Skuse, the forensic scientist whose faulty evidence helped imprison the Birmingham Six.)

Goldsmith's press ambitions were foiled at every turn. He tried to buy the *Observer* and the *Daily Express* and when both attempts failed launched *Now!* in September 1979. The latest in a long line of would-be British rivals to *Time* and *Newsweek* it lasted for a mere 19 months and cost Goldsmith an estimated £6 million, finally convincing him that he had no future in this country.

France meanwhile had become a no-go area following the election of the Socialist François Mitterrand. According to Olivier Todd, then employed on his magazine *L'Express*, 'Jimmy became convinced that if Mitterrand won it would only be a matter of time before the Russian tanks started rolling up the Champs Elysées.' America beckoned, along with a new lady, Laura Boulay de la Meurthe, to add to his collection. Goldsmith was a polygamist who by the time of death had reared eight children by four separate wives and mistresses – a further indication of his innate inability to plough a single furrow.

During the 1980s he dabbled in oil drilling in Guatemala, American supermarkets and timber, in the process making himself even richer. Then in 1987 he cashed in most of his assets ahead of the October stock market crash (making an estimated £2–3 billion) and decided to devote his energies to preserving the environment which up till then he had been successfully plundering for his own gain. Like his ecologist brother Teddy and his friend John Aspinall, Goldsmith was a natural merchant of doom who could easily persuade himself that the End (environmental, political or economic) was Nigh. He now bought 30,000 acres of land near the village of Zapata on the coast of Mexico and constructed an elaborate fortress-style home with accommodation for servants, chefs and even its own private hospital. Guests, who included Robert Redford and Henry Kissinger, were accommodated in lodges scattered round the estate, each with its own moat to protect them from scorpions. This Mexican bolt-hole, taken in conjunction with the similarity of his name to Goldfinger and his resemblance in voice and appearance to Charles Gray as Blofeld in the film *Diamonds Are Forever*, helped to foster the caricature of Goldsmith as the villain of a James Bond film intent on world domination.

In his final gamble he tried once more to pursue a political role, this time as the opponent of the Maastricht Treaty and what he saw as the dangerous advance of federalism in Europe. As a natural autocrat, an archetypal cosmopolitan whose business interests ignored all natural boundaries, Goldsmith scarcely struck a convincing figure as the champion of the nation state and democratic freedoms. Still, in 1994 L'Autre Europe Party (formed with Phillipe de Villiers and General de Gaulle's grandson), won 12 per cent of the vote in the French European elections and he became an MEP. He then turned his attention to Britain, launching his Referendum Party with the help of a motley gang of Tory discontents, the ever-faithful Aspinall, David Bellamy and the actor Edward Fox. Ignoring complaints that his party would only split the Tory vote and ensure the election of the firmly pro-Europe Labour Party, Goldsmith who, unbeknown to all but his private circle, was already suffering from cancer, threw himself into the campaign, making speeches and canvassing on the streets of his chosen constituency of Putney. It was another expensive disaster. Goldsmith himself lost his deposit and the last unforgettable glimpse the British had of him was early on the morning of 2 May, as he stood on the platform at the count, his face contorted with hatred, shouting abuse at the defeated member David Mellor. It was an enduring image of frustration, the frustration of a man who had never succeeded at anything except making money. Having no fixed abode he was regarded as an outsider wherever he went. Even in later life when he launched his Referendum Party he seemed to have no understanding of the British way of life.

Many people (women especially) were said to find him charming and unfailingly courteous. His far-from-critical biographer, Geoffrey Wansell, said of him that he 'eternally displays the courtesy of a Medici prince'. Those of us who crossed his path, however, saw another Goldsmith – a steely eyed predator, ruthless and singularly lacking in charm. Combined with his ferocious energy, he had more than a hint of megalomania and liked to expound his theories, like some latterday Oswald Mosley, on 'what should be done' to prevent catastrophe.

We should ultimately be grateful that his gambling urges and chronic restlessness prevented him from ever getting to a position where he could start to put his ideas into practice. •

13 February 1997

Dennis Barker

Forever young

The actor Barry Evans, who has died aged 53, was ideal as the sex-starved hero in *Here We Go Round the Mulberry Bush*, the 1967 film which Hunter Davies scripted from his own novel. He was funny and touching as a boy who finds it ludicrously difficult to lose his virginity.

Evans made his fame with his youthfulness – he was 18 when he made *The Class* in 1961, while claiming to be 16. Yet that youthful image became a millstone as he got older and wanted more mature parts. In 1970 he was starring in *The Adventures of a Taxi Driver*. In the 1990s he was driving his own minicab in Leicestershire.

In 1970, he appeared in BBC television's version of Shakespeare's *Much Ado About Nothing*, a line of acting he would have liked to develop; but it was the taxi film rather than the Shakespeare role which had the resonance, attracted the fan mail and proved the trap.

As the 1960s ended, Evans was doing well enough in London Weekend Television's *Doctor in the House* comedy series, which he followed with *Doctor at Large*. In 1977, he was again successful as the innocent foreign language teacher in ITV's *Mind Your Language*. He did try to broaden his range with *Thirty Minute Theatre* on television and on stage for two years with the Young Vic company.

In the harder-edged 1980s he increasingly found the image of desperate youth turning desperately sour. Helen Malone, his agent for 20 years, found him not only a good actor but a nice man; but it was difficult to get him the sort of parts he now wanted and needed. Her nephew Malcolm Knight, who took over after her death, had encouraging talks with Evans at the end of last year. Evans made it clear that he was now looking for straight parts where he could play his real age.

His death, alone in a dilapidated bungalow where he lived in a Leicestershire village, tragically intervened before that could happen. Perhaps tragedy had always stalked him. Though born in comfortably middle-class Guildford, he was nevertheless in a Twickenham orphanage until he was 17. Though he won a John Gielgud Scholarship to the Central School of Speech and Drama, his life ended before he could achieve many roles of the sort that would have impressed his patron. His was indeed a story of youthful innocence gorged and then destroyed. •

Martin Godwin

A last service to a friend . . . Peter O'Toole and Sean Connery carry the coffin of the actor Ronnie Fraser to his grave in a Hampstead church on 20 March

· ·

22 March 1997

James Wood

A great master of the short story

S ir Victor Pritchett, V. S. Pritchett, who has died aged 96, was almost as old as the century, but much more benign. His remarkable longevity meant that he died into posterity while still alive, and his reputation became cloudily venerable. But Pritchett was one of the century's most distinguished short-story writers in English, and one of the century's great literary journalists. As a story writer, he influenced writers as diverse as Harold Pinter, William Trevor and Martin Amis; his American admirers include Eudora Welty, Richard Ford and the late Raymond Carver.

Pritchett was a great inheritor of Dickens's comedy, which he saw as reflective of the truest English character. As an essayist, he wrote memorably – and self-definingly – about Dickens's solitary fantasists. They are 'solitary pronouncers . . . They are strange, even mad, because they speak as if they were the only persons in the world.' Dickens, he wrote in a characteristically jewelled phrase, saw people 'whose inner life was hanging out so to speak, on their tongues, outside their persons'. Pritchett's own characters are just such solitaries, going through life on a cushion of inner fictions.

Pritchett was born into Dickensian circumstances, in lodgings above a small toy shop in Ipswich. Or at least, Pritchett would make this world Dickensian in his marvellous autobiography, *A Cab at the Door* (1967). It was a family of small means and large pretensions, dominated by Pritchett's ebullient father, whom his son likened to Mr Micawber – a small businessman, shopkeeper, travelling salesman or Christian Scientist, depending, it seems, on the time of year and the vigour of his whim.

Pritchett once said that his father was a man with no imagination but bottomless fantasy (his bedroom was crammed with tinned food in readiness for Armageddon), and he was clearly the model for Pritchett's fictional fantasists. His mother was illiterate but nevertheless a great storyteller; her habit of laughing in the middle of sad stories may well have given her son his love of comic pathos.

At home, the bookish Pritchett became a tolerated joke; he was known as 'the professor'. At 16, he left Alleyn's School in Dulwich (his family had moved to London) and went into the leather trade. But he was restless to travel and spent his late teens and early twenties moving around Ireland, Spain and France. He recalled reading one of the very first editions of Joyce's *Ulysses* in a Paris street, in 1922. His first book, *Marching Spain* (1922), was an account of a long walk from Badajoz to Vigo; travel and writing about travel remained one of his recreations. But it was his short fiction, which began to appear in the 1930s, in which he found his true voice.

The world of these stories never really changed, in 50 years of writing. His last new collection, *The Careless Widow and Other Stories*, which appeared in 1989, still inhabited the England of his earliest stories: a land of travelling salesmen, barbers and cocky executives; bad teeth and tired municipal lawns; petty satisfactions and rebellious comedy. Pritchett went to Dickens and to the nineteenth-century Russian short-story-tellers – Gogol, Turgenev and Chekhov – for his sense of comedy. He recalled arguing at a dinner with H. G. Wells, who insisted that one could only write about the working classes satirically. But in place of H. G. Wells's breathlessly cocky 'little men', Pritchett put something more like a Russian clerk out of Gogol; instead of comedy, he saw the pathos of yearning.

In 'The Fall', one of his most famous stories, Charles Peacock, a drab accountant, is attending an accountants' annual dinner in a nameless Midlands town. Charles's brother has become a celebrated film actor, and the vicarious celebrity Charles draws from this is the only colour in his monochrome life. Peacock has a party trick, which is that he can imitate his brother's famous stage-fall. He starts performing at the dinner, and as he gets drunker, so his fall becomes sloppy, repetitive and unfunny. Accosting strangers in the bar, he crumples to the floor. Each time, he stays a little longer on the ground. The beauty of the story, and its perfect melancholy, is that we know exactly what Peacock's friends think of him – that he is an embarrassing bore – but that Peacock does not. He goes on falling, now lost in his own drunken fantasy, until there is no one left in the bar. As the story ends, he is falling by himself – and for himself, because he has become his audience. As Pritchett wrote of Dickens's characters, 'our comedy, Dickens seems to say, is not in our relation with others but in our relation with ourselves'.

Pritchett's second great career was as a critic. At the beginning of the war, the literary editor of the *New Statesman* asked Pritchett if he would like to contribute a weekly essay on one of the classic authors. At the time, Pritchett was travelling around the country by train, collecting evidence for a government pamphlet on the future of the railways. He had a lot of free time (he read the whole of *Clarissa* on the Great Northern Line).

The result was a series of essays on most of the great Russian, British and French novels that would feed such celebrated critical books as *The Living Novel* (1948) and *The Truth-Tellers* (1962). Pritchett would go on to have a 40-year relationship with the *New Statesman*; in America he wrote regularly for the *New Yorker*, which took most of his reviews of American fiction.

Pritchett is as great an essayist as Virginia Woolf and Henry James, and he is a much more complete critic than either. The 1,300-page *Collected Essays*, which finally appeared in 1991, is certainly one of the great achievements of criticism in English. What awes, initially, is Pritchett's regal range. It was natural for him to think in terms of entire literatures, because he was deeply read in the entire literatures of Britain, Russia, Spain and France (he spoke these last two languages fluently).

Some of his finest insights have a monumental sweep: 'We recall that the greatest Russian novels of the nineteenth century arose from the failure of a class, whereas the English sprang out of its success.' Though Pritchett's tone was always softly modest, his breadth of reading and the acuteness of his insight were often formidable. When writing on Russian nationalism in nineteenth-century literature, for instance, he observed, 'We are moved by it because of the strangeness of meeting a nationalism rooted not in pride but in humility.' English essay-writing generally flows from two channels: metaphor and aphorism. Few critics mix these waters. Dr Johnson and Chesterton are aphorists; Coleridge, James and Woolf are metaphor-makers. Pritchett, wonderfully, was both. He felt and wrote about literature, pressed into its textures, instinctively through metaphor, because metaphor seemed to him the truest way of speaking fiction's own language; of allowing, as it were, fiction to speak to itself. Yet Pritchett's metaphors are often so compact that they have the snap of aphorism. Woolf criticised E. M. Forster for too often interrupting his novels with his own commentaries, 'like a light sleeper disturbed by noise in the next room'. Pritchett produces an even more exquisite variant on this when he laments the fact that Ford Madox Ford 'never fell into the determined stupor out of which greater novelists work'. Pritchett's criticism reveals his deep humility and wisdom. As he got older, and as he produced less fiction, so he lavished his literary power on his essays. His criticism became his velvet funnel, a muted form of self-description and autobiography.

One could trace Pritchett's own humane aesthetics in his generalisations: 'One of the reasons why bad novels are bad is not that the characters do not live, but that they do not live with one another. They read one another's characters' minds through the author.' 'For Boswell stumbled soon upon the vital discovery that experience is three parts hallucination.' 'With all his mastery, Trollope is interested only in what people are like, not in what they are for.' In his 1969 Clark Lectures at Cambridge, on Meredith and English comedy, he wrote that Dickens's characters draw on a sense of themselves as walking histories or legends. His own essays are walking histories: they have the density and the poetry of his short stories, but use literature rather than life as the anvil against which to shape themselves.

V. S. Pritchett was a writer who earned all his deepest literary resources by the age of 50, and used the next 30 years genially spending them. So it often seems that the second half of his life was without literary development – stories that resembled his earlier ones; biographies of Balzac, Turgenev and Chekhov; reprints of earlier travel books on London and Ireland; a knighthood in 1975; the Presidency of International PEN; and the occasional visit from Raymond Carver or Eudora Welty. He wrote very little after 1990, but lived in grand retirement in Regent's Park, with his wife of over 50 years, Dorothy; journalists, writers and ordinary readers who visited him there were welcomed with vigorous hospitality by Lady Pritchett and with shy amusement by Sir Victor. But it was an astonishing life-work partly because of its rare perfection: he knew how to develop as a writer and he knew when to stop.

The result is that in over 3,000 pages of fiction, criticism and travel-writing there is not a dull sentence or a wounded paragraph. As Martin Amis once put it, 'As an artist, Pritchett is exceptionally pure.' Modest and kind, he was a far greater literary sensibility than much noisier writers of his age. The English forest has one less tree now. •

24 April 1997

Frank Keating
Great talisman of hope

The timing, impeccable to the last, was poignant. The news came on the morning the cricketers of England were preparing to call 'Play!' on the first day of 1997's county championship. Then, one by one, the pavilion flags were lowered to half-mast and young men in cream flannels, who knew him not, stood to attention for a minute because they knew who he was all right, and what he had contributed everlastingly to the innate goodness as well as the grandeur of their game.

Compton was an all-time great and as those standards dipped at Canterbury, Chelmsford, Old Trafford, Trent Bridge and Hove – which in his bonny prime he had sunnily beguiled – bells metaphorically tolled the world over at places happy to accept that team-game players can lift spirits by their skill and chivalry.

Because of the drab days he so illuminated, Denis was almost a cultural icon to Britain of the immediate post-war, a valorous talisman of gaiety and of hope. As Chesterton had it, 'There is a great man who makes every man feel small. But the really great man is the one that makes every man feel great.'

I was always awestruck in the presence of this cigarette-card monarch of my infancy. We last spoke when Alec Bedser won his New Year knighthood. 'No doubt about it,' said Denis, 'Alec was the best medium-pacer I ever saw, and the greatest trier of the lot.' And then he added, 'Lovely chap too.' There were very few men Denis remembered of whom he would not add, 'Lovely chap too.'

We spoke as well that day of the death a few months before of Jack Robertson, the opening batsman who had laid down the markers for the entrance of Compton and Edrich and their string of voluptuous partnerships for Middlesex ('Dear Jack . . . lovely chap with it') and Denis at once became croaky and saddened with age. 'There are very few of my vintage left any more. The awfulness of age is that every day you wake up and quite expect to hear another lifelong chum has gone . . .'

Fifty years ago this week, at his beloved Lord's, he set forth on his summer of summers and scored 73 for MCC against Yorkshire, the champion county. Not that he burst resplendently from the bud after that – his next eight innings brought only 200 runs and one half-century. At the end of May, the sun got up and Middlesex played the touring South Africans. Compton hit 150. He went on to score five more centuries against the tourists, four of them in Tests, altogether smithereening Jack Hobbs's records for a single season, with 3,816 runs and 18 centuries. Both still stand. 'I did love the sun on my back,' said Denis.

England was still war-cowering and uncertain: scant, skint lives being put back together in monochrome. In glorious Technicolor, Compton's genius – the whistling happy-go-lucky errand boy, his feet on the handlebars – lightened the load, and on these pages Neville Cardus acclaimed, 'Never have I been so deeply touched on a cricket ground as in this heavenly summer of 1947, when I went to Lord's to see a pale-faced crowd, existing on rations, the rocket bomb still in the ears of most, and see the strain of anxiety and affliction passed from all hearts and shoulders at the sight of Compton in full sail . . . each stroke a flick of delight, a propulsion of happy, sane, healthy life. There were no rations in an innings by Compton.'

One who was to follow Cardus here, John Arlott, wrote his first cricket book in that summer of 1947. It ended, 'To close the eyes is to see again that easy, happy figure at the wicket, pushing an unruly forelock out of the eye and then, as it falls down again, playing off the wrong foot a stroke which passes deep-point like a bullet . . . never again will the boyish delight in hitting a ball with a piece of wood flower directly into charm and gaiety and all the wealth of achievement.'

His own favourite innings that year – 'probably the most memorable of all, I think' – was for Middlesex against Kent at Lord's, 'a run-chase, 390-odd at over 100 an hour; we just failed, but it was such glorious fun going for them'. Typical Compo, great good Compo. His 300 in three hours in Benoni, South Africa, was always passed off with a chuckle and 'Ooh, great fun'. Of his 17 Test match centuries he would not disagree when you said that context was all and best of all was 145 at Old Trafford in 1948, at the beginning of which a bumper from Ray Lindwall ('The greatest I faced; Bill O'Reilly next') had cut his eyebrow – splat! – like a boxer's.

Movietone News next week gave over its whole bulletin to that innings and Leslie Mitchell's evocative dulcets ended the commentary, 'Shaky and ill as he must have been, Compton plays like an utter master. Great as Compton is, never has he been greater.' Denis would tell how, groggy, he only continued that epic innings after a few slugs of doctor's-orders brandy.

It was apt too that yesterday was St George's Day, because, Chesterton again:

St George he was for England
And before he slayed the dragon
He drank a pint of English ale
Out of an English flagon.

Lovely chap, too. •

Denis Compton

Voices from elsewhere

'In the 1960s, I was the darling of the blue-rinse spiritualists;
in the 1970s, the hippies found me and made me their guru . . .
The 1990s have brought them all – and more.'
Diary of a fortune-teller

'My lover is . . . a Thatcherite. Is this the end?'
Dulce Domum

'I spent last weekend deciding whether to smuggle out my favourite puppy.'
64 days in an animal-testing laboratory

23 April 1997

Liz Whittaker

Diary of a fortune-teller

Mrs A arrived at 9.15 a.m. She wanted to see me before work, hoping I would tell her she could find the courage to walk out, letting her boss know what she thought of him. Of course, she didn't tell me this before we started, but it emerged anyway during the reading, as so often questions do, quite naturally.

I told her that she will most probably tolerate it for a while longer out of financial necessity. We talked about it after the reading. Sometimes a half-hour sitting, like this one, goes on to an hour or more. I don't charge any extra. People have got so much to worry about these days that it is much harder to be precise about time than it used to be.

At one time, when my father first taught me the skills of palmistry, tarot, runes and astrology he had learned from his mother, I thought that fortune-telling was a joke and that he was pulling my leg when he said people of all ages, intellects and backgrounds would consult me in the future. He was obviously a psychic himself, because the fact is he spoke the truth.

There are no boundaries of age, intellect or wealth to the kind of people who find their way to my door. In the past 30 years, I have looked into the future for businessmen, teachers, politicians, doctors, lecturers, housewives, journalists, insurance salesmen, drop-outs, actors *et al*. Fashions come and go, though, and at different times different groups have predominated in my client list. In the 1960s, I was the darling of the blue-rinse spiritualists; in the 1970s, the hippies found me and made me their guru; in the 1980s, it was commodities men and media types; but the 1990s have brought them all – and more. Everyone wants to know their future.

I have flirted with other careers, in teaching, journalism and local government, and I write children's stories and plays and do my share of community work. I am derided by some for my fascination with the strange, inexplicable world of the psychic, but loved by my friends and appreciated by my clients.

I used to go to church, but the establishment is not happy with what I do, and though some vicars are more tolerant than others, there are many who would still have me burnt at the stake, so I avoid religion of any kind.

Psychics go back centuries in my family and, despite my early scepticism, I now feel that my role is to help keep people sane, to enable them to see some continuity in life, and to look at their past and their future in order for them to gain a solid foothold in the present.

As a natural optimist, I always look for the best in people, but I find it harder now to give optimistic forecasts than I did 20 or even 10 years ago. I rarely see creativity and spiritual enlightenment as people's central goals in the way they once were. Nor do I glean a strong sense of commitment to collective improvement, which I used to see frequently. Political activity nowadays is more about careerism and personal reward. All too often I seem only to see an obsession with money: will they have it, will they lose it, will they find work, will they be able to afford their daughter's wedding, will their investments be secure, will they win the lottery or lose their house?

Sometimes I find it depressing, but most often I am aware it is only another phase in our slowly developing social history, and I exercise my psychic curiosity by trying to glimpse a more positive long-term scenario. For all that, love is still a favourite topic – even though it seems to have taken a back seat to sex in the media – and that inspires hope for the future.

At 11.30 a.m., Mr B. from Swansea rang. He is supposed to be here for an appointment at noon but can't make it because of traffic on the M5. Can I do the runes over the phone? Just a single question? The company are downsizing. Is he in or out?

I suggest he make another appointment where we can look at the whole picture. There is nothing to be gained by using precognition on a yes/no basis. Life is about cycles, not single events. What looks bad today can be the source of something brilliant for tomorrow. He laughs and says, 'What are you trying to tell me, Liz?' •

19 February 1997

Richard Phillips
Diary of an NHS patient

The man in the bed opposite me had two days to live though neither of us could have known that. I was about to witness the accident which would lead to his death.

He had never been in hospital before. 'I'm into keep-fit,' he told me. 'It shows,' I said. He was in his early seventies, but looked 20 years younger. Being half his age created no barriers. We chatted between our crossword clues. We got on well.

Both of us had been admitted with stomach pains. Mine had gone, because my appendix had been removed, but his seemed to be getting worse. We exchanged symptoms. While he still suffered pain, I whinged about the discomfort of a drip in my arm and the unpleasant experience of being fitted with a catheter. Then, in the early hours of the morning, everything changed.

We were both feeling thirsty and uncomfortable. For nearly an hour we made admittedly feeble and apologetic attempts to get help from the nurses. Our needs didn't seem like priorities after one of the nurses had told us they were hopelessly short-staffed and it was going to be 'a hell of a night'. We both felt sorry for the nurses and didn't want to add to their already gruelling workload. There were just three looking after more than

20 of us. Finally – despite the sign above his bed saying 'nil by mouth' – my new companion decided to reach out for a drink of water. He leant over too far and fell out of bed. The saline drip, preventing him from dehydrating, crashed down on top of him.

It was like watching a slow-motion replay. The clattering of the bedside table and the look on his face as he hit the floor are etched on my mind. He came to rest with his feet in the air, the drip trolley and tube tangled up around him. Those words about a 'hell of a night' had been prophetic.

I climbed out of bed, carrying my equipment with me into the corridor. I shouted at the top of my voice for a nurse. She came straight away. 'Oh, shit!' she shouted. 'Crash! Crash!' Nurses appeared from other wards. Consultants, doctors and auxiliaries appeared within minutes. For nearly three hours, there, in front of me, they struggled to keep him alive. There were 10 or more people around the bed. 'Can you hear me?' asked one doctor. 'Do you know where you are? Do you know who I am? Do you feel pain anywhere? Just do as we say and we'll help you.' But there was little, if any, response.

Frantic phone calls were made to find an intensive treatment bed. There was none available in the hospital. Lively discussions about what to do next soon turned into irritable arguments.

Components from my own drip were taken to use on my friend, and as the nurse passed my bed she apologised for not having time to empty my catheter bag. I had visions of terrible things happening, but my mind was on my friend.

Finally, in the early hours of that morning, he was transferred to a hospital more than 30 miles away. Less than 24 hours later, he was dead. I only discovered this when I read my local newspaper. His family's obituary notice read '. . . thanks to all the doctors and nurses involved . . .'

Now I face a horrible dilemma. Do I contact the man's family to make sure that they know their loved one fell out of bed after an hour of calling for help, or do I allow them to be happy and contented in what is likely to be comforting ignorance? Even if they have already been told that he fell out of bed, they can't know how fraught and grossly understaffed it was that night. They are unlikely to know what a direct influence the shortage of nurses had on those tragic events. Part of me feels duty-bound to tell them about it all, yet I don't want to disrupt their lives.

The nurses did everything they could within the pathetic circumstances, but I suspect their 'hell of a night' was by no means unique. I believe that what I witnessed highlights unacceptable shortages of staff and facilities in hospitals throughout the UK.

When my friend's family hear reports of health service cut-backs, I can imagine them responding with glowing accounts of how he was treated. Do I allow them to perpetuate a myth or do I carefully and sensitively put them straight? •

1 January 1997

Peter Hetherington
The bleat goes on into the New Year

Somehow they managed a swift New Year meal late last night, as bitter easterlies piled the snow high around their rolling border acres. But it wasn't much of a celebration at Gallows Hill Farm. Almost every mouthful of fillet steak was interrupted by more bleating and another potential emergency in the nearby barn.

'You can't afford to relax with such a valuable commodity in the shed,' croaked Audrey Porksen, farmer's wife, fighting off a flu bug with antibiotics as her husband, Hans, shivered outside under the flimsy cover of the maternity wing. 'You need your wits about you.'

In mid-Northumberland, where a coastal plain meets the foothills of the north Pennines, their extended lambing season began this week – four months before most upland farmers start preparing for the most testing time of the year.

By yesterday, five more pure-bred Suffolk lambs were born on the family's 340-acre hill farm, near the pleasant National Trust village of Cambo; by the end of the week around 60 should have emerged in a large rearing barn, carefully segregated for triplets, twins and singles.

Hans Porksen, who is German-born, runs the enterprise with Audrey, supplemented this week by their daughter Vicki. They have turned the farming calendar on its head for commercial reasons. 'Prices have been going up rapidly,' says the enthusiastic farmer, a former agricultural college lecturer. 'Many more people are eating lamb, and we all know why.'

With consumers still wary of beef as the BSE crisis rumbles on, butchers are finding that demand often outstrips supply – even with a 30 per cent increase in sheep production over the last 10 years alone, pushing the population up to 43 million. Adventurous farmers have now set barns and outhouses aside for early lambing, with some erecting long, greenhouse-style polythene tunnels to house the newborns until the weather improves.

Hans and Audrey, who have farmed at Cambo as National Trust tenants since 1990, produce some of Britain's fastest-growing pedigree Suffolks in collaboration with scientists from the Scottish Agricultural College. The animals are sold as breeding stock, with maturing rams fetching at least £600 in sales later this year (1997).

'We are making use of the most advanced genetic programmes available,' says Hans, proudly flourishing promotional leaflets proclaiming that his flock is the finest of its kind in the country. 'This is probably the fastest-growing breed in the UK, with the highest weight gain. They give us good muscle, with less fat – a very attractive animal.'

They are, in short, 'super sheep', engineered to perfection. But they also need round-the-clock care from the farmer and his small team. 'We have to give them a lot of attention,' he warns. 'They are delicate animals.'

Although he has been farming in England since 1963, Hans says he still gets great excitement from the lambing season. Easing another lamb from a mother's womb yesterday afternoon, he had to shake the animal to life with the help of daughter Vicki. 'It is still magic, isn't it?' he enthused as the animal took its first, tentative steps. 'They have a never-ending fascination.'

By late March, they will have to contend with another lambing season – out on the surrounding hills, which rise to 600 feet, where 500 Blackface ewes are grazing. Although their offspring will be born out of doors, Hans can see huge potential in round-the-year lambing – provided the prices are right.

Audrey, meanwhile, confesses to a little sentiment. Lambs might occupy almost every acre on the farm, but she still can't bring herself to eat the stuff – particularly the variety reared at Gallows Hill. 'I am far too attached to them,' she says. •

22 February 1997

Barbara Cartland and Richard Hoggart
Head to head

Dear Richard,

I am astonished at the Department of National Heritage's conclusion in its review this week that British libraries have become over-concerned with entertainment and not enough with 'high seriousness'. More alarming still were earlier reports, clearly fed to the press by a Government minister, in which romantic literature was made a particular target.

This is political correctness gone mad – again. The implication in the Government's line is that an élite committee will censor the books stocked by public libraries in order to favour educational tracts and weed out so called 'light literature'.

We could almost imagine now the composition of such a committee. Censorship, we all believed, was a thing of the past (although I would entirely favour its reintroduction to control the flow of pornography and over-violent material on the market that is doing so much damage to our children).

My fear is that popular fiction will be made a scapegoat for what the Government calls 'entertainment'. Is it just because romance is so popular in the libraries and borrowed by women more than any other category of book that it is so resented? Every year romantic authors, such as myself, come top of the league tables in public lending rights. Women enjoy reading romance, as I have found from so many letters. In romance they find a world away from their humdrum lives.

I write historical romances and I go to great pains to make sure that my historical information is correct. If, in the reading of one of my books, someone is encouraged to study the history of the times in which the novel is set, then that must surely have educational value. This week's events amount to a potential attack on popular preference. If the public want fiction – the 'easy read' if you like – then just who is to say that they do not deserve to get it?

Yours sincerely, Dame Barbara Cartland

Dear Dame Barbara,

In your anger against 'censorship' by public libraries you have, I'm afraid, gone for entirely the wrong target. Let's establish two incontrovertible points.

First, libraries were set up a century and a half ago so that many more people could have access to the 'best that has been thought and said'. Second, the greatest achievement of British culture has been its literature, from Chaucer to the present.

Here we can spot your faulty aim. No one is suggesting that what you defend as 'light' literature should be censored. Quite the opposite. The Department of National Heritage is implying that many libraries – their budgets badly reduced – are carrying out censorship by no longer attending to the claims of books of quality, from whatever period they come.

In some places, great nineteenth-century novels have been taken off the shelves; it is unlikely that you will find more than one copy of those contemporary novelists who do challenge our imaginations. You will be likely to find multiple copies of the latest Mills and Boon formulaic offerings.

Why do the librarians (not all of them, of course) do this? Because they confuse democracy with populism. Populism suggests that we provide lavishly by attending chiefly to a head-count of demand.

Democracy also recognises other and better criteria: that we all have a right of access to the best, and that we needs must love the highest when we see it. In other words, good books from all periods must have a full right of access to the shelves.

Yours sincerely, Richard Hoggart, Author of The Way We Live Now

Dear Richard,

If public libraries, some created almost two centuries ago, still do not by now stock the basic classics, then I would be somewhat surprised. Literature of all sorts is not static, but is growing and changing every year. New books can become classics in every field, but my basic argument is choice. Members of the public who visit libraries must be allowed to choose freely the writers and the type of book they like best. When I was a girl the schools I attended had no books at all and I remember a strong hunger to read and I have read all types of literature ever since.

Our schools today are producing many pupils who are barely literate and therefore everything must be done to encourage them to read. If someone started reading any romance, not necessarily one of mine, and ended up with Jane Austen, all the money spent on education in this country might be considered worthwhile.

Yours, Barbara

Dear Barbara,

You say that libraries should offer unrestricted choice. No public library in any part of the world can offer that. There are far too many books, let alone other demands on money, for that to be possible. So, yes, limits – which must include decisions not to stock some books – have to be set, on clear criteria.

Your problem is that you don't like to hear that a lot of libraries today are buying too many of your kind of novel, at the expense of stocking works of greater literary value. Other people don't see why head-counting should be the dominant criterion.

You question whether any libraries have ceased to have 'the basic classics' on display. I have seen library staff removing the major Victorian novelists so as to make space for videos and software. This week the Evening Standard *toured 10 public libraries in London. The results show you are mistaken here also.*

You then invoke a common myth: that reading ephemera leads on to better authors such as Jane Austen. I am glad you do recognise a difference of quality there.

Yes, a very few children, fascinated by words, will start with sauce-bottle labels and move on and up. Virtually no one else, habitual readers of your novels and others like them, is led to do that.

They, naturally, keep asking for more of the same. There are plenty of authors and publishers to provide that. This is not an 'onward and upward' progress but the 'round and round' reality. Shakespeare hit the spot: 'The appetite grows by what it feeds on.' Most popular fiction belongs to the Consumer Society, not to a truly Literate and Literary Society.

Yours, Richard

Dear Richard,

We would both agree in this debate that public libraries are in existence to provide a public service and this means that they must respond to public demand. If someone goes to a public library and asks for a popular romance, only to be told that she can only have Shakespeare or Byron, the public library service is not doing its job properly.

The history of the last 20 years has proved one thing, and that is that market forces and popular demand can move mountains. The service of British Telecom has improved immeasurably since competition and privatisation and now we have dozens of TV stations giving the public what they want instead of Auntie BBC telling us what we should watch.

If only there was some effective way of privatising the public libraries, then it should be done. I am sure that some entrepreneur can come up with a good idea that will increase the scope of libraries and make them more accountable to public demand. That would be much better than a faceless quango laying down the law about which books people should and should not be reading.

It is my guess that the public would want a lot more romances and popular fiction rather than less.

Yours, Barbara

Dear Barbara,

I don't wish to be impolite but I have to say that your latest letter is the most misguided mishmash I've read in many a day.

Of course libraries must respond to public demand. But they mustn't help set public demand in concrete by making available only material we know we already like. Good libraries show us that the world can be a lot wider and more interesting than we have thought. Your preferred vision – of libraries stuffed with popular romantic fiction because that's all we can take – is out of 1984.

Broadcasting: Britain introduced the idea of broadcasting for public service rather than profit-making. Hence the BBC is internationally regarded as the benchmark for the best practice. Or was. It is now under immense pressure from those who aim to make their audiences into tame masses. In come more game shows, low-level soaps and the rest. Of all of which you seem to approve.

Finally: surely a professional novelist should never indulge in trite clichés: 'Auntie BBC' and 'faceless quangos'; inaccurate 'boo' phrases. Good language and so good thinking have to be kept up – especially today, and especially by writers.

Yours, Richard. •

---

15 July 1997

Linda Grant

Country mutters

On Thursday night, as the country folk of Britain turned their backs on London and returned home to their villages after their great march on the capital, I was standing in an alley which ran between two rows of terraced houses in Newcastle upon Tyne. The countryside wasn't far; from some vantage points in the city, you could even see it. The alley was full of a dozen or so figures, like swarming rats with black and white markings. The black and some of the white was on their bodies, the ubiquitous Newcastle United strip. The rest of the white came from the extreme, dead-white waxy pallor of their faces. They resembled animate corpses.

They seemed to be children, but not quite. The cheekbones stuck out at peculiar angles as if the bones hadn't formed properly in the womb or were subject to some post-natal wasting disease. The features of the face were lopsided or too big or too small. Terrible eyes. I recognised what I was seeing: the extreme effects of malnourishment, of a diet consisting entirely of junk food, of the very cheapest burgers made from the worst meat, oven-ready chips formed from reconstituted potato with any vitamin C leached out before they ever reached the plate, meals that consisted of nothing but sweets. No fruit, no fresh vegetables.

There is an existing iron deficiency anaemia in 3–5 per cent of British adolescents. The compassionate give money to Oxfam to stamp out malnutrition in the Third World and here it was in Newcastle and, I'm sure, in every other town and city in the country. For I'd seen kids like this before, cruising the shops, looking at pairs of trainers that cost the whole of their family's monthly food budget.

On the train going back to London, rural England – dressed in flax and linseed and corn flagged by the strident red of poppies – flashed past at a hundred miles an hour, delightful to look at in a chocolate-box kind of a way as if it had been thoughtfully provided by the railway company for the pleasure of its passengers. As it passed, all the thousands of words I had read last week philosophically for or against fox hunting receded with it. During the journey I came to the conclusion that I simply did not care about the rights of the fox or of farmers or of ramblers or of those who wish the countryside to be preserved in some traditional way. I could not care less. As the week ended and it got to Sunday, those children spread like a malignant tumour across my mind's eye. I couldn't get rid of the awful, ugly sight of them.

What I do care about is why we have an agricultural policy which does not produce a wholesome nutritious diet that the poor can afford. For while campaigning food writers such as the admirable Joanna Blythman rightly argue that we should buy more organic, ethically reared foods, millions cannot even afford the waxed, gas-ripened, chemically blasted, genetically engineered specimens the supermarkets offer us unfresh from the intensive farming that is modern agri-business. If adulterated foods are too dear, what hope is there that they will buy cruelty-free eggs or traditional varieties of apples? The disastrous diet of Britain's poor is partly the responsibility of farmers who have seen easy money in producing cheap nutritionally void food for the masses, creating a hunger for the industrially extruded, breaded chicken cutlet that to many palates actually tastes good. The craving for the comfort of sugar and fat (when God knows there's little else pleasure and control in your life) results in the amazing new food sensation which has just reached Newcastle – the battered, deep-fried Cadbury's Creme Egg.

But it is not just the farmers who are to blame for the nutritional ills we suffer. The cult of the countryside must also take a bow. I come from generations of urban dwellers. My grandfather, driven for a day out in the country, would look at a field – that gap between the towns without books or betting shops – and say in disgust, in his broken English: 'Here they could build houses for the workers.' I almost never visit the countryside for pleasure, nor do I enjoy the company of animal companions. Without this deep-rooted British attachment to the land and to four-legged friends, I ask what is the countryside for? Is it a place of refuge for weary townsfolk? Is it a place of recreation? Is it a form of out-relief for other species? Is it the bearer of the nation's traditional ideas of its pre-industrial self? It may be all of these but as far as we are concerned the bottom line is that it is the place where our food comes from and without that food we cannot live at all. In the countryside's remembered golden age, before the war, wheat waved in the breeze serenaded by the Hovis brass band. Why can't we go back to that? Because the horror of factory farming has given us cheaper food. Where the poor of today eat too much junk, the poor of the 1930s had too little of anything to eat. Modern farming at least has eliminated hunger as the poor's appetiser.

The nutritionally conscious middle classes, especially the animal lovers, are unknowingly complicit in ensuring that the poor are denied marginally better food than they would otherwise get. In my local health food shop, on Saturday afternoon, I was invited to sign a petition against the proposed arrival of a McDonald's in our neighbourhood. I hesitated and then left without adding my name. For those on benefit, for the past few months the McDonald's chain has been their only chance to eat non-British beef. Compared with the cheapest economy pack of burgers available at a corner shop, the Big Mac is the equivalent of corn-reared, Aberdeen Angus steak. And they throw in a leaf of iceberg lettuce. If there is no McDonald's, will the poor buy lentils at the health food store? No. They will continue to eat their burgers at local kebab shops where the provenance of the meat doesn't even bear thinking about and is only meat at all if you count cows' tongues and lips and the contents of their hooves as beef.

Something just as drastic as the diet of the children in the alley in Newcastle has happened to politics in Britain. In the last 10 years we have begun to assume that we cannot do anything about poverty and so various secondary debates have flooded in to fill the vacuum left by the grand intentions inaugurated at the end of the war. An alternative discourse has grown up in which human beings – wasteful, greedy, ignoble – are villainised in favour of the sentimental purity of the rural idyll, where endangered species roam in a vision of freedom and oneness with nature we can only envy.

The kids in the alley can never be the winners in the compassion auction if they have to compete against the beauty of a newborn lamb or the sorrow and the pity aroused by a fox about to be torn to pieces by hounds. They will be elbowed aside by ramblers, shouted at, those little vandals who, if they were to be let loose on the countryside, would no doubt only burn it down. Loving every species except our own, saving whales and dolphins and baby seals, you (because I personally have never contributed a penny to the salvation of a single animal) are condemning human children to short lives ended by cancer and heart disease. At least the fox mangled by hounds dies fast. At least it had a life before the dogs got it. You look at the kids in the alley, fathers and grandfathers before them never knowing work, and you wonder who is happier, they or the foxes? •

26 November 1996

John Casey *

Don's delight: the book that changed my life

The dominant image of Spinoza is that transmitted through the Romantic tradition – of a mystical pantheist. Goethe and Lessing, Coleridge and Shelley admired Spinoza immensely for his ability (as they saw it) to understand the whole world as divine, and for the noble view of human potential that seemed to entail.

Yet in his own lifetime Spinoza was widely regarded as a dangerous atheist, a man who denied the transcendence of God, free will, responsibility and hence morality.

Little of his work was published during his lifetime – which was probably just as well for him.

My own interest in Spinoza was first aroused by this very ambiguity: was he *Gott Tronken* (God intoxicated) or an atheist? A prophet of human freedom or a dismal determinist? His work is genuinely two-sided. He tried to draw a picture of the world by the most austerely impersonal method ('more geometric'), and yet you always feel that the whole scheme is driven by passion.

No philosopher is more rigorous than Spinoza. Everything in his system proceeds from a particular doctrine about substance – that the universe does not consist (as Descartes thought) of two substances, mind and matter, but of one substance which under one aspect is mental and under another material.

Spinoza used this idea to depict human beings as aspiring towards the mental, or spiritual, by becoming ever more active in mind, body and emotions. The more spiritually active we are, the less are we 'in bondage to nature' and the closer we come to freedom. None of this is pious uplift, but follows a rigorous argument.

Spinoza's 'free man' is a man of strength of mind and nobility (*fortitudo et generositas*). He is someone whose actions proceed from himself in the fullest sense, rather than from unacknowledged obsessions, fears and desires.

Spinoza suggested to me the possibility of a genuinely secular ethic which stresses human autonomy, while at the same time making room for that tradition of intellectual contemplation which runs from Plato and Aristotle, and which in Spinoza himself plausibly issues in the *amor intellectualis dei* – the 'intellectual love of God'. •

Spinoza's *Ethics*, edited by G. H. R. Parkinson (Everyman, £5.99).

John Casey is an English lecturer and Fellow of Gonville and Caius College, Cambridge.

27 May 1997

Deborah Cameron[*]

Don's delight: the book that changed my life

n the final term of my English degree I had to write a long assignment for a course in twentieth-century literature. Unfortunately I didn't much care for the giants of modernism. I was a passionate if still rather ignorant feminist, and I preferred linguistics anyway.

I brought cynical calculation to bear on the problem, and decided I would choose as my subject an author who was female (on political principle), obscure (so my tutors would know as little as possible about her) and not too prolific (to save on the reading). I went to the course tutor, told him candidly that this was my plan and asked who might fit the bill. He considered for a moment and then said, rather doubtfully, 'Well, there's always Dorothy Richardson. She only wrote one book, and it's not even in print.' I asked him if he had read it and he admitted he had not.

'Perfect,' I thought, and trotted off to the library.

There I discovered that this 'one book', *Pilgrimage*, is actually a multi-volume work of inordinate length. Once I had started on it, however, it turned into an obsession. I persuaded friends to read it too, and we sat around discussing what impelled Dorothy Richardson to write this text that just went on and on and on. We considered whether she was right in the observations about gender difference which she put into the mouth of her protagonist, Miriam Henderson, whether Virginia Woolf was right to say she had invented a 'feminine' sentence, and why her work had been so neglected. Naive though they doubtless were, these discussions opened up new horizons and I recall them as high points in my literary education.

When *Pilgrimage* was reprinted as a Virago Modern Classic I read it again. It didn't stir the same passions, and I was rather disappointed. But I think there's a more general moral to this story, which I try to bear in mind as a teacher: never write off the cynical student. Something you start reading in total bad faith can grab you unexpectedly and lead you to new insights. ●

Dorothy Richardson's *Pilgrimage* is published by Virago Modern Classics in four volumes, price £10 (approx.) per volume.

*Deborah Cameron is Professor of English Language at Strathclyde University.

. . . .

3 April 1997

Harold Jackson
How to go like the clappers

The Central Council of Church Bell Ringers is appealing for 10,000 volunteers to learn the peculiarly British art of change-ringing, and the Millennium Commission has backed the drive by donating £3 million to get hundreds of bells into good enough condition to ring in New Year 2000.

It all sounds thoroughly blood-stirring but, as a recent volunteer, I wonder if the commission has any idea what it is unleashing. My band practises for about two hours a week and I've been assured it will take at least a year, probably longer, before I can regard myself as a competent ringer.

So, if the target volunteers actually come forward it will mean 10,000 more or less incompetent bell-ringers treating the public to 4,000 man-years of out-of-beat jangling. How's that for an issue to drop into the election campaign? However, relief is at hand in the shape of a well-thought-out computer program enabling novices to practise ringing at their keyboards – silently if necessary. At the very least its authors, Chris Hughes and Simon Feather, should be in the running for the Noise Abatement Society's gold medal.

The aim of change-ringing is to sound the bells in as many sequences as mathematically possible. The maximum number is calculated by multiplying up the number of bells – 1 x 2 x 3 x 4 and so on. St Paul's Cathedral, with 12 bells, can encompass 479,001,600 changes. Our village church, with six, offers a mere 720.

The simplest way to work through them is known as a plain hunt, achieved by transposing the ringing sequence of each pair of bells for one strike, of the two middle pairs for the next strike, each pair again for the third strike, the middle pairs again for the fourth and so on. This produces the sequence:

```
1 2 3 4 5 6
2 1 4 3 6 5
2 4 1 6 3 5
4 2 6 1 5 3
```

If you follow the diagonal paths of bells 1 and 3, you can see that each is moving up one position in the sequence. Bells 4 and 6 are moving down one position and Bells 2 and 5 are in the throes of changing direction.

That will, in fact, give only 12 variations before you're back to 123456, so there's some arithmetical jiggery-pokery known as a bob at the twelfth variation which sets the ringers up for the next 12 changes, then another bob, and so on until they complete all 720 possibilities.

Now it's one thing to sit quietly musing over your graph paper. It's something else to keep track of the permutations while you're chucking around 650 lb of obstinate metal at the end of 15 feet of rope.

The bells are attached to a wheel around which the rope runs. For ringing, the mouth of the bell is raised skyward. Then, as the ringer pulls the rope, the wheel and the bell travel through 360 degrees until the bell mouth again faces skyward. Another pull reverses the process.

This means that several hundredweight of bell starts moving at the slightest tug and there's nothing you can do to stop it. The ultimate sin is to let go of the rope so that it careers randomly round the belfry. Veterans in our band have vivid memories of one which wrapped itself round a radiator, yanked it off the wall and swung it towards some fast-vanishing ringers.

The joy of Chris Hughes's software, which he has called Abel, is that it allows you to make all your mistakes without injuring a soul. It can be adjusted to show any standard number of bells on the screen and the speed and pitch at which they are rung. The program will do all the work if you wish, which is useful for learning the 'tune' of a particular method, but you can also nominate the bell (or bells) you wish to operate manually. Even more valuably, you can program in some of the commonest mistakes (coming in too early or late, for example) so you recognise their sound and learn how to dig yourself out of them. There's a library holding many of the standard methods for practice, and software allowing you to write your own.

In the end, of course, there is no substitute for reality and the program certainly can't train you in the mechanics of the art. My current problem is not so much ringing as stopping (by standing my bell mouth upwards). If you ever hear one lonely bell chiming mournfully as you pass through Suffolk, do give me a wave. •

....

4 March 1997

Matthew Norman
Diary

Further evidence of the fragility that afflicts the monarchy. Centenarian Maud Neal of Harrow has attempted to reject her telegram from the Queen in favour of a pound of chocolates. Told by staff at her nursing home that they would be contacting Buckingham Palace, Mrs Neal said that, although she had nothing personal against Her Majesty, she had little use for a piece of paper and would prefer the confectionery, raising her fists and threatening to 'duff up' the offending member of staff should the telegram arrive. •

....

5 April 1997

Dulce Domum
Bad housekeeping

Harriet: 'Mummy, can I stay with Kate next weekend? She's, like, my best friend and she's really, like, beautiful and witty, and we're writing this, like, play, right? So can I?' 'Like, yes, right?' If she goes to Kate's next weekend, I shall be half-way to an adult 48 hours with James Campbell. Haven't seen him much recently. He's been designing mockeries for a rock star. Dag Zitzone really digs his garden – though not, like, literally. James hopes to interest him in a potager and, eventually, in an arbore-tum. My own modest orchard is also taking shape. Last weekend, James waded about spraying.

I hovered indoors in a froth of anxiety. How toxic is Roundup? Who shall I vote for? And can you really get natural progesterone from the yarrow plant? If so, could James give me some seeds? Forget the orchard, let's have a progesterone plantation. Horti-cultural Replacement Therapy. *Hortus hormonalis matronalis lubriciiii.*

If I had such a blessed acre, I suspect the middle-aged women of England would rise as a man and descend with secateurs. The Yarrow Marchers. The main difficulty of our medieval dalliance is not the antiquity of the equipment but the disapproving scrutiny of the young.

'Mummy, is James staying the night again? I don't like it! I can't come into your bed in the morning! Besides, it'll make Daddy jealous!' So Kate's invitation to a weekend of, like, dramaturgy couldn't be more convenient. Now there's only Henry to get rid of. Although his presence here every other weekend is now only virtual. The moment he arrives, he locks himself in his attic and puts on rap music. Soon he's going to want a kind of cat-flap through which I will be required to push pizza and chips at intervals. Still, I'm told he does the same thing at his dad's place, so at least he's being scrupulously impartial in his anomie.

'Mum?' The lad himself, a husky baritone these days. 'Do you mind if I stay in Lon-don this weekend? Blind Pew is doing a gig at Hammersmith and I want to go.' Express melodious regret and cheerful acquiescence, and assure him I shall look forward to see-ing him again when he can find the time, with his wife and children if necessary. He makes a noise suggestive of disgust at the thought of so tacky a destiny and rings off.

Hurrah! The fledgelings have left the nest and preparations for the dirty weekend can begin immediately, starting with the extensive marinating necessary to bring out the full gamey flavour of the ripe old bird.

James arrives with a bunch of flowers. I receive them with a sardonic sense about how tiresome it is when men bring their work home, then rush out with them to the kitchen where I go dewy-eyed in private.

Flowers! Nobody's brought me flowers since Tom. But how am I to retain the interest of a sexily crumpled 50-year-old man? I am, after all, a repulsively crumpled 50ish woman. Console myself with the thought that it would be even worse were I an omelette. I suppose he'll have to close his eyes and think of crumpet.

While the chicken is roasting, he asks if he might have a bath and whether I would mind soaping his back, or, as it turns out, his front. Afterwards, as they used to say when novels were more tasteful, I wonder aloud who I am to vote for. He sighs in sympathy.

'Yes . . . the Tories are all rubbish since they ditched Maggie. What a woman!'

Make excuse and lock myself in the bathroom, where I feel sick for several minutes. My lover is a . . . Thatcherite. Is this the end?

'It's not her politics,' he explains. 'It's just bossiness in stockings, I'm afraid.'

I used to revile fetishism, but now it may be my only hope. Wonder if they do black stockings at the village shop, and whether a youth could bring them round, piping hot, on his bike. •

· ·

2 July 1997

Paul Evans
A country diary

The Wrekin: From afar, the Wrekin and its surrounding wooded hills have all but vanished under a shifting, smoky cape of cloud. Inside, the woods are dank and gloriously sodden. The air is spicy with the sharp green scent of bracken, the sticky sweetness of honeysuckle drapes and hidden stinkhorn. Within this humid wood-mist, the fungi are stirring early from damp loam and rotten logs. Out in the open, in the regenerating quarry valley in Maddocks Hill, is a spectacular display of common spotted orchids. An ooze from the quarry floor determines a new path, joining run-off from woods and lanes to drain into a little wet woodland. Beneath a canopy of alders these trickles merge into a narrow stream, which leads to one of those uniquely secretive places: an old yew tree twists out of the stream bed surrounded by a muddy pool with tussock sedge. From this swamp, the stream passes under the road to plunge into the narrow gorge of the Forest Glen. Water from the north end of the Wrekin flows north through the Forest Glen, into the old reservoir, out through Cluddley and along the west side of Wellington, as the Beanhill Brook, before entering the River Tern in the Weald Moors and eventually the Severn at Atcham. Here in the woods of Hazel Hurst, at the foot of the Wrekin, the recent rains begin that journey with a strange and rare song. This is the wild, indecipherable song of nameless streams, where few paths cross but none follow. A song which bubbles and pours over stones, roots and mossy logs; deep and throaty in its narrow trough; thick and leafy under a green shade. A rare song because summer rains have in recent years been ephemeral, but this year's are persistent, strident, scouring the stream beds in a cleansing tide. This is the cold clear life-blood the ancient may have drunk here from a skull. •

26 March 1997

Zoe Broughton

64 days in an animal-testing laboratory

Ever since I was young I used to wonder what went on behind the high barbed wire of the huge animal-testing laboratory down the road. I'm not opposed to animal testing if it's done to advance medical science, and if in the process the animals are kept well and treated compassionately. I decided to apply for one of the lab's many vacancies advertised in the local paper, to see for myself.

A few days later I got an interview for a job as an animal technician. The pay was about £120 for a five-and-a-half-day week. I made myself sound keen and stressed that I had experience of working with animals. They checked my name to see if it appeared on any animal campaign lists. Before I'd come to terms with what I was about to involve myself in, I was working in one of Britain's largest animal-testing laboratories.

Day 1   I don't know what to expect, not even which department I will get sent to or how I will respond to seeing animals in pain. To fit in, I make up a false past. I can hardly reveal I am a film-maker. But I am worried that I may say something that might blow my cover.

I am assigned to the dog toxicology unit. I've always had pet dogs, but as we enter the building the noise and smell hit me. I cannot stop my face showing the shock. I notice immediately that the little puppies are keen to play, whereas the older dogs are wary of human touch. Some stay at the back of their cages and don't even move when I give them their food. My job is to look after a room of 32 puppies. On the first afternoon I am asked to check the health of my dogs. I am shown how to do it, but trying to check teeth and paws on a wriggling little beagle puppy seems almost impossible. Later I read the Home Office Guidelines and it states that it has to be done by a competent person – how can I be competent on my first day at work? All the dogs had their own distinctive characters and I was shocked to find out that they would all be put down. By the end of the day I was mentally and physically exhausted.

Day 4   The hardest job is putting the young puppies away after their one hour of exercise in the small concrete corridor between the two rows of cages. They paw at me with their shitty feet. I pick one up, read the number tattooed in its ear and walk the length of the room to find its cage, all the while trying not to tread on paws and slip in the fresh shit.

It's repulsive and by the end of each day my lab clothes have turned from white to brown.

Day 8   I have to help take blood samples. They call it 'doing a bleed'. I bring the first dog out and sit her on a chair beside me, holding both front paws in one hand and holding the chin up with the other. The animal technician shaves the dog's neck and then plunges the needle in. She continues bleeding afterwards – I get blood on my arm and I see the other dogs look and know what is coming. Some grip the floor cringing and a couple try to dart past me and escape. Often the technicians can't find a vein. I count one needle being put in three times and once under the skin prodded in different directions 15 times before finding a vein. I feel pretty queasy.

Day 10   I am told not to use so much sawdust – 'One shovelful is enough and it needn't be piled up.' There is no bedding and this is all the dogs have on the concrete floors. The Home Office inspectors turn up. I don't see them look in any of the units I deal with – they just stand outside the dog rooms and chat with the technicians.

Day 15   Another visit from the Home Office inspectors. This time I see them outside in the corridor – a technician tells me to sweep the floor – I sweep it, but they don't enter my side of the laboratory. I've now seen them arrive twice, but I haven't seen them look at a dog yet.

Day 18   I still feel physically sick with nerves. The Independent Television Commission (ITC) has granted me permission to film what is going on. The camera equipment is strapped to my body. It is very bulky and I am worried because it is visible every time I bend over.

Day 29   The worst day yet, as the experiments started on my 32 puppies. The test involves putting each dog in a sling and injecting a chemical used in the scanning of human livers. Two are sick as they are being injected, some of their legs swell up and on top of this the puppies have 10 blood tests each through the day. The technicians keep saying that 'these dogs are too young for this type of experiment as their veins are too small' – so why have they got them so young? If the puppies wriggle, they are hit or shaken by the scruff of their necks. I feel like a torturer. I hold them and soon get their blood on my hands.

Day 30   I help prepare the doses for another experiment – it is an agrochemical toxicity test for a Japanese company. A lot of the tests in my department were testing for the toxicity of herbicides and fungicides. The man I am working with measures out the compound and I put it into capsules. He is meant to print out the weight of each dose on a computer so it can be checked. What he actually does is measure out one dose correctly, print this out seven times and then make the next six doses for the week far more quickly and with less accuracy. This means the dogs are not getting the right dose; these experiments may be invalid.

Day 32 Walk into my unit and one of my puppies, number 1,619, has half a pint of congealed bloody faeces around his cage. The vet looks at him and says it is all right to continue with the daily doses.

Day 33 I'm finding it hard to watch these needles being repeatedly put into the dogs' legs, over and over. One technician gets so angry when he can't find a vein that he shouts, and quickly jabs the needle in repeatedly, often going right through the vein. Twice I have seen him give up and squirt the rest of the liquid into the bin.

Day 40 I have had plenty of opportunities to read the files. I have been writing notes on scraps of paper and have now established which experiments are in which rooms, who's sponsoring which companies, the compounds being tested and how each is being administered.

Day 45 Today I film the pictures of the animal technicians' pets on the wall – many of them talk non-stop about their lovely pets and then go back to work.

Day 56 We have now finished the experiment with my puppies and today we have to go through the whole blood-testing rigmarole again. I cannot believe the animal technicians' attitudes – they are messing around while trying to take blood. One technician pokes, tickles and fools around with the man he is working with. This makes the process of finding a vein take even longer.

Day 57 They've started the post-mortems on my dogs. Today I carry my favourite puppy along the corridor to what are known as the Death Row cages. I spent last weekend deciding whether to blow this whole project and smuggle her out – but I must think of the future of the other animals here and hope that my film will help all of them.

Day 64 I have just walked out of the laboratory for the last time. I wanted to say goodbye and pet the dogs, but I've found it so hard loving those about to be put down that I kept my distance at the end. I don't think anybody suspects me.

I have followed the whole process with my puppies, from the settling-in weeks, through experiments to the post-mortem. As I was leaving, they told me my chores for the next morning – nobody knew I would not be there, but in the edit suite, assembling the evidence of their cruelty. •

A postscript

My main worry three months ago about the treatment of beagles at one of Britain's largest animal-testing laboratories was that nothing would happen after my article was published in these pages and then my film was broadcast. Happily, it did. The *Guardian* and Channel 4 both received hundreds of complaints, the Home Office and the RSPCA were inundated with phone calls, and the animal-testing establishment was shaken.

Huntingdon Life Sciences Ltd (HLS) is the largest contract testing laboratory in Europe, and my film suggested that their tests on dogs were not to be relied on, that the data – due to the technicians' short cuts – was inaccurate. Some of the company's clients withdrew their work and the share price plummeted from 121p to 54p. Those shown allegedly 'controlling the dogs' in a rough manner were sacked. The Home Office began a full investigation.

On 24 July, Home Office Minister George Howarth told Parliament in a written answer: 'Shortcomings relating to the care, treatment and handling of animals, and delegation of health checking to new staff of undetermined competence, demonstrate that the establishment was not appropriately staffed and that animals were not at all times provided with adequate care.' As a result, he has revoked the company's licence, with effect from November 30, unless 16 conditions are met. In other words, these laboratories – which, according to Home Office estimates, are currently using 1,000 beagles, 200 marmosets, 450 macaques, 13,000 mice, 35,000 rats, 2,000 rabbits, 4,000 guinea pigs, 3,000 birds, 4,000 fish and smaller numbers of other mammals such as cats and baboons – could be closed down.

Huntingdon Life Sciences has associated laboratories in Korea, Japan and America. While I was investigating HLS in the UK, unknown to me another woman was scrutinising HLS Inc in East Millstone, New Jersey, for the organisation People for the Ethical Treatment of Animals (Peta). The alleged violations witnessed included puppies being killed in the same room where post-mortems were being carried out, as a power saw was being used to cut the skull of a dead puppy on the next table. Another case alleged that a puppy was cut open from neck to groin, exposing its ribcage. It then howled, threw its head back and writhed from side to side, obviously still alive. HLS Inc have taken Peta to court and they have now been injuncted. Peta has been barred from using the videotapes and documents in their campaign against HLS Inc. They say they are unable to get the US Department of Agriculture to follow up the case due to this ruling.

I still get flashbacks of the gruesome images and sounds I witnessed, the post-mortems of the hounds I felt so much for, and the constant high-pitched barking. To calm down, I have taken to living on a houseboat. Aptly, my floating home is named *The Beagle*. •

Editorial Footnote: On 18 September, two HLS employees admitted charges under the Protection of Animals Act of 'cruelly terrifying dogs'. They were given community service orders by Huntingdon magistrates and ordered to pay £250 costs. The prosecution followed Channel 4's film and Zoe Broughton's *Guardian* article.

The Arts: ancient faces and lonesome songs

2,000 years on from the paintings above, we give prizes for portraits like this. What's gone wrong?

1 July 1997

Adrian Searle

A miracle of ancient faces

'**W**e know nothing of the artists,' says the catalogue to the British Museum's beautiful exhibition *Ancient Faces: Mummy Portraits from Roman Egypt*. Of the portraits themselves, and their sitters, who lived in the first couple of centuries AD, we know a bit more. Many were the descendants of Greeks, of mercenaries who fought for Alexander the Great and the early Ptolemaic dynasties in Egypt. Painted in hot wax and pigment, and drawn either from life or soon after the subject's death, the portraits were buried with their sitters, and have been found all along the Egyptian Nile, from Fayum, near the delta, to Thebes in the south. Descendants of settlers, the subjects of the paintings were dedicated followers of Roman fashion, young men and kids from the gymnasia who died with their puppy fat. We recognise the tanned, overweight yuppies of the time and their wives, a man with a tic, his mouth dragged down on one side, proud soldiers and freed slaves.

How modern they look. Just like you and me, except for their *I Claudius* hairdos and jewellery, their nicely trimmed beards, their Roman poses. Nowadays, they'd be sporting retro-beat goatees and designer baldness, or dressed by Armani, shod by Nike, Walkman headphones casually slung around their necks. What a way to go. The ancient funerary portraits are head-and-shoulders shots, like passport snaps, with no attempt made to contextualise the figure within anything other than a cursory, plain background. And so we concentrate on the face. Contemporary portraiture, as exemplified in the annual BP award show at the National Portrait Gallery, loads its subjects with the impedimenta of everyday life and a lot of symbolic clutter. I would bury most of it, but wouldn't want to be buried with any of it.

Here's new-lad writer Nick Hornby, pictured at his desk with his laptop, pretending to be busy on the phone, ashtray and pack of Silk Cut to the fore. The painting has all the candour of a bad public relations set-up. And a prize-winning portrait of spy-writer Phillip Knightley, with a budgie on his head and with his unnamed Indian wife hovering to one side with a bottle of wine. He's about to enjoy a little snack. The painting fails to be witty, and makes you never want to read any of the man's books. The faces here are, by the way, mere compositional details. Knightley, painted by Kevin Cunningham, is trying to keep a straight face. If I were the budgie, I'd know what to do next.

Unlike the anonymous painters of the works in *Ancient Faces*, we know who the perpetrators of the BP award portraits are, though from year to year they're largely interchangeable. Why is it that so much contemporary painted portraiture is so bad? Many of the artists here, I think, are trying to show off their skills rather than bring their subjects to life, and they prefer props to confrontation, signs of modernity to life itself. Most, it seems, have been taught to paint rather than think. Also, unlike their anonymous

The Arts: ancient faces and lonesome songs

forebears, they refuse to take a dispassionate stance towards their subjects – letting the paint describe not just the physiognomy of the person who is painted, but also the painter's journey around the chin, across the cheek, into the folds of the face, the orbits of the eyes. One might describe the activities of the painters of the Mummy portraits as affectless observers and recorders, documentarists rather than commentators. Strangely, however, their paintings have more presence than anything in the National Portrait Gallery.

The ancient portraits, painted on imported wooden panels and on linen shrouds, were set over the faces of the dead, like masks, and preserved *in situ*, along with the wrapped bodies, the cocoons of flesh and bone and resin and tar, swaddled in ornamented caskets in their tombs. The portraits themselves are remarkable and, to our eyes, remarkably modern and sophisticated artworks.

They have a kind of presence that does not depend on the impedimenta of an age. And, as paintings, it is difficult not to see them as the products of the same artistic canon that includes the portraits of Titian and Rembrandt, Van Dyck, Sargent, even Lucian Freud. Many are painterly in a peculiarly modern way, with their modelling, their shadows and highlights, the paint often almost sculpted on against the cursory backgrounds, the clothed shoulders rendered with dragged, thick, shorthand strokes. It is as if these 2,000-year-old painters had already seen Venetian painting, late Rembrandt, Picasso's Classical phase. Their plainness, as images, has a directness unfiltered by sentiment, precocity or flashiness.

And there they are – blam – in the painted flashlight of the recorder's eye. Painting, I suppose, was their photography, and a kind of magic documentary. We appreciate it now in a way I doubt they ever would. These people wanted to live for ever, and in a funny way they achieved their aim. Here they are, we look at them, and the portraits look at us. They have achieved their immortality. They are among us. They aspire to nothing more than a sense of liveliness and likeness. Everything else falls away.

What passes for contemporary painted portraiture, on the other hand, often feels it has to compete with photography by disowning it, by larding up the picture with paint, private symbolism and kitchen-sink detail. It is already out of date before it's even dry. It is still possible to paint a face, and to deal with something as basic as recognition. The human image remains compelling. But where's the compulsion at the National Portrait Gallery? Portraiture here descends too often into vanity painting, and it isn't always certain where the vanity of the sitter ends and that of the painter begins.

One might say that the funerary portraits of Roman Egypt were formulaic, but their limited aims had some kind of purpose beyond the manufacture of anodyne images. They also didn't have the need to compete with photography. They were part of a culturally recognised symbolic order and system of beliefs, something most modern painted portraiture signally lacks. Likeness and painterliness here are confounded by a terrible gimmickry, flashiness and self-conscious painterliness that gives many of the works an utterly fake sense of value. This annual award exhibition is a constant reminder of how smug and dismal and worthy and dull much British contemporary portraiture is. And when it tries too hard, it just looks arty. The best works are the most direct. The winner of the BP Portrait Award, James Lloyd, depicts a young woman in the corner of some dingy studio watching a hand-held TV. It is a hard-won image, in the Slade School tradition of dour figure painting, but it is more about studio dinge and boredom than portraiture. Somehow, I'm more interested in what she's watching on the little screen than in the sitter herself.

The best at the BP awards, to my mind, is James Baylay's *Leaning into the Mirror*. A face set against blankness, its contours uncertain, the colour leaking and flaring around the edges, the face seen as though it were an alien object, seen directly. This portrait is little more than a trace of one who will pass on. It has a kind of fleetingness, caught by the painter. There's a lesson in this somewhere. ●

● ●

25 February 1997

Michael Billington
A critic purified

C ritics have a lot in common with vampires: both, as P. G. Wodehouse suggested, 'come out after dark, up to no good'. Which is rather the point made by Conor McPherson in his eerie, obsessive one-man play, in which a Dublin drama critic in the throes of a breakdown falls in with a south London vampire and emerges purified by the experience.

Brian Cox, bulky in a typically baggy critic's suit, takes the stage with commanding ease and, for the first half at least, keeps one riveted. He describes how, as a critic, he turned himself into a 'character' through his abrasive reviews and drunken behaviour. But one day he fell in love with Helen, an actress playing Salome at the Abbey, crazily lied to the director at a post-first-night pub party about the tone of his review and, abandoning wife and family, eventually followed Helen and the cast to London, claiming that his eulogistic notice had been rewritten by his editor.

Can such things be? McPherson persuades you that they can. He captures very well the feuding intimacy of Dublin life where, unlike London, critics and artists regularly collide. He also conveys the self-loathing and romantic obsessiveness of an ageing hack who finds in Helen a Homeric ideal. I don't know of any critic who has actually destroyed his life through his fixation with an actress; but it would be nice to think it could happen.

For me the play goes off the boil only when the degraded hero is taken up by a vampire and acts as his pimp, nightly luring London's glittering young back to his pad. I presume this is intended as inner fantasy rather than stark reality: a metaphor for the critic's kinship with these parasitic nocturnal bloodsuckers and a symbol of his attempt to revivify himself through the elixir of youth. But McPherson's writing, so good when rooted in Dublin reality, loses its narrative grip when it explores the turmoil of nervous breakdown.

Never mind – Cox is always fascinating to watch. He has a remarkable ability to buttonhole an audience, confiding in us as if we were sitting in his front room. He also has the capacity to convey inner grief: it was there when, as a young actor, he played the distraught, silent hero of David Storey's *In Celebration*, and it is here now in this loquacious critic when he confesses he dare not respond to his wife's care because 'you open those floodgates, Christ knows what the hell is going to come pouring out'.

Cox colours the performance with humour and irony, but at its heart lies the strange sadness of a man in the grip of a Faustian fantasy about the exchange of his soul for power. The play may not be as spellbinding as McPherson's *This Lime Tree Bower*; but Cox, under the author's immaculate direction, leaves behind an ineradicable image of middle-aged melancholic yearning. •

11 January 1997

Nik Cohn

Are you lonesome tonight?

Ian Pollock

'**I**s Elvis in me? His spirit living?' Staring at his hands on the table top, Paul Chan ponders. 'Sometimes I think so, yes,' he decides. 'I feel him inside. Sometimes, yes, I feel him move.' Tracking down this man has been a long quest. Many months ago, while walking near the Pantiles in Tunbridge Wells, I passed a Chinese restaurant called Graceland. The windows were covered with glossy pictures of a Chinese Presley, dressed in a white suit of lights, Las Vegas-style. Paul 'Elvis' Chan, the captions announced, but the restaurant was shut.

A passer-by told me that it opened only at weekends; the rest of the time Chan could be found in the Old Kent Road. Further inquiries, phone messages, even letters brought no response. Then, tonight, finding myself adrift in south London, I rang on the off chance and Chan answered. 'I not sing tonight,' he told me gruffly. 'Talk, maybe, a little. But if you expecting Elvis, he not be here.'

The Arts: ancient faces and lonesome songs

The Old Kent Road is not a thoroughfare that I've ever thought of as having a fashionable end, but by the time I reach its version of Graceland, I know where the other end is. There's a tower block on one side, a railway bridge almost overhead and an unlit alley out back. The restaurant is deserted, the kitchen closed. Nothing but empty tables and the reek of disinfectant. Paul, sitting alone and surrounded by Elvis photos and movie posters, does not look a happy man. Slim and neat, with longish hair swept back at the sides and a jet-black forelock trained to flop loose across his forehead, he doesn't take after Elvis so much as the King's first English disciples, Billy Fury and the young Cliff Richard. 'Why you here?' he demands, his upper lip curling with just the right surly twist. 'If you want to write about Elvis, you better think deep. You don't do this for fun, understand? Only if you have need.'

His eyes are red-rimmed; he looks spent. For a testing moment, he stares me down, then the tension in him breaks and he starts to talk. 'I am born in Hong Kong, that's where it begins. It is 1956, I think, and I'm hearing "Teddy Bear". This voice is very soft, so much beautiful, I believe: "Here is the King of Kings." ' From that moment, the pursuit of Presley consumed him. 'At school, when I start my education, I am not really concentrate or work hard on my study, my only care is Elvis. I take money from my mother, I go to the cinema, *Love Me Tender*, *King Creole*, this is my whole life, understand. This is all I am.'

He came to England in 1970. By this time, he was married. 'We get income, we have got house. We have everything. Two children, first daughter, second son. We work; we work and sing. We are the one happy family.'

But now a strange pattern began to take shape. More and more, Chan's life echoed his idol's. 'Our marriage, similar, not too much different. My wife, she not respect me truly, never listen to my deep wishes. At the end she leave me, gone. Bring me a divorce and she give me my broken heart.'

After the split, his wife kept the house and children, while Chan restarted from scratch. 'I work in Chinese restaurant, also living there. Year goes, then one day I say, "Chinese restaurants, too many, too much boring, they need a song." So I'm saving three years, more four years, and I open here. For Elvis, understand? To bring us together, same place, same time.'

Eight years after launching his first Graceland, he now owns three. Each weekend, he starts off his evening by appearing at the one in Sevenoaks, then moves on to Tunbridge Wells, before finishing up at Elvisworld Central on the Old Kent Road. The rest of the time, he lives alone in a big house in Bexley Heath, also named Graceland, with a one-acre garden, a Cobra in the garage that he never drives and gates decorated with clef notes, just like the original in Memphis.

'Same as Elvis, I did all right. I only small, he so big, but not all different inside. We make it, fine, but everything is not all right. In our heart, we both lonesome tonight. Sometimes when I sing, I feel upset, I cry. In my opinion, Elvis, he was not a happy guy. He have money, but he can't go to restaurant, get Chan's good food. He must have hamburger and Coca-Cola, this make him sick. I am not 100 per cent believing he take drugs. I just think he sad to be alone, all the time alone.'

As he talks, he stares. His dark eyes are lustrous, velvety, and they keep nailing me. 'Don't drag my heart around,' he says at one point, then jumps up from his seat and ducks behind the bar. Fumbles with a cassette, then vanishes, leaving me alone with the Dettox and the hundred faces of Elvis on the walls. Ghostly faces stare in through the windows. There's a leaking tap somewhere.

Suddenly, the silence breaks. 'And now, the moment you've all been waiting for,' a canned voice intones. 'Ladies and gentlemen, please put your hands together for . . . Mr Paul . . . Elvis . . . CHAN!' As the taped multitudes roar, he erupts from behind the bar, magnificent in his suit of lights, into this dark and deserted room. 'Well, it's one for the money, two for the show . . .'

Two nights later, I'm back again, to watch Chan in serious action. This time, the restaurant is packed with punters, wolfing down platefuls of Chinese food and swilling away the aftertaste with warm Liebfraumilch. The crowd has a sloppy, jeering look. When the canned voice makes its announcement and Paul Chan comes bounding out, the first response is laughter. One drunk pulls slit-eyed faces behind the singer's back, and three women go off in hysterical screeching. If Chan notices, however, he gives no sign. He's lost so deep in Elvis that he can't be reached.

Though his voice is thin and his accent garbled, he tackles each number with utter conviction. 'Heartbreak Hotel', 'Don't Be Cruel', 'All Shook Up' – one classic after another. And gradually, the mood starts to shift. The crowd stops laughing and starts to smile. Women get up and dance; a skinny boy with adenoids borrows the mic to murder 'Suspicious Minds'. Then another Elvis walks in, this one from the Elephant and Castle, and renders 'Return to Sender'. By the end, the place sounds and feels like a revival meeting: unholy rollers singing along; enemies hugging; lovers entwining; total strangers yelling the choruses into each other's faces.

Wrestling with 'American Trilogy', Chan works himself into such a froth that he almost collapses. When the number ends, he staggers off into the shadows, but the crowd will not let him go. He has to come back for 'Blue Suede Shoes'. 'I die for this King, no problem,' he told me the first night we met. 'He's making me miracles.' •

* * *

28 June 1997

Andrew Clements
The devil's in the detail

At the Royal Festival Hall on Wednesday Alfred Brendel offered his own exceptional bicentenary tribute to a composer whom he has championed steadfastly throughout his career. Brendel is the pre-eminent Schubert pianist of our time. In the past four decades he has constantly returned to the sonatas for further exploration, refining his interpretations as he uncovers more in each work.

What he has exposed in the sonatas has almost always been a more complex musical personality than history sometimes ascribes to Schubert, so that even in the early works 'the image of the unselfconsciously lyrical composer simply does not fit', as he wrote in an introduction to the programme for this recital.

The result is that compared with other outstanding Schubert interpreters (Sviatoslav Richter, Clifford Curzon, Rudolf Serkin), who have hymned the melodic purity and dance-like exuberance of these works in glorious contemplation, Brendel's recital is more nervously expressive, full of dark undercurrents suddenly illuminated by brilliant shafts of light, but finding the intensity within the music rather than applying it cosmetically.

That does not always make for comfortable listening. His first work was the early A minor Sonata D537, in which he was on the look-out for harbingers of the later, more ambiguous masterpieces.The first movement was taken deliberately, hardly an allegro at all. The melody of the central allegretto had a halting expressiveness, although Brendel's careful shaping of the theme on each of its reappearances was a lesson in how a great pianist can do so much with nuance. The finale had a real dash to its exuberance, but still picked out the shadows. The ending was almost brusque, thrown away as if such high spirits could not be sustained.

The Four Impromptus D935 then offered a sequence of sharply delineated portraits, the first in F minor charged with *Sturm und Drang*, the A flat phrased as naturally as breathing, the variations of the B flat full of classical air, the F minor wittily buoyant and breathtakingly incisive. But both these works, fascinating as they were, turned out to be only a prelude to a quite awe-inspiring account of the great B flat sonata that followed the interval.

There are some performances that have greatness stamped on them from the first bar. The spellbinding way in which Brendel unfurled the opening melody, allowing it space to breathe, yet always paying close attention to the left hand, conjured up the whole world of the sonata in a matter of moments.

Everything in the first movement was placed with faultless precision, every detail contributing to the whole. The slow movement unfurled with the same organic inevitability, a detail intensified here, a phrase sung out there, yet all welded into a perfect whole. The scherzo sparkled, its central section darkly introspective, and the finale, with each return of the main theme subtly altered by the accumulated experience of what had gone before, was eased through to an unhurried discharge of the tension. The emotional map was complete.

After such an overwhelming performance, encores were almost superfluous, but there were two: the Moment Musical in C sharp minor, all glinting half-tones, and the G flat movement from the other set of Impromptus, full of singing melody and crystalline accompanying figures. Altogether an extraordinary, privileged experience. •

Tom Stoppard

The Persons of the Play: Tom Stoppard, Knight of Denmark; Mia Farrow, Daughter of Polonius; Felicity Kendal, the Player Queen; Woody Allen, the gravedigger
(Rosencrantz and Guildenstern are dead)

Act 1, Scene 1. Enter Mia and the Knight.

MIA: Absent thee from Felicity awhile.

SIR TOM: I shall in all my best obey you, madam. (*They embrace. Exeunt pursued by paparazzi. Enter Rosencrantz and Guildenstern*)

ROSENCRANTZ: Zounds, I thought you were dead!

GUILDENSTERN: I thought *you* were dead!

ROSENCRANTZ: Have you heard?

GUILDENSTERN: About him? Yes. Read it in *Ye Daily Male*. Etchings of the happy couple walking together in Ireland. Before my God, I might not this believe without the sensible and true avouch of mine own eyes. But soft, lo where he comes again. (*Enter the Knight*) Wot ho, Sir Tom, is it true that you and Princess Mia, lately wife of yon Woody, are walking out?

SIR TOM: Blast you! Anyway you are both dead. (*Runs them through with rapier*) O!/that this/too famous flesh too/would melt,/Thaw, and resolve itself into a dew;/Or that the Everlasting had not fixed/His canon against extramarital sex. Oh God, Oh God. (*Exit Sir Tom, pursued by* Observer *profile writer. Enter Benetton-like gathering of assorted children*)

FIRST CHILD: Mother, you are not going to marry another playwright?

MIA: Hush, my little ones. Ask yon peasant boy if he needs a mother! (*Exeunt children in pursuit of orphan. Enter R&G, again*)

R&G: (*together*) My lady! The players are come!

PLAYER QUEEN: (*hissing*) For Stoppard and the trifling of his favour,/Hold it a fashion and a toy in blood,/A violet in the youth of primy nature,/Forward, not permanent, sweet not lasting,/The perfume and suppliance of a minute,/No more! (*Exit Player Queen. Enter Sir Tom*)

MIA: Darling!

SIR TOM: Darling! I'm sorry. I saw her. She was wretched to you.

MIA: Oh God. It's *him*! (*Points at gravedigger, polishing glasses*)

GRAVEDIGGER: (*to Sir Tom*) Hi, you guys. Am I interrupting?

MIA: Aaaagh! (*Grabs Sir Tom's rapier and drives into gravedigger*)

GRAVEDIGGER: Alas, I am dead. You should watch her, she's crazy, Sir Tom. (*Dies*)

MIA: Darling!

SIR TOM: Darling! (*Looks worriedly down at corpse*) I'll lug the guts into the neighbour room! •

• •

13 February 1997

John Berger
What the fingertips know

When Memory Dies, by A. Sivanandan, 411pp, Arcadia Books, £9.99

We live today in a culture which has no faith in any future and which pretends that the past is obsolete. (Watch the delivery of newscasters on the telly to discover the nature – and the poverty – of the instants which are left.) Much fiction is written to suit the special appetite of this instant culture. Yet there are writers and books who resist and perform a holding action – awaiting the time when a future tense will reappear.

Such books often listen attentively to the dead who are still here. Their attention is neither morbid nor nostalgic but simply – in contrast to the surrounding culture of infantile regression – adult. To quote four who come to mind because I have read them recently: the first great book about the Vietnam War by the North Vietnam writer Bao Ninh; Bernardo Atxaga's book about the Basque countryside; Anne Michaels's masterpiece recalling the Holocaust; and now Sivanandan's quivering and haunting novel about this century on the island of Ceylon which became Sri Lanka.

Sivanandan, as editor of the journal *Race and Class* and as director of the Institute of Race Relations, is well known as a polemicist and a trenchant political commentator. Perhaps to some readers who know him as such, this book will be surprising, for it does not argue, it watches helplessly – as does most poetry – and with an immense tenderness. After you have read it, you understand that the militant's insistent vision of social justice has its origin in an extraordinary poetic sense of tact. (A quality found in certain ancient rules of hospitality.) The novel covers three generations of an extended family and is divided into three books. Each one begins with the promise of the monsoon rains and ends with a violent death, the violence being generated first by British colonialism and later by the ethnic war between Sinhalese and Tamils. The family is Tamil and their last adopted son is Sinhalese.

The ethnic war destroyed what the island was, not so much because it claimed territories but because it divided people's selves, the selves created by the island's own past life. Men began to forget until they betrayed all that they once knew. Then they killed the designated 'enemy' and, very soon, each other.

Because of its understanding of this tragedy, the book reveals what happens inside people when an ethnic war is instigated between close neighbours anywhere in the world. (The former Yugoslavia, for example.) Listen: 'When memory dies a people die.' 'What if we make up false memories?' 'That's worse, that's murder.' Such were the times into which Saha and Rajan and Vijay and Lali and Meena were born. But the book's story is not a history; it is a close-up narrative of their lives, the stories they tell themselves about themselves as they fall in love, forgive, fight, eat.

How to convey the flavour of its narrative? It is unhurried – hence a certain nineteenth-century air. Yet this is not the essential. If you are a story-teller in a culture where karma is a popular commonplace, you are bound to tell stories differently. The story is woven rather than driven. No story, however, ever crashes. Every story is accepted – even by those suffering it – because it is held in the hands. Nothing is far from what the fingertips know.

Sahadevan is with his aunt: 'Prema joined him on the stoop and, gazing up at the night sky, muttered inaudibly. Sahadevan leant forward to catch her words. Just then the moon, lifting itself up from a cloud, caught her in its light, and Sahadevan could not help noticing how ugly her face was in repose: featureless and pudgy like the rest of her. And he realised then that it was her smile which made all the difference. It was her smile that somehow rearranged her face at a moment's notice and made it so beautiful, made all that pudginess comforting . . .'

This description of an old woman's smile (she will die soon) is also a description of the extraordinary poetic tact of this book, and of what will make it unforgettable. •

....

31 March 1997

Jonathan Romney
A famous boy 38 years on

Early in Olivier Assayas's recent film *Irma Vep*, currently on release, there's a sudden irruption of natural dynamism. Jean-Pierre Léaud appears and simply hijacks the film's energy flow: he furrows his brow, prowls, declaims, stalks off, reappears, falls into a heavy silence that no one seems to dare interrupt. Watching this extraordinary display, flamboyant yet introspective, you sense that this is a man who can get away with anything, and knows it.

If you haven't seen a French film for the last 40 years, you may be shocked to realise that this mercurial presence is the same person whose candid 14-year-old features glared defiantly from the closing freeze-frame of François Truffaut's *Les quatre cents coups* in 1959. It's practically impossible now to detect in Léaud any traces of that boy. But what you can see is the distance he's travelled since then, which is not the poignant travelogue we usually read in the faces of former child stars. Léaud's history, his public growing-up, is unusually complex: there's evidence of that in Truffaut's 1979 film *L'amour en fuite* (*Love on the Run*), now released on Artificial Eye video.

This was number four and a half in Truffaut's series of Antoine Doinel films. In *Les quatre cent coups*, he enlisted Léaud, a rebellious boy, to be Doinel, the mirror of his own stormy youth, and having re-created Léaud in his own image, became a surrogate father to him, helping with his education, lodging and, later, training in film. In 1962, Truffaut used Doinel and Léaud again to recount one of his own early amours, in the short *Antoine et Colette*.

Léaud remained inseparable from Doinel, playing him in *Baisers volés* (*Stolen Kisses*, 1968) and *Domicile conjugale* (*Bed and Board*, 1970). The series tends to be viewed warmly as quasi-autobiography in a tender romantic key, but it also carries unsettling overtones of entangled mutual dependency – a director who couldn't let go of his character, and needed one actor, ostensibly his creation, to be at once that character and the director's own double.

And Léaud's problem was partly that if Doinel was modelled on him, equally Doinel was his role model, his excuse for being a loose cannon – the character was an irresistible, disastrous role model for young men who wanted to get away with being charmingly unreliable for as long as they could. To complicate matters, Léaud was being remoulded through the mid-1960s by Truffaut's old friend, later adversary, Jean-Luc Godard, in his own image, as the impassioned political agonist of *Masculin-féminin* and other films.

In *L'amour en fuite*, Truffaut revived Doinel one last time, partly because he'd run out of ideas, partly perhaps to free both Léaud and himself from the character. The film updates Doinel's story, cutting in sequences from the earlier films.

Antoine at 35 is still a scurrying, unkempt adolescent, but Léaud's presence, once so natural-seeming, is bizarrely stylised, stagy: he acts entirely in his own space, obliging everyone else to meet him on his terms. He seems to be playing both Doinel and 'Jean-Pierre Léaud', and grappling with the problem of which one is more fictional. This may be the pathological outcome of living with a character for 20 years, and carrying the burden of the public's fondness for a long-vanished boy; it may partly be the result of those Brechtian lessons he'd learned from Godard. This effect, and the complex flashback structure, give the film the feel of an uneasy exorcism.

Who knows whether the loss of Doinel in this film didn't mark Léaud as powerfully as Truffaut's death in 1984? Through the 1980s the actor, always prone to depression, experienced more serious mental problems. When he appeared in Aki Kaurismaki's *I Hired a Contract Killer* (1990), playing a man burned out by life, he fitted the part almost too well – he offered a study in exhaustion, a sort of walking self-autopsy.

Today, Léaud may be hard to control as an actor, may be indulged by directors as a national treasure – he may get away with murder as Klaus Kinski or Brando used to. But his cameo in *Irma Vep* rather justifies that – he seems to have regained such a fund of pent-up energy that you can't wait to see him devouring other films.

Léaud's history is such that writing about his career can feel like preparing an obituary – not for him, perhaps, so much as for his past selves, all of which, when you see them again, suggest different potentials that were never met as expected. Léaud has never been the image of the fine actor in control (a Daniel Auteuil, say), and he'll never be a trustworthy elder statesman. But his appearance in *Irma Vep* is a blast of pure, intransigent self, and makes you realise what a succession of strange, unruly old men we can look forward to from him. •

1 April 1997

Michael Simmons
Grosz indecency

With piquant timing, George Grosz has arrived at the Royal Academy. He will surely feel at home haunting a society polarised between fat cats and the very poor, where there is corruption among the ruling class, an obsession with sex, a gung-ho truculence towards foreigners and a leader of the left who occasionally wears the right's clothes with apparent equanimity.

What you see on the usually staid Academy walls should be accompanied by a health warning. There is sleaze aplenty in Grosz's work, as well as rollicking orgies and plenty of pubic hair. The exhibition demonstrates that the polarised Berlin of the 1920s, like parts of Britain in the 1990s, was not a haven for the morally or politically squeamish.

Looking at these pictures, it is hard to credit that the city was to become something Grosz could dispense with. What you have here is 'his' Berlin, concentrating on his savage depictions of a highly charged society and an age for which he formulated, in Ezra Pound's words, an image of its accelerated grimace. Hitler was writing *Mein Kampf* at the time and tomorrow's Nazis were already at work in the streets.

Street in Berlin (1922), by Grosz

Royal Academy/DACS

'Man,' Grosz wrote in 1922, 'has created an insidious system – a top and a bottom. A very few earn millions, while thousands and thousands are on the verge of starvation . . . To show to the oppressed the true faces of their masters is the purpose of my work.' A year later he wrote that his acerbic, almost merciless drawings of high and very low life were performing what he considered an important educational and social service.

In the 1914–18 war, he twice enlisted and was twice discharged – first with a debilitating sinus infection; then, towards the war's end, as mad. But he bounced back to foist the shock of Dadaism on the viewing public, calling himself Propagandada, and, despite the organisation's reservations about Dada, joined the newly formed Communist Party. Outside, on the Kurfürstendamm, Grosz said, there was a public-lavatory atmosphere and the smell of very rotten teeth; he sought, in his drawings, to depict this atmosphere.

The works were so tellingly explicit that maulings from the establishment were inevitable. It was not just that he portrayed sex, criminality and sleaze so graphically – the cauldron of Berlin could stand for that – but that he satirised the army (charged in 1920, found guilty and fined 5,000 marks); that, in a work called *Ecce Homo*, he 'made and distributed sexually explicit images' (charged in 1923, found guilty – with others – and fined 6,000 marks); and that he blasphemed (charged in 1928–31, and, despite several appeals, fined 2,000 marks).

Berlin's 'golden' 1920s were for many anything but. Grosz saw a ubiquitous and distasteful arrogance and a hypocrisy in 'society' settings – places littered, as he put it, with grotesque corpses and lunatics among the ruling class and the pillars of society. And yet, running through his seemingly irrepressible castigation and condemnation, there was an inescapable tension festering between him and his subjects. Something had to give.

That something was Grosz himself. His few intimates had long known that this provincial publican's son was a practical joker, a fastidious person who liked assuming false identities. It was his own real identity that had become increasingly difficult to define; and, as he acknowledged after the Great War, he had no home. In the mid- to late 1920s it all caught up with him: he withdrew from the fray, preferring moral argument to hand-to-hand fighting.

Grosz's friends and his wife, Eva Peter, whom he married in 1920, knew he hated Germany and things German, that he had always identified with America. As the chasm between hard left and hard right widened and the polemics and the violence escalated around him, he softened, painted more and more commissioned work and became a father. Then, when an offer to teach in the US came along, he accepted it. Though he had met Lenin and had received his membership card from the great Rosa Luxemburg herself, he had long since left the Communists.

The big problem, as he admitted, was that he identified with the people he distorted – the bad and the ugly as well as the poor and the deprived. 'In reality,' he wrote in his autobiography, 'I myself was everybody I drew: the rich man favoured by fate, stuffing himself and guzzling champagne, as much as the one who stood outside in the pouring rain, holding out his hand. I was, as it were, divided into two.'

Inevitably, his path frequently crossed that of Bertolt Brecht. Grosz illustrated Brecht's children's book, *The Three Soldiers*, and they worked together on stage sets for Erwin Piscator's Berlin production of the satire *Good Soldier Schweik*. By 1933, when both fled Berlin and their Nazi persecutors, Grosz was the first to be stripped of German citizenship, within days of reaching the US. Brecht, more intellectually incisive and therefore more dangerous to the Nazi cause, got the same treatment two months later. After exile, the two met briefly in Denmark in 1935, by which time Grosz's output had already mellowed, though Brecht still had some of his best work before him.

Arriving in the US (a week before Hitler became chancellor), Grosz subsided into taking photographs, adapting only with difficulty to his new life. His work became softer but somehow uneasy, his self-portraits discomforting. The Nazis destroyed many of the works he left behind, though they included 15 in the Entartete Kunst exhibition of 'degenerate' art in Munich. Grosz mused on 'burning a part of his past', on 'far-away conflagrations and the smell of blood'.

In the words of one German critic, Wieland Schmidt, Grosz in the US wanted to 'live only for art, for pure art – and from that moment on his art was dead'. Somehow, between the anodyne paintings and the heavy drinking, he survived, producing some bizarre 'stick men' pictures and speaking, in the late 1950s, of discovering serenity and joy. Then, in 1959, he finally yielded to pressures to return to Berlin. He did not go east, where his friend Brecht had somehow got by until he died in 1956, but to the glitzy, sleazy West. Within weeks Grosz had drunk himself to death.

So who was the real George Grosz? Not, certainly, the artist whose works are now on show at the Royal Academy, for they are only part of him. A more apposite question might be: was there a real George Grosz? •

Eric Cantona: deified April, retired May 1997

More important than life and death

• •

19 April 1997

David Lacey

Cantona arises from the tomb . . . titter ye not

S ince being sent off for fighting hardly amounts to martyrdom, it must be assumed that the canonisation of Robbie Fowler has been put on hold. He would not have won many admirers at Goodison on Wednesday by claiming that there had been no contact with the opponent in question. Not to worry. By the time Fowler fell out with Everton's David Unsworth, football had already discovered a divine alternative.

One's initial reaction on seeing Eric Cantona depicted, in an oil covering 80 square feet, as Christ arising from the tomb was that both painter and purchaser must be several shades short of a full palette. Then again the artist was joking and presumably Cantona bought the picture for the same reason Marilyn Monroe snapped up as many of those nude photos of herself as she could.

The clergymen who attacked the Cantona painting surely missed the point, which was that the work was not really trying to make a point at all. How could it when the mighty Eric presented a figure more reminiscent of Frankie Howerd in *Up Pompeii*?

But do not titter. Oh titter ye not. Portraying famous football people in biblical scenes could set a trend. Joe Kinnear might feature in the miracle of the loaves and the fishes, Kenny Dalglish could deliver the sermon on the mount and George Graham cleanse the temple. And who better than Paul Gascoigne to turn water into wine?

The most intriguing feature of Michael Browne's painting *The Art of the Game* was not so much his image of Cantona, based on Piero della Francesca's *Resurrection of Christ*, as his inclusion, in the background, of Andrea Mantegna's Julius Caesar on his Triumphal Chariot. Except that, in this case, Caesar is Alex Ferguson, the first consul of Manchester United.

Historically, the juxtapositioning of the two characters is inaccurate, Julius Caesar having died in 44 BC. But Browne could hardly have portrayed Ferguson as the ruler of Rome at the time of the resurrection since Tiberius eventually went mad. And Julius did do well in Europe, particularly when winning on away Gauls.

Yet, compared to old Jules, Fergie has the edge in getting past 15 March without a scratch. Since the security of a manager is roughly on a par with the emperors Nero and Caligula, this is no small feat.

The current season presents a scenario worth considering as football's answer to *I, Claudius*. Arsenal sacked Bruce Rioch as the first ball was kicked, Howard Wilkinson left Leeds United while the leaves were still green, Ray Harford parted company with Blackburn Rovers before the clocks went back, Frank Clark was replaced by a consular horse at Nottingham Forest and Kevin Keegan took the Brutus way out at Newcastle.

Tomorrow, on BBC2, Alan Hansen, *Match of the Day*'s Virgil, will be talking to a number of modern managers in a documentary, *The Sack Race*. Tommy Docherty (dismissed by Manchester United after they won the FA Cup because of his love for the club physio's wife) is interviewed, as are two other managers who could be said to have been more seriously involved with affairs of the heart, Graeme Souness and Barry Fry.

Souness, while manager of Liverpool, had a triple heart bypass and during the 1992 FA Cup semifinal with Portsmouth had a doctor at his side on the bench. Fry has had two heart attacks but still went out and bought Peterborough.

This season has seen around 50 managerial changes in England and Scotland. Three of them involve one man, Iain Munro, late of Hamilton, St Mirren and Raith. Colin Murphy was dismissed by Notts County four weeks after taking part in the programme. Has Michael Browne ever thought about depicting certain club chairmen in a reproduction of *The Last Supper*?

The public have only another week to view the resurrected Cantona before he takes it home. But do not despair. Supporters of Leeds United are believed to be commissioning another to depict Eric in a role which acknowledges his Frenchness and sums up their feelings towards him. It will be based on the *Death of Marat*. •

* * *

14 April 1997

David Lacey

Zola flair lights up the way to Wembley

The short outwitted the long and the tall at Highbury yesterday as Chelsea reached their fifth FA Cup final, and their second in four seasons, to leave Wimbledon with nothing but a field of wistful dreams.

The all-round craftsmanship of Gianfranco Zola, aided by the marksmanship of Mark Hughes and the footballing sagacity of Dennis Wise, not only brought Chelsea a decisive victory but rescued the day's first semifinal from scrappy mediocrity. In the end Wimbledon could not live with the skill and vision these players brought to Chelsea's football.

Hughes, his presence in doubt because of a groin injury, gave Chelsea the lead at a significant psychological moment shortly before half-time and scored their third goal in the game's dying seconds. In between times Zola virtually put the contest beyond Wimbledon's reach with a piece of artistry which had the losers' manager Joe Kinnear observing that 'the hallmark of a great player is producing the goods when it matters, and he did just that'.

So Ruud Gullit and his dreadlocks will lead out Chelsea at Wembley on 17 May; a Chelsea team, moreover, who should be in a more sanguine frame of mind than the relatively limited side who lost 4–0 to Manchester United in the 1994 final. To start with, Hughes will be wearing Chelsea blue this time. Yesterday's match, however, belonged largely to Zola, who carried on rather where Dennis Bergkamp had left off for Arsenal the previous afternoon. Seldom if ever can Highbury have witnessed two such displays of individual talent in 48 hours.

Once Wimbledon had to chase the game, or to be more specific the ball, on rapidly tiring legs they were done for. The pursuit of two cups and a place in Europe has strained the stamina of even Kinnear's muscular athletes.

All might have been different had Chelsea's goalkeeper and central defenders lived down to their pessimistic pre-match billing. Frode Grodas and Franck Leboeuf, it was felt, would wilt under Wimbledon's aerial bombardment. This never happened. Wimbledon's football reached for the sky from the outset, with free-kicks, corners and the prodigious throw-ins of Vinnie Jones landing in Chelsea's goalmouth like howitzer shells. But Gullit's defence held firm.

Catching high balls against Wimbledon must be rather like collecting conkers amid falling trees. But Grodas's handling seldom wavered and, with Leboeuf showing impressive calm in front of him, the panic factor never came to Wimbledon's aid.

Interestingly, five of Chelsea's six survivors from the 1994 final (Wise being the other) were either defenders or midfield players with defensive leanings. Yesterday Johnsen was the best of these because he not only challenged Ekoku and Gayle for high balls with consistent success but denied Wimbledon the second ball, from deflections and ricochets, which brings them so many goals.

The only success Wimbledon achieved was in hustling Chelsea out of their usual smooth passing patterns during the opening 20 minutes. But once Wise began to find space in midfield and down the flanks, and even without the injured Petrescu, Chelsea were able to get behind their opponents and put pressure on the Wimbledon centre-backs Perry and Blackwell.

After an anonymous start Zola became a steadily growing influence. Earle had gone close a couple of times for Wimbledon, preserving the thought that the long ball might yet win the day, but it was Leboeuf's long pass to Zola, three minutes before half-time, which swung the game in Chelsea's favour. With exquisite timing the small Italian held the ball until he could release Wise to his left. With Sullivan beaten, Kimble got in front of Burley as the cross dipped towards the net, but his clearance was chested down by the incoming Hughes, who then scored from close range.

The match was always Chelsea's after that. Three minutes past the hour Wise and Di Matteo worked the ball in to Zola from the left, Zola's first touch was impeccable, Blackwell was beaten by a deft turn, and Sullivan by a firm shot.

Just before that Kinnear had brought on Holdsworth to give himself an extra striker, but what Wimbledon really needed were new legs. Zola hit a post with a deflected shot and in stoppage time a weary Perry misjudged Grodas's huge clearance and mis-headed the ball straight to Hughes, who scored gleefully.

'Everybody was saying we couldn't cope with Wimbledon's strength and hassle,' said Gullit, 'but we played good, patient football.'

Zola was delighted. 'I have finished my vocabulary,' he said. Yesterday, so far as Wimbledon were concerned, he knew too many long words. •

14 April 1997

Martin Thorpe
Suffering Spireites dream on

This was very nearly the greatest FA Cup tie in the competition's 125 years. In the end it had to make do with being one of the greatest. Put together for £320,000, the fourth-oldest club in the world were 20 minutes away from beating a Middlesbrough side that cost £21 million to become the first team from outside the top two divisions to play in an FA Cup final. And had the referee David Elleray not controversially ruled out what appeared a good Chesterfield goal when the Spireites were 2–1 up, they probably would have achieved that.

In the sixty-eighth minute Howard found himself free in the area with the ball at his feet. He turned smartly and hammered a shot which hit the bar and came down over the line. To everyone's surprise, Elleray blew for an infringement, but no one was clear what the offence was, least of all the referee.

After the game he at first said that the whistle was for an offence by Morris after the ball had hit the bar and rebounded off the pitch, implying that he did not feel the ball had crossed the line. Later he had a different story: 'I've seen the replay and I accept the ball crossed the line,' he said and added that he had blown up for an infringement before the ball hit the bar.

It was the sort of refereeing controversy which has plagued this season, and one which gallant and spirited Chesterfield did not deserve. But Middlesbrough's escape was not all about good fortune. Ravanelli and Juninho have shown the doubters since they arrived here that they really are prepared to sweat as well as swagger. Having been 2–0 down after 60 minutes, they helped to pull their shell-shocked side to 2–2 after 90 minutes and one goal ahead with only one minute of extra-time remaining.

Chesterfield had given everything and looked dead on their feet. Then Beaumont, a late substitute with more strength than his team-mates, hoisted a last hopeful long ball into the Boro area. Kevin Davies, Chesterfield's biggest threat all afternoon, jumped with a defender and the ball fell to Jamie Hewitt on the penalty spot. With one last summoning of will, the defender leapt higher than the red shirts gathered around and

More important than life and death

Over he goes . . . Chesterfield win a penalty as their striker Andy Morris, scorer of his side's first goal, is sent flying under the challenge of the Middlesbrough goalkeeper Ben Roberts

steered a looping header past the flat-footed goalkeeper Roberts into the top corner.

It is Hewitt's thirtieth birthday on 17 May, the day of the Cup final, and he made sure that Chesterfield at least have a chance of being there to play Chelsea. They must replay this fixture at Hillsborough a week tomorrow.

Chesterfield had calmly asserted themselves from the whistle but the first real turning point came after 37 minutes. Vladimir Kinder had already been booked for kicking the ball away needlessly at a free-kick when the skilful Davies beat him down the right. Kinder twice pulled back the striker and was sent off for a second bookable offence.

Nine minutes after half-time Chesterfield took advantage of the extra man when Howard got past the substitute Blackmore down the right and fired in a cross to the ubiquitous Davies. His shot was deflected past the keeper, and the six-foot-four-inch striker Andy Morris had only to tap the ball in at the far post.

Six minutes later Chesterfield went 2–0 ahead. Morris again steamed into the area and was upended by, or fell over, Roberts's diving body. Elleray judged it to be the former and Dyche hammered in the penalty.

Chesterfield went wild. It is difficult to blame them but they probably went too wild and found it impossible to clear from their minds the dream of achieving the impossible. They paid the price.

Within four minutes Boro had pulled a goal back: Emerson sent Blackmore clear down the left and Ravanelli bundled in the cross for goal No. 28 of the season. When, two minutes later, Elleray gave a penalty to Middlesbrough after Juninho seemed to run into Dyche, it only compounded the injustice in Chesterfield's minds. Hignett duly equalised from the spot, squeezing the ball under Mercer's body.

Thirty minutes of extra-time was a daunting prospect to tired Chesterfield, and Boro duly applied a firmer grip to the game. The impressive Mercer produced a flying save from Juninho and blocked well from Ravanelli. It was inevitable that Boro would take the lead; Mustoe's shot cannoned off the bar, bounced over the head of the advancing Juninho and fell to the defender Gianluca Festa, who drilled the ball past Mercer.

But Chesterfield come from defiant stock and were not about to give up then. 'I'm so proud of my players and everybody associated with the club,' said their manager John Duncan. 'It was an extraordinary, emotional day, the best of my career.' •

* *

4 December 1996

David Hopps
England brought low by the vicar's son

Among the many innovations that David Lloyd has introduced to try to rejuvenate English cricket – dressing-room maxims, Churchill speeches and fitness camps, to mention but three – he has yet to turn to the power of prayer, but that might seem his best option today after another humbling experience at the start of the Zimbabwe tour.

England's latest setback came at the hands of James Kirtley, son of a Sussex vicar, and the fact that he was from their own parish did not make the experience any more palatable. When you are struggling to remember which end of the bat to hold, being given the run-around by a fringe county player is about as embarrassing as it gets.

Not that Kirtley is a fool: far from it. He had an auspicious debut season for Sussex last summer and is blessed with a consistent outswinger, but four cheap wickets yesterday for Mashonaland, which left England fortunate to finish a rain-disrupted first day on 175 for nine, hardly seemed a divine intervention.

England had reasonably blamed rustiness for their defeat in a one-day match against a President's XI on the same ground on Sunday, but with only two four-day matches before the first Test they can no longer take refuge in that excuse.

Such is the shortage of preparation time that they have already confirmed their intended Test side, to allow the preferred XI maximum playing opportunity. That such practice is sorely needed was underlined as England collapsed to seven for three, Kirtley dismissing Atherton and Hussain in his first three overs, and again to 94 for seven before Robert Croft's unbeaten 66 displayed overdue resourcefulness.

Discovering Kirtley bowling for Mashonaland invited the suspicion that he might have some Zimbabwe ancestry. Not a bit of it: he had simply approached Grant Flower, the Zimbabwe opener who was playing club cricket in Sussex last summer, and inquired about the possibility of wintering in Zimbabwe to be near the England team.

In Kirtley's most optimistic moments he imagined that his proximity to England might be worth a spot of net bowling, a learning session in the bar and the chance to relax in the sun and watch some Test cricket. Instead he was called up from his club, St George's, for his Mashonaland debut in the Logan Cup last week, took seven wickets in the match and was a late replacement yesterday when Eddo Brandes withdrew with a finger injury. He ran in with verve all day and was further rewarded with the tail-end wickets of Gough and Mullally.

Atherton's faith that England will benefit from their extensive rest is being sorely tested. In the nets the captain has found even the physiotherapist Wayne Morton unplayable, and yesterday he barely survived his first ball, a confident lbw shout from Kirtley, before steering to the wicketkeeper the third delivery he faced. •

5 March 1997

Paul Weaver
Last hiccup of a cricket winter

England's last match of a long and sometimes frustrating winter was not so much a last hurrah as a last hiccup. Their defeat by New Zealand in the fifth one-day international, letting the hosts level the series at 2–2 with one tie, was a less than grand finale.

It would hardly be surprising if these England players turned out to be related to the marathon runner who was helped over the winning line and then disqualified, or the grand prix driver who ran out of fuel in sight of the chequered flag. Good finishers they are not.

This defeat was hardly surprising, though. In cricket, as in any sport, it is difficult to regain the initiative once it has been lost, and England, perhaps distracted by thoughts of home, had surrendered their supremacy in the previous match, the defeat in Auckland.

It is disappointing to end a largely successful tour with successive defeats. Unlike in their 3–0 defeat by Zimbabwe, however, they have played enough good cricket here to be forgiven.

If these defeats help change their sniffy attitude to one-day internationals, so much the better. In evolutionary terms England are somewhere between the Mesolithic and Neolithic periods and have been left behind. If they are to have any chance in the 1999 World Cup they must find younger players with more all-round ability. This summer there can be no room in the one-day team for John Crawley, Nasser Hussain or even Michael Atherton. Adam Hollioake could captain a side that should also include Mark Ealham and Dean Headley – and Chris Lewis and Graeme Hick, if the selectors can trust themselves not to disrupt a settled-looking Test side on the evidence of one-day performances.

England need much more than a change of personnel, though. Dated tactics need to be reappraised and so does the threadbare homily that the priority is given to winning Test matches. From now on the priority must be to win Test matches and one-day internationals. The purist will tell you that Tests are the real thing, which is true, but the purist is in a minority through the turnstiles. •

9 June 1997

Mike Selvey
England sprint to Ashes victory

Even by the standards of an already remarkable summer, the scenes here last night were the stuff of dreams. The pavilion clock was edging round towards seven o'clock when Alec Stewart clubbed Shane Warne, the demon Warne, to the extra-cover boundary to win a match that had been England's for the taking since the astonishing events of the first morning.

Australia, in their second innings, were dismissed for 477, with three wickets apiece to Darren Gough, Robert Croft and Mark Ealham. The last nine wickets fell for 150, the last four within two overs, against an attack that never wavered in its endeavour.

It left England an entire day plus 24 overs last night – and an additional eight if a result were on the cards – to score 118 runs. That target is three fewer than Australia made when they chased 151 in 1981 and Botham charged England to victory. Perish the thought: 11 came from Glenn McGrath's first over and, although Mark Butcher was lbw to Michael Kasprowicz, the run-rate never wavered.

Michael Atherton's boundary brought up 50 inside nine overs, Stewart's clip to mid-wicket off Warne the hundred inside 20. The win came at a gallop from 21.3 overs with 15 balls of normal time left.

It was heady stuff, roared to the rafters by an ecstatic crowd. Chariots were swung low and of course the Ashes were coming home. It is early days for that theme yet, but the margin of this win, following the one-day victories, shows that at last England has a side to compete with the best. Neither will the Australians need reminding that the last five Ashes series have been won by the side winning the opening Test.

Atherton, equalling Peter May's record 41 matches as captain, wants this series and he wants it badly. He played majestically at times, never better than in the penultimate over, when he drilled successive balls from McGrath on the rise through extra cover. He hit nine fours in his 57, having added 90 in 18 overs with Stewart, who made 39. On the way a two clipped off Kasprowicz took Atherton past 5,000 Test runs, something achieved by only 11 other Englishmen.

With Australia 256 for the single loss of Matthew Elliott overnight, Atherton opted to take the new ball from the start and, although Greg Blewett was occasionally beaten by Andrew Caddick, he completed his century, his third in three Ashes Tests, with driving which matched that of Nasser Hussain earlier in the match.

It was Croft, a giant now in the England side, who made the breakthrough when Taylor misjudged his flight, stopped his shot and offered a return catch that the bowler flung almost to the Bull Ring. Taylor's 129 had taken more than six and a half hours of defiance and he and Blewett had taken their second-wicket partnership to 194.

Waugh then received a snorter that brushed his glove on the way through to Stewart and, when his twin, Steve, was stranded on the crease in front of his stumps, Gough had blown away the middle order in an inspired spell broken only by a 70-minute break for rain.

The end of the innings was unexpectedly swift. Atherton persisted with Ealham, whose opening over conceded 10 runs, and when Healy swung at a wide long-hop, the captain held a low catch in the gully. It transformed Ealham. Kasprowicz edged a beauty to second slip and after the injured Jason Gillespie had been run out in a mix-up involving his runner, Warne chipped a return catch to end the innings. From nowhere Ealham had taken three for nought. It was that sort of a day; it had been that sort of match. •

· ·

15 April 1997

David Davies

The power and the glory of Tiger Woods

After Tiger Woods had hit his second shot to the seventy-second hole at Augusta National on Sunday, the crowds surrounding him went crazy. They recognised, if he did not, that he could take 13 putts and still win, and their hootin' and hollerin' told of their joy at the crowning of a new and glorious talent.

The object of this delirium walked on to the green, about to win his dreamed-of green jacket in his first major as a professional, and surveyed the scene. All around him people were going potty, shouting, chanting, clapping their hands above their heads, but Tiger Woods barely saw any of it or heard it at all.

Asked later what he felt as a 21-year-old walking on to that green, knowing that he could not fail to win the championship, he said, 'Do you want an honest answer? I thought, "Boy, what a tough putt I've got left."' Then, realising what he had said, he went on, 'My focus never left me. I concentrated until I'd won.'

If one incident sums up the 1997 US Masters, that surely is it. Woods, a young man who set a dozen different records last week, is a golfer not only without parallel in terms of obvious ball-striking talent but with the ability to close out the distractions and concentrate wholly on the business in hand.

Amongst the things that Woods was not thinking of was that by two-putting for a round of 69 and a total of 270, he was setting a new record aggregate for the Masters of 18 under par, beating a mark set by two of the game's great names, Jack Nicklaus and Raymond Floyd.

He was not thinking that by two-putting he would win by 12 shots, another record, or that by playing the last three rounds in 66, 65, 69 he was setting a record of 200 strokes for the last 54 holes. Likewise those middle rounds of 66, 65 set a new mark for a second-third-round total and he also became the youngest winner ever. He took that record off Severiano Ballesteros, who won in 1980 as a Beatle-browed urchin of 23.

Other things to elude him as he faced his tough putt were the fact that he would win for the fourth time since turning professional in August of last year, in only his fifteenth start; he would earn $486,000 (£300,000) to move to $966,350 for the season and that he would now be averaging $117,130 per tournament. All he could think of was 'Boy, what a tough putt.'

It was too – a nasty, slippery, slidy one of some 20 feet which he did well to stop six feet below the hole. He did even better to hole the return. It would have been a severe anticlimax had he missed. It would not have been a fitting finish to one of the great displays, reminiscent of the days when Nicklaus was in his pomp and demolishing fields in precisely the same way as had Woods.

This was a benchmark performance. Woods knows that he will not be able to play to that level every week and that there will be courses less accommodating to his immense length. But he now also knows that, whatever the strength of the field and whatever the level of pressure, he has the skills and maturity to overcome them, and by a substantial margin at that.

There was, inevitably, immediate talk of a Grand Slam. In the moment of victory and with the extreme confidence of youth, Woods refused to rule out such a possibility. He said, 'I can't tell you whether it's realistic or not, but I can tell you that Phil Mickelson won on the [PGA] tour four times last year, so really it's only a matter of getting hot four times and having a lot of luck at the right time. What I can also tell you is that, if I enter a tournament, winning that tournament is my goal.'

Woods's strength is his extreme length but there are courses where this will not be the asset it was at Augusta. Some of his hitting last week was, in the literal sense of the

word, awesome. A drive and nine-iron at the 555-yard second hole is almost unbeliev-
able; a three-wood and nine-iron to the 485-yard tenth is ridiculous. •

11 August 1997

Mike Selvey

England expire to lose the Ashes

With little more than a whimper and a bit of perfunctory sabre-rattling, England lost the fifth Test by 264 runs yesterday, surrendering the Ashes, the
series and any reason to be considered in the same breath as the Australian
cricket team.

Required to make 451 to take the match — a winning fourth-innings total that would
be unprecedented in Tests — or to bat for more than four sessions to keep the series
alive, they lost their openers in the space of four deliveries either side of the tea interval
and the remainder of the wickets over the next two and three quarter hours, as batsmen
crossed the thin line between a positive approach and a reckless one.

The match finished on the dot of seven o'clock when, with seven balls remaining
of the extra half-hour that can be claimed if a result looks possible, Devon Malcolm
edged Glenn McGrath to Mark Waugh's fly-paper hands at second slip. England had
been bowled out for 186 in less than 49 overs and only a bristling, unbeaten 82 in 93
balls from Graham Thorpe saved them from the ignominy of being dismissed inside little more than a single session of normal time. The final Test at the Oval now becomes
an irrelevance; England will very likely win it.

On a dry, dusty fourth-day pitch, against the world's best exponent of wrist spin, disasters can happen. But this was no Shane Warne benefit. Until a meek tail-end surrender brought him three bonus wickets, Warne's twirling from the Radcliffe Road End
had been a red herring.

The first wicket – that of Mike Atherton – and the last two went to McGrath and that
of Alec Stewart to Paul Reiffel. But the heart of the innings was torn out by Jason Gillespie who, in 20 deliveries in the middle of eight overs of unadulterated tripe that cost
65 runs, picked off Nasser Hussain, John Crawley and Adam Hollioake.

Afterwards, Atherton declined to give clues as to his continuation in the captaincy,
which is inevitably called into question after three successive comprehensive defeats.

Earlier, England's bowlers had surrendered the initiative as the Australian wicketkeeper Ian Healy, a worthy Man of the Match, jutted his jaw and pummelled them all
round the ground, making 63 from 78 balls after Andy Caddick's second ball of the day
had confounded Steve Waugh.

Healy helped Australia from 167 for four overnight, a lead of 281 that was not invincible, to 336 all out and a lead that most certainly was. •

7 July 1997

Stephen Bierley

Sampras sweeps Pioline aside

Rationing was in force the last time a Frenchman appeared in the Wimbledon men's singles final, Yvon Petra winning the title in the grey austerity of 1946. Cedric Pioline had hoped to emulate his fellow countryman yesterday but Pete Sampras imposed his own strict quota, winning his fourth title on Centre Court by 6–4, 6–2, 6–4 in one hour and 34 min of implacably controlled dominance.

This was the 25-year-old American's tenth Grand Slam tournament victory, placing him fourth overall with Bill Tilden of the United States – one behind Rod Laver of Australia and Sweden's Bjorn Borg and two short of another Australian, Roy Emerson. His fourth Wimbledon title in five years equalled Laver's total and, of the modern winners, places him one short of Borg.

This was vintage Sampras – not a trace of self-doubt or a hint of weakness. The only time he became a fraction tentative was while serving in the third set at 4–3. His right arm tightened a little as the trophy glinted on the near horizon. At deuce he double-faulted for the first time since his quarterfinal victory over Boris Becker.

And how the Centre Court cheered, attempting to rouse the subdued Pioline for one huge and final effort to extend the match and perhaps take a set off the world's undoubted No. 1.

The opportunity was there but Pioline mishit a forehand and as quickly as the chance arose it disappeared. Two more serves and the two-game gap had been reinstated; one more service game and the title belonged to Sampras.

'For me it all boils down to just four tournaments a year,' he said. 'I just love winning the major championships and, if I stay fit and happy, I believe I can beat Emerson's record.' Few would doubt him. He has now won his last three Grand Slam finals in straight sets. He usually has at least one awkward match per tournament but clearly peaks for the finals to such an extent that his opponents are rapidly demoralised. Here it was Petr Korda, the Monte Carlo-based Czech, who extended Sampras to five sets in the fourth round, although even then the left-hander's resistance served to sharpen the American's backhand. Pioline tried to attack it yesterday and was given short shrift.

Sampras's one current regret – apart from having to play too much tennis – is that he does not have a constant rival, particularly now that Andre Agassi has turned his back on the game. For Sampras the real final here was against Becker, who after his quarterfinal defeat announced that this would be his last Wimbledon. There are only

More important than life and death

between a dozen and 20 players in the men's game who are genuinely comfortable on grass, and none can compare with Sampras at yesterday's exalted level.

Sampras will always be open to criticism about his bland off-court personality but he is rarely anything less than affable and it is his tennis that people pay to watch. Yet such is his unbending excellence, hinging on what must be the best serve in the modern game, that some even view his style of play in a critical light. This is totally unreasonable. The fault is not in Sampras but in the grass.

Pioline, who lost the 1993 US Open final 6–4, 6–4, 6–3 to Sampras in the Frenchman's only other major final, must have feared what was coming – and when it did there was precious little he could do.

Above all Pioline needed a good start, an hors-d'oeuvre that would zing off the palate and carry promise of an extended feast. But he double-faulted immediately, which felt akin to sitting down in a French restaurant and being served a meal from the microwave.

The Frenchman, his nerves as raw as those of his quarterfinal opponent Greg Rusedski, managed to cling on to that opening service game but then lost his second, the American clinching the game with a scintillating backhand which seared down the line. One break was enough, as it was in the final set. In all Pioline won only 16 points on the Sampras serve.

It was obviously disappointing, as Pioline had won a marvellous semifinal against Germany's Michael Stich, the 1991 champion, on Friday by virtue of a peacock's tail of vivid returns. Sampras's serve was simply too powerful and varied to permit a second helping.

Just occasionally Pioline's backhand flashed a potent reminder of happier days, one in the second set being the hardest-struck shot of the final. But this was only a tiny glint of the Frenchman's unquestionable talent; the rest was hidden by Sampras's massive shadow.

On one occasion Cyclops, the electronic device that measures the length of a serve, went off with no ball in play. It was as if the ghost of Yvon Petra had suddenly strayed on to Centre Court to offer Pioline encouragement.

In truth it needed a malevolent poltergeist to strike Sampras's right arm numb in order to save him, although Pioline could perhaps comfort himself that nobody else in the original draw, seeded or unseeded, would have done much better. •

31 January 1997

Emily Sheffield

My mate Iva has been very quiet since I went to the gym

I recently gave my best mate Iva a black eye when aiming for her arm. Fisticuffs are a normal part of our drunken bonding sessions, but her ability to deliver a vicious dead arm at will usually gave her the upper hand. Her black eye balanced things out, but she swore revenge. I thought it might be the perfect time to take up boxing.

I assumed I would get hit during my first lesson but Akay quickly convinced me that this might not be sensible. 'Imagine the full force of someone's body weight centred in a fist which smashes straight into your stomach or face,' said the owner of the All Stars gym. I thought for a second, visualised how long the queue at casualty might be and was relieved when he added, 'No one spars till they are skilled enough to defend themselves and fit enough to take the punishment. That takes at least three months.'

The gym is in an old church, and a saint casts a benign eye on the proceedings from a fresco above the ring. Numerous punchbags provide the purgation. I had arrived early to find a room of sweaty men and rapidly backed out, my fears that boxing gyms were testosterone zones confirmed. I hid in the corridor until fetched back in to meet the coaches, Colin, Clayon and Chip, who assured me half the class usually were women.

After a 20-minute warm-up I was taken up into the ring to learn the basics. Akay was my coach. 'First, hands. Fist clenched, thumb resting over your bent fingers and tucked in where they won't get broken. Hold them up either side of your face to protect it at all times, except when delivering a punch.' Your body has to be turned to the side, to present a narrow target. 'Feet apart, with your body weight centred to absorb the force of a hit.'

We then ran through the three basic punches: jabs, hooks and uppercuts. Jabs are fairly self-explanatory; with right or left hooks, you make a move to hug someone then punch them in the side of the head; and uppercuts are vicious little numbers where you ram your fist upwards to make contact with the chin.

The preliminaries out of the way, I got to don the gloves and whack pads that Akay held up. This is fantastic for releasing pent-up energy and beats hitting your head against a wall (or smacking your best mate). Akay shouted instructions and said I improved once I had worked out the difference between my left hand and right.

Defence was next: parrying and blocking. Parrying involves deflecting a straight jab at your face by knocking it away from you. Blocking is used to prevent right or left hooks. You merely throw your arm up in its path.

I was soon jabbing, cutting, hooking, blocking and looking a total prat. Akay sent me to the punchbags to practise. They brought on a serious sweat but I could not say

Frank Baron

Rum punch ... 'It beats hitting your head against a brick wall – or smacking your best mate'

the same about skipping, which seemed to play a major part in the get-fit regime.

This body-improving took on a surreal air when a couple intent on serious abdominal tightening lay down with legs entwined and alternatively sat up while passing a huge orange ball between them, as if involved in some fertility ceremony. I was glad to see that this was not expected of us all.

For the last 45 minutes the coaches take it in turns to inflict pain on various parts of your body. Weights are used to muscle up your arms before you are commanded to drop to the floor and do 100 press-ups (I got to five). Flipping on to your back to complete 1,000 or so tummy-lifts finishes off the torture. But after it is over Akay and the boys are all heart: they provide free tea and biscuits to enjoy while your sweat dries and you work out which bits of your body will refuse to work in the morning.

My mate Iva has been very quiet since I went to the gym. I described to her in detail my new punches and defence tactics and invited her round for dinner for a demonstration. She seemed very keen, but an hour before dinner she suddenly developed the flu. Which was a shame, because I thought a matching pair of black eyes might look rather fetching. •